Gold from Dragon City 龙城之金

辽宁三燕文物选萃
337—436

City Masterpieces of Three Yan from Liaoning, 337–436

Edited by Willow Weilan Hai

海蔚蓝　主编

Liu Ning

刘宁　著

With additional essays by Annette L. Juliano and Tian Likun

附论文者：朱安耐　田立坤

China Institute Gallery

华美协进社中国美术馆

Liaoning Provincial Museum

辽宁省博物馆

Liaoning Fine Arts Publishing House

辽宁美术出版社

This catalogue is published to accompany the exhibition:

Gold from Dragon City: Masterpieces of Three Yan from Liaoning, 337–436

Organized by China Institute Gallery and Liaoning Provincial Museum

该图录为配合"龙城之金：辽宁三燕文物选萃，337—436"展而出版。该展览由华美协进社中国美术馆与辽宁省博物馆共同组展。

The exhibition is presented at:

展出地点如下：

China Institute Gallery

100 Washington Street

New York, NY 10006

212-744-8181

September 5, 2024 to January 5, 2025

华美协进社中国美术馆

华盛顿街100号

纽约，纽约州10006

电话：212-744-8181

展期：2024年9月5日至2025年1月5日

General Editor and Project Director: Willow Weilan Hai

Exhibition Curators: Liu Ning, Bai Baoyu, and Liu Zhiyong

English Editor: Anita Christy

Chinese Editor: Willow Weilan Hai

Translators: Chen Mi and Jade Chuyu Xiong

Exhibition Designer: Perry Hu

主编暨艺术总监：海蔚蓝

展览策划：刘宁 白宝玉 刘志勇

英文编辑：柯安霓

中文编辑：海蔚蓝

英文翻译：陈觅 熊楚钰

展览设计：胡维智

Notes to English Reader

Chinese text is romanized in the pinyin system throughout the text. Dimensions are given as height (H), width (W), and depth (D), for most three dimensional objects. Measurements of length (L), diameter (Diam), and thickness (T), are given where appropriate. Explanatory comments and interpolations added by the English editor to the translated Chinese essays and catalogue entries have been enclosed in brackets.

Front cover illustration: Hat ornament (detail, cat. no. 59), Liaoning Provincial Institute of Cultural Relics and Archaeology

Frontispiece illustration: Hat ornament, (detail, cat. no. 58), Liaoning Provincial Museum

Back cover illustration: Seal of the Duke of Fanyang (cat. no. 29), Liaoning Provincial Museum

封面插图：花树状步摇（图录第59号局部），辽宁省文物考古研究院

扉页插图：花树状步摇（图录第58号局部），辽宁省博物馆

封底插图：范阳公章（图录第29号），辽宁省博物馆

目录
Contents

图 63

录 Catalogue

附 263

录 Appendices

Gold from
Dragon City

龙城
之金

Masterpieces of
Three Yan from Liaoning
337–436

辽宁三燕文物选萃
337—436

Prologue　序章

Sponsors of the Exhibition
展览赞助者

This exhibition, related programming, and catalogue have been made possible in part through the generous support of the following*

LEAD SPONSORS

Virginia Kamsky
In memory of Didi Pei

Anonymous

BENEFACTORS

E. Rhodes and Leona B. Carpenter Foundation
New York City Department of Cultural Affairs

Laurie and David Ying
Anonymous

PATRONS

Chen Chunyang
In memory of the internationally known photographer Wang Wusheng

Dame Jillian and Dr. Arthur M. Sackler Foundation
for the Arts, Sciences and Humanities
Joseph Tse Foundation
Angela H. King
Anonymous

CONTRIBUTORS

Diane Schafer

SUPPORTERS

Wang Gongwang

Sarah Jane Prinsloo

New York State Council on the Arts

This program is made possible by the New York State Council on the Arts with the support of the Office of the Governor and the New York State Legislature.

INDIVIDUALS

Qian Wan

Mynoon and Stephen Doro Family Foundation, a Donor Advised Fund of Renaissance Charitable Foundation

Christiana Dittman and Bruce McInnes

Mrs. Geraldine S. Kunstadter

Margro R. Long

Jane Cao

IN-KIND SUPPORT

Care-way Fine Art International Logistics Co., Ltd.

Zhou Xiaolu

Hai Tao

*at time of printing

Message from Liaoning Provincial Museum

Wang Xiaowen

Director of Liaoning Provincial Museum

During the period of Wei, Jin, and the Sixteen Kingdoms (3th–5th centuries CE), in the northern part of China, the Murong Xianbei founded Former Yan and Later Yan, and Feng Ba, a Han Chinese who adopted Xianbei culture, founded Northern Yan. The three regimes are collectively called the "Three Yan." All three Yan states had Longcheng ("Dragon City," present-day Chaoyang, Liaoning Province) as their capital, and their remains form the Three Yan culture archaeological site centered on Longcheng.

The Three Yan remains are characterized by the culture of the Murong Xianbei clan as well as traces of various other cultural influences, demonstrating a diversified and distinctive cultural profile. A large number of unparalleled treasures have been unearthed from the Three Yan archaeological site, including goldware exemplified by *buyao* hat ornaments, equestrian accessories represented by wooden stirrups covered with gilded bronze sheets, and a collection of vivid murals. We are proud of this cultural heritage. The three Yan regimes not only created their own history, but also promoted the integration and cultural exchange of various other ethnic groups. They greatly influenced the social development of northern China and wrote an important chapter in the history of the Chinese nation.

Following the 2008 exhibition *The Last Emperor's Collection: Masterpieces of Painting and Calligraphy from the Liaoning Provincial Museum*, this is the second time Liaoning Provincial Museum has held an exhibition in China Institute Gallery. For this occasion, Liaoning Provincial Museum will not only display its own collection of Three Yan treasures, but also collaborate with Liaoning Provincial Research Institute of Cultural Relics and Archaeology and Chaoyang County Museum to create a comprehensive collection reflecting the rich history of the Three Yan.

I would like to thank China Institute in America for inviting us again after sixteen years, and our colleagues of China Institute Gallery for their dedication and hard work. I hope that American audiences will enjoy this exhibition, learn about the history of the Three Yan, and experience the diversity of Chinese culture through visiting it. I wish the exhibition great success.

May 2024

致辞

王筱雯
辽宁省博物馆馆长

魏晋十六国时期（公元3—5世纪），在中国北方地区鲜卑族慕容氏相继建立了前燕和后燕，鲜卑化汉人冯氏建立了北燕、前燕、后燕、北燕三个政权合称"三燕"。三燕均以龙城（今辽宁省朝阳市）为都城，形成了以龙城为中心分布的考古学文化遗存。

三燕文化遗存以鲜卑族慕容氏部分为主体，受到了多种文化因素的影响，形成了多元交汇且独具特色的文化面貌；出土了以"步摇"为代表的三燕金器、以"木芯钉鎏金铜片马镫"为代表的三燕甲骑具装和丰富多彩的三燕壁画等一大批震惊世人的艺术珍品，成为我们引以为傲的文化遗产。三燕不仅创造了自己的历史，还推动了古代民族的融合与文化交流，影响了中国北方地区的社会发展，在中华民族历史上书写了浓墨重彩的一笔。

本次展览是继2008年"末帝宝鉴：辽宁省博物馆藏清宫散佚明清书画"展览后，辽宁省博物馆第二次赴华美协进社中国美术馆举办的文物展览。与上次办展有所不同，在本次展览中，辽宁省博物馆不仅将馆藏三燕文物珍品悉数展出，还联合了辽宁省文物考古研究院、朝阳县博物馆共同鉴选展品，将辽宁省内的三燕文物精品集结，力求展品丰富充实，全面展现三燕的精彩历史。

感谢华美协进社再与辽宁省博物馆结缘，十六年后再次相邀，也感谢中国美术馆同仁的付出与努力，希望美国的观众朋友能够喜欢此展览，通过欣赏展览了解三燕的历史，感受兼收并蓄、多元包容的中国文化。

预祝展览圆满成功！

2024年5月

Preface

Willow Weilan Hai
Senior Vice President, China Institute in America
Director and Chief Curator, China Institute Gallery

Learning from the past is crucial to understanding the cycle of human history. Less than one-tenth of human history, however, may have been recorded in writing and passed down, often in an incomplete or vague manner. In the absence of written records, the rise of modern archaeology and new archaeological discoveries continue to bring surprises, not only filling gaps in our knowledge but even rewriting history, providing new evidence for understanding the past and present. This is precisely the eternal allure and charm of archaeology.

One of the achievements of archaeological discoveries in the Liaoxi region over the past seventy years has been the revelation of the Three Yan culture established by the Murong Xianbei. The discoveries reveal the transition of this nomadic people from pastoralism to agriculture and their transformation from a non-literate society to one influenced by the literature of the Eastern Jin dynasty (317–420). Their dazzling gold *buyao* ornaments and distinctive horse tack had a profound impact on later developments in gold craftsmanship and cavalry. Additionally, Roman glassware unearthed from the tomb of the noted official Feng Sufu bears witness to the ancient traffic and cultural exchange along the Steppe-Silk Road more than 1,600 years ago. Through archaeology, the vibrant century of the Three Yan, once submerged in the currents of history, is brought back to life.

This exhibition was organized on an abbreviated timetable. When the exhibition on Nanjing's Great Bao'en Temple was unable to proceed as scheduled for fall 2023, the Liaoning Provincial Museum, known for its high-quality exhibitions in recent years, came to our attention, especially its exhibition *Age of the Dragon City: Three Yan Culture's Archaeological Achievements*. This exhibition was recognized as one of China's top ten most exquisite exhibitions in 2021. We would like to express our gratitude to Dr. Liu Ning, Deputy Director of the Liaoning Provincial Museum for leading the curatorial effort. With the assistance of the Liaoning Provincial Research Institute of Cultural Relics and Archaeology and Chaoyang County Museum, the curators quickly selected exhibits and reconstructed the exhibition. Special thanks to the Gallery Committee of China Institute in America, which named our exhibition *Gold from Dragon City: Masterpieces of Three Yan from Liaoning*. We are also extremely appreciative to scholars Annette L. Juliano, Tian Likun, and Liu Ning for contributing enlightening catalogue essays under tight deadlines.

This exhibition, introduced for the first time in the United States, uses the latest archaeological discoveries to offer a more artistic perspective on the fascinating hundred-year history of the little-known Murong Xianbei. Whether admiring the variety of artifacts, exploring the intertwined ancient history of Xianbei and Han peoples, or tracing the origin of dragon culture in the Year of the Dragon in 2024, audiences will find numerous points of interest and commonality.

More profoundly, this exhibition showcases a model of ethnic integration and cultural exchange. Just as in today's world, cultural exchange serves as the most important bridge to promoting mutual understanding and integration. Only through continuous cultural exchange can civilizations complement each other and progress together. It is, therefore, our hope that this exhibition will contribute to unity and world peace. Over three decades of serving China Institute Gallery, I have sought an exhibition theme like this one to illustrate the importance of this perspective. The realization of this exhibition brings me great satisfaction.

That the exhibition could be organized on such short notice was greatly facilitated by our ability to dedicate funding remaining from contributions of private sponsors to the previous exhibition, *Flowers on a River*, as well as funds intended for the Great Bao'en Temple project. The Institute is also blessed with enormous encouragement from loyal supporters of China Institute Gallery, especially from the leading sponsor, Virginia Kamsky. A special acknowledgement is owed to Virginia Kamsky, the former Chairman and CEO of China Institute. During her decade-long leadership, from 2002 to 2012, Ms. Kamsky's wisdom and cultural vision enabled China Institute Gallery to develop a partnership with Chinese museums and present to the world a unique series of thematic Chinese art exhibitions. These in-depth exhibitions built on the Gallery's historic reputation for small, thematic exhibitions and enhanced its reputation in the field, enabling this organization to fulfill its mission in accordance with its highest standards. I am forever grateful for Ms. Kamsky's leadership, encouragement, and support. Her generous support of this exhibition is dedicated to the memory of Didi Pei, the late, deeply missed Chairman of China Institute. All the sponsors of this special exhibition deserve gratitude from the bottom of my heart. Together we witnessed and proved again the power and benefit of cultural exchanges that can unite people and enrich humankind.

Organizing this exhibition and the accompanying catalogue on a short lead time required extremely hard work from all the teams. My special gratitude goes, again, to Dr. Liu Ning, the Deputy Director of Liaoning Provincial Museum, and lead curator of this exhibition. Not only was this exhibition adapted from Liaoning Provincial's award-winning exhibition *Age of the Dragon City*, but she proved herself a reliable professional who worked around the clock and at any hour answered calls, WeChat texts, or emails, then promptly took action. To all the colleagues from Liaoning Provincial Museum, Liaoning Provincial Institute of Cultural Relics and Archaeology, and Chaoyang County Museum who worked on this project, thank you for your hard work and cooperation. Thanks to Liaoning Fine Arts Publishing House for trying their best to design and print a beautiful catalogue to accompany this exhibition. Thanks to Care-way Fine Art International Logistics Co. Ltd., for over twenty years of dedication and care shipping all the China exhibitions to China Institute Gallery.

Thanks to the Board and CEO of China Institute, the Gallery committee, and all my colleagues at China Institute for your support. To the gallery staff, Xige Xia, gallery manager, Yue Ma, director of art education, and Tracy Jiao, gallery coordinator, goes our gratitude for your hard work and assistance; to all the docents, volunteers, and interns of China Institute Gallery, I am grateful for your enthusiastic help in introducing exhibitions to public visitors. My special gratitude goes to the Gallery's talented consultant specialists: to Anita Christy, for her elegant English editing; to Perry Hu, exhibition designer, who always designs and installs exhibitions that showcase the Gallery at its best; to Nicole Straus, Margery Newman, and Kristin Guiter, for their PR efforts in connecting with the media to reach a broader audience; and to Chen Mi and Chuyu Xiong, for the clarity of their translation of the catalogue.

The journey of carrying out the mission of introducing Chinese art through exhibitions at China Institute Gallery has been accompanied by sunshine as well as wind and rain. I am forever indebted to all my friends: to Liu Dan and Wang Huiyun, to Dame Jillian Sackler, Angela King, Michael and Winnie Feng, Laurie Ying, Mr. and Mrs. Robert Gow, William and Terry Carey, Annette Juliano, Sharon Crain, Marie-Hélène Weill, Lillian Schloss, Ingrid Ehrenberg, Matthew Edlund, Xu Huping, Cheng Zheng, Lu Mei, Zhou Xiao Lu, and Lu Hao, among many others; to my teachers Jiang Zanchu and Zhang Bing; and to my parents Hai Xiao and Zhao Renbao; my siblings Hai Shuhong, Hai Lang, and Hai Tao; and my sons, John Jingshan Chang and Jeffrey Haiqing Chang, for their love and care, which sustained me through all the difficulties of engaging in this sacred cultural mission. We all share the steadfast belief that true art can help us cultivate greater humanity and contribute to peace in the world.

This mission, and the journey to advance it, have been memorable. Together, we did it. Thank you all.

序

海蔚蓝
华美协进社高级副社长
华美协进社中国美术馆馆长暨总策展人

鉴古知今，是人类历史循环往复的一个智慧环节。然而人类历史得以借记载而传承的，或许十之一二，或许语焉不详。近代考古学的兴起、新的考古发现，不断带来无数惊艳，不仅拾遗补阙，甚而改写历史，为鉴古知今提供了新的佐证。这恰是考古学永恒的魅力和诱惑。

辽西大地七十多年来的考古发现，其中的成果之一，就是揭示了慕容鲜卑所建的三燕文化的面貌：一个马上民族从游牧到农耕，从没有文字到浸润东晋的书风，其灿烂夺目的金步摇和极富特征的马具，对于尔后的金饰工艺和骑兵队伍的完善都有着深远的影响。此外，冯素弗墓出土的罗马玻璃器，更是见证了一千六百年前草原丝路的交通往来，东西方文化交流的源远流长。那曾经淹没于历史洪流中的活生生的三燕百年，借着考古学而重现人间。

这个展览可谓"急就章"。在 2023 年秋的南京大报恩寺展览未能如期进行之际，近年来有制作优质展览声誉的辽宁省博物馆，其 2021 年荣获当年全国博物馆十大陈列展览精品推介优胜奖的"龙城春秋：三燕文化考古成果展"吸引了我们。感谢辽宁省博物馆副馆长刘宁博士领衔策划，以及辽宁省文物考古研究院和朝阳县博物馆的协助，让我们能于极短的时间内重选展品和重构展览；感谢华美协进社美术馆委员会给这展览命名为"龙城之金：辽宁三燕文物选萃，337—436"。我们也感谢朱安耐、田立坤和刘宁诸位学者在如此短促的时间内，贡献了启智的学术论文。

这个首次在美国介绍三燕文化的展览，更多从艺术的角度来审视和推介鲜为人知的慕容鲜卑百年间的精彩历史，将最新的考古发现分享给观众，使他们无论是欣赏丰富的各类艺术品，还是探索错综交融的古代历史，或是应对 2024 年龙年之际对龙文化的溯源，都可以找到自己的兴趣点。

更深刻地，这是一个民族融合和文化交流的例子，一如当今的世界，唯有文化交流，是促进彼此理解和融合的桥梁；唯有如此不断地文化交流，人类文明才得以取长补短，互相激励和精进；或许，亦可期待得以促进世界和平与大同。服务华美协进社中国美术馆三十多年，我一直想有个这样的题目来阐述民族融合与文化交流的重要性，这个展览使之得以实现，令我深感欣慰。

该展能于如此短暂的时间内实现，首先要感谢私人赞助者自"河上花"和"大报恩寺"两展的余款资助，以及美术馆忠实的支持者对该展的慷慨赞助。特别是领衔赞助者甘维珍女士。我要特别感谢甘维珍女士——华美协进社的前董事长和首席执行官。在她领导下的 2002 年到 2012 年的十年里，她的睿智和文化视野，使华美协进社中国美术馆得以与中国博物馆建立合作，向世界展示了一系列富有创意的中国艺术主题展。这些具有相当深度的特展，使这个以小型主题展知名的美术馆，赢得了业界的瞩目，高水准地完成了传扬中国文化的使命。我永远难以忘怀甘维珍女士的领导、鼓励和支持。甘维珍女士对该展的慷慨赞助，也是对刚离世不久的华美协进社董事长贝建中先生的特别缅怀。我内心激荡着对所有支持该展的赞助者的无尽谢意，我们一起努力实现该展，再次见证文化交流得以团结众人和鼓励人性的公益力量。

在如此短促的时间内组织和落实该展，以及编辑出版展览图录，实有赖于各团队难以想象的辛苦工作和竭诚合作。我特别再次感谢辽宁省博物馆副馆长刘宁博士，她作为该展的客座策展人，不仅授权该展基于辽宁省博物馆的获奖展览"龙城春秋"来改编，并且为该展各项事宜不分昼夜地回应电话、微信、邮件并立刻执行，充分体现了敬业的专业精神。我也要感谢辽宁省博物馆、辽宁省文物考古研究院和朝阳县博物馆的同仁的辛劳和配合，感谢辽宁美术出版社领导和编校、设计人员全力制作出版精美的展览图录，感谢北京开尔唯珍品国际物流有限公司二十多年来兢兢业业地为所有华美协进社中国美术馆中国展览的安全运输竭诚服务。

感谢华美协进社董事会、首席执行官、艺术委员会和所有华美协进社同仁的支持。感谢华美协进社中国美术馆主任夏熙格、艺术教育主任马玥和美术馆馆员焦宇晨的努力工作和协助。感谢美术馆的讲解员、义工和实习生的热情协助，将展览诉诸更多观众。我要特别感谢美术馆富有才华的专家顾问，感谢柯安霓雅致的英文编辑；感谢展览设计师胡维智，他的用心设计和细心陈列，总令展出出彩；感谢妮柯尔·斯笏丝、玛姬瑞·纽曼、柯斯顿·吉特尔的公共宣传、联系媒体以广视听，也要感谢陈觅和熊楚钰为图录的专业翻译。

华美协进社中国美术馆以中国艺术展览为媒介来传扬中国文化的征程，沐浴着阳光，也伴随着风雨。一路走来，我深为所有友人的不懈支持而感动，如刘丹和王慧芸、吉莉安·赛克勒女爵士、徐棋、冯英祥夫妇、应赵美玉、罗伯特·高夫妇、威廉姆·凯瑞夫妇、朱安耐、雪莲、玛丽·卫尔、莉莲·史洛斯、艾英格、马修·艾德隆、徐湖平、程征、陆楣、周晓陆和卢浩等，恕未能一一提及更多名字。还有我的恩师蒋赞初和张彬，我的父母海笑和赵仁宝，我的姊妹海曙红、海浪和海涛，我的儿子张静山和张海青。感谢所有友人和家人的爱护和关怀，鼓励着我排除万难，努力完成这神圣的文化使命。因为我们坚信，真正的艺术有益于人类的修为并将为世界和平做出贡献。

这个文化使命，这个履行征程，将被铭记。因为我们的共同努力，我们完成了。感谢大家。

Chronology of Chinese Dynasties and Historical Periods
中国历史年表

Xia dynasty　夏 — ca. 2070–1600 BCE

Shang dynasty　商 — 1600–1046 BCE

Zhou dynasty　周 — 1046–256 BCE

    Western Zhou　西周 — 1046–771 BCE

    Eastern Zhou　东周 — 770–256 BCE

    Spring and Autumn Period　春秋 — 770–476 BCE

    Warring States Period　战国 — 475–221 BCE

Qin dynasty　秦 — 221–206 BCE

Han dynasty　汉 — 206 BCE–220 CE

    Western Han　西汉 — 206 BCE–25 CE

    Eastern Han　东汉 — 25–220

Three Kingdoms　三国 — 220–280

    Wei　魏 — 220–265

    Shu Han　蜀汉 — 221–263

    Wu　吴 — 222–280

Jin dynasty and Sixteen States(or Kingdoms)　晋及十六国 — 265–439

    Western Jin　西晋 — 265–317

    Eastern Jin　东晋 — 317–420

    Sixteen States(or Kingdoms)　十六国 — 304–439

Cheng-Han　成汉 (304–347)	Former Zhao　前赵 (304–329)
Later Zhao　后赵 (319–351)	Former Yan　前燕 (337–370)
Later Yan　后燕 (384–407)	Northern Yan　北燕 (407–436)
Southern Yan　南燕 (398–410)	Former Liang　前凉 (317–376)
Later Liang　后凉 (386–403)	Northern Liang　北凉 (397–439)
Southern Liang　南凉 (397–414)	Western Liang　西凉 (400–421)

Former Qin 前秦 (352–394)   Later Qin 后秦 (384–417)

Western Qin 西秦 (385–431)   Xia 夏 (407–431)

Southern and Northern dynasties 南北朝 ——————— 420–589

    Southern dynasties 南朝 ——————— 420–589

        Liu Song 宋 ——————— 420–479

        Southern Qi 齐 ——————— 479–502

        Liang 梁 ——————— 502–557

        Chen 陈 ——————— 557–589

    Northern dynasties 北朝 ——————— 439–581

        Northern Wei 北魏 ——————— 386–534

        Eastern Wei 东魏 ——————— 534–550

        Northern Qi 北齐 ——————— 550–577

        Western Wei 西魏 ——————— 535–557

        Northern Zhou 北周 ——————— 557–581

Sui dynasty 隋 ——————— 581–618

Tang dynasty 唐 ——————— 618–907

Five dynasties 五代 ——————— 907–960

Song dynasty 宋 ——————— 960–1279

    Northern Song 北宋 ——————— 960–1127

    Southern Song 南宋 ——————— 1127–1279

Liao dynasty 辽 ——————— 907–1125

Western Xia 西夏 ——————— 1038–1227

Jin dynasty 金 ——————— 1115–1234

Yuan dynasty 元 ——————— 1206–1368

Ming dynasty 明 ——————— 1368–1644

Qing dynasty 清 ——————— 1616–1911

Republic of China 中华民国 ——————— 1912–1949

People's Republic of China 中华人民共和国 ——————— 1949–

Gold from
Dragon City

龙城
之金

Masterpieces of
Three Yan from Liaoning
337–436

辽宁三燕文物选萃

337—436

Essays 论文

A Note on Nomads in Northern China: the Murong Xianbei

Annette L. Juliano

Research Associate, Institute for the Study of the Ancient World, New York University

China's northern geography is characterized by fertile, agricultural plains with deep layers of yellow loess soil that gradually transform into unforested grasslands (known as steppes) into Inner Mongolia and across Eurasia. Here, China's stable agrarian culture yielded to a more mixed economy of pastoral herds and the mobile horse-dominated cultures of the steppes. In addition to Chinese peoples, "Numerous large and small ethnic tribes inhabited a vast arc of the marginal land that extended from Gansu province, the Ordos Desert (part of northern Ningxia) through north China and southeast Inner Mongolia to northeast China, encompassing forests, mountains, deserts, and grasslands"[1](fig. 1).

Fig. 1   Hunlunbuir Grassland, Northern Inner Mongolia. *Photo courtesy of Sergio Tittarini* (https://www.flicker.com/photos/8603336@N05/9758870183/).

Even with the construction of the Great Wall, an iconic bulwark, stretching more than 1,500 miles across the north, the northern nomads repeatedly succeeded in breaching this artificial border. Along the Wall, the relationship between agriculturalists and the horseback-riding nomads was ambivalent, ranging from the hostile to the hospitable[2] (cat. no. 91). During peaceful periods, these peoples freely exchanged commodities and goods in active border markets sharing livestock breeding and trading, including agricultural products, such as grains, along with jade, silk, leather, and rock crystal moving into China: "mules, donkeys, horses and camels entered from the frontier in long lines bearing furs of sables, marmots, foxes and badgers." [3] The symbiosis of this complex relationship involved not only lucrative trade but also military alliances, and intermarriage.

Xianbei 鮮卑 refers to a powerful, multi-ethnic confederation of nomadic tribes or clans, the first in the region to eventually establish an empire controlling all of northern China and the Mongolian plateau. Assessing available textual and archaeological evidence, scholars believe this confederation to be most likely of Mongolic-Turkic roots. Recent DNA analysis (published in 2023) seems to confirm the Xianbei's

Mongolic-Turkic origins and support the hypothesis that they originated from the Amur River basin and the Great Khingan mountains in the Amur region during the Neolithic period.[4] Apparently, the evidence also confirms that the Xianbei moved south in several migrations and settled in proximity to Han society. Most of the ethnic active in the north came from this area of China as well as from the area of Inner Mongolia and the northeast.[5]

Sporadic citations about the Xianbei, including other aggressive tribes such as the Xiongnu 匈奴, appear in Chinese texts attributed to the Han dynasty (206 BCE–220 CE). Some scholars cautiously point to the earliest mention of the Xianbei as 49 CE as well as two later dates in 120 and 127 CE recorded in the *Hou Han Shu* 后汉书 (Book of the Later Eastern Han Dynasty, 25–220 CE).[6] Since the Xianbei and their tribal rivals had no written language, the documentation of nomadic activities, customs, military exploits, and interactions with the Chinese along the far northern border and into Inner Mongolia survives almost exclusively through the perspective of Chinese texts, particularly the dynastic histories.[7]

Although their genetic origins remain enigmatic, DNA processing has supported scholars' preliminary assumptions about *who* the Xianbei were and *where* they originated. These questions also still apply to the other clans in the Xianbei confederation as well as to most of the northern nomads. This uncertainty is exacerbated by the absence of narratives written by the tribal people themselves and by their practice of forming confederations; smaller tribes merged with other larger ones to gain greater protection, economic stability, and military strength. For example, when the Xianbei defeated another powerful tribe such as the Xiongnu, the Xiongnu survivors joined the winners and changed their identities, calling themselves Xianbei. Today, this situation has begun to gradually shift with the application of DNA analysis to the increasing accumulation of archaeological finds from nomadic cemeteries in the north; the contents now permit new techniques of analyses of the imagery on gold plaques and amplify connections with ancient goldsmithing techniques.[8]

As mentioned earlier, the Xianbei tribal group emerges in the Han as part of a larger earlier confederation called the Donghu 东胡 (Eastern nomads). In 177 BCE, when the Donghu was defeated by the Xiongnu, the Xianbei and another closely allied nomadic tribe, the Wuhuan, broke away and fragmented into groups that migrated north and west. The Xianbei regained power when the vigorous leadership of Tanshihuai 檀石槐 (? –181) finally united the splintered Xianbei tribes. Since ruling over such a vast area presented considerable challenges, Tanshihuai divided the territory into three administrative-military sections, although he was most interested in two regions, the Ordos Desert in the west and the southern part of northeast China. The western region that stretched from Dunhuang in Gansu to northern Hebei (in the area of today's Huailai county), was managed by the Tuoba Xianbei;[9] the central section, controlled by the Murong Xianbei, was smaller and situated in the center of northern Hebei (today's Tangshan to Huailai); the third or eastern section stretched northeast of Hebei to Jilin (between Tangshan and Liaoning), and was ruled by the Yuwen Xianbei clan. Several brief power struggles and external military threats, however, caused the confederation to collapse. For a short period, the confederation was reunited, only to fall apart again in 235 CE with the Xianbei tribes dispersed. The Murong Xianbei settled within China around the Chaoyang area in Liaoning and, eventually by 342, controlling most of the northeast where they established overlapping states, all designated as "Yan." The Murong Xianbei's culture, often described as hybrid, was shaped by their strong connections to Chinese culture as well as to nomadic customs.

This exhibition focuses on the art, culture, and society of the three Yan states—Former Yan (337–70 CE); Later Yan (384–406 CE); and Northern Yan (407–36 CE)—the most sinicized state. The Northern Yan was conquered in 436, by the Tuoba Xianbei which went on to conquer and unify northern China (439) under the banner of the Northern Wei dynasty (386–534 CE).[10] By now thoroughly sinicized, the surviving Murong were assimilated into the mixed multi-ethnic population of north China.

Focusing on the archaeological finds from the three Yan states unearthed in and around the city of Chaoyang 朝阳市, this exhibition reflects the rich multi-faceted culture of the Murong Xianbei; its selection of objects demonstrates the intertwining of these three cultural threads. As mobile horseback-riding nomads, the Murong Xianbei invested heavily in horse gear and fashioned the earliest stirrups and produced saddles embellished with gilt bronze openwork designs. In fact, gilt openwork is a hallmark of Murong horse accessories—which, interestingly, the Murong shared with Koreans and Japanese of the time.

Extensive use of gold also characterizes a significant part of nomadic art (fig. 2) from plaques with deer and fantastic animals to earrings, headgear, and pectorals. Among Murong gold works are the "step and sway" ornaments constructed of thin leaves attached to branches that quiver with movement and were most likely worn on a hat (cat. no. 61). Clearly identifiable Chinese objects include bronze mirrors (fig. 3), inkstones, gold seals, and belt plaques with openwork dragons, as well as underground tombs with extensive wall paintings. Finally, the exhibition displays cross-cultural connections with such objects as two early Buddha images, a glass bowl made in Rome, and clay heads that capture different foreign faces.

Fig. 2   Gold pectoral (cat. no. 80). Sixteen Kingdoms, Former Yan (337–70), excavated in 1980 from tomb No. 6 at Wangzifenshan, Shiertaixiang, Chaoyang, Liaoning Province. *Photo courtesy of Chaoyang County Museum.*

3a

3b

Fig. 3a and 3b (detail)   Han-Jin bronze mirror (cat. no. 27). Han and Jin dynasties (202 BCE–420 CE), excavated from a tomb in Sandaohaozidong, Liaoyang, Liaoning Province, 1993–97. *Photo courtesy of Liaoning Provincial Museum.*

Notes

[1] Annette L. Juliano and Judith A. Lerner. *Monks and Merchants, Silk Road Treasures from Northwest China*. New York: Harry N. Abrams, Inc and Asia Society, 2001: 51.

[2] The Great Wall has a long history actually beginning as a series of defensive walls built during the Eastern Zhou period by competing feudal states; these walls were built to deter incursions of northern nomadic tribes and to fend off periodic attempts by neighboring states from acquiring more territory. See Arthur Waldron. *The Great Wall from History to Myth*. Cambridge, England and New York: Cambridge University Press, 1990.

[3] Ying-shih Yü, *Trade and Expansion in Han China: A Study in the Structure of Sino-Barbarian Economic Relations*. 1967:251. Henry Serruys, "A Note on China's Northern Frontiers," *Monumenta Serica*. 1969: 50.

[4] Cao, D., Zheng, Y., Bao, Q. et al. "Ancient DNA sheds light on the origin and migration patterns of the Xianbei Confederation," *Archaeological and Anthropological Sciences*. November 24, 2023.15: 9–10.

[5] Charles Holcombe, "Foreign Relations," Chapter 13:297. Edited by Albert E. Dien and Keith N. Knapp. *The Cambridge History of China: II: The Six Dynasties 220–589*. Cambridge University Press, London, 2019.

[6] Charles Holcombe, "The Xianbei in Chinese History," *Early Medieval China*, 2019. Fan Ye 范晔 , Hou Han shu 后汉书 (Beijing: Zhonghua shuju, 1965), 90.2985. This history of the Later Han was not compiled until the fifth century and therefore should be consulted with caution. An earlier appearance of the term, Xianbei, in the *Chuci* 楚辞 (472–221 BCE) refers to a type of ornamental belt buckle, rather than to a people. See Lin Gan 林幹 , Dong-Hu shi 东胡史 (Huhehaote: Nei-Menggu renmin chubanshe, 2007), 71–72.

[7] See Sarah Laursen's dissertation for a list of the other textual sources, containing commentary on the Xianbei and other nomadic groups; however, the Weishu was the best resource. See "Leaves that Sway: Gold Cup Ornaments from Northeast China," University of Pennsylvania, 2011: 13–14 (UMI Number 3463014).

[8] Ibid., 186211.

[9] Yuwen were descendants of the nomadic Xiongnu, who became assimilated with the Xianbei.

[10] After the Northern Yan fell in 439, the Tuoba Xianbei consolidated their control of north China by conquering Gansu province; at the time several nomadic states occupied the province.

Juliano and Lerner, *Monks and Merchants* 2001: 113.

中国北方游牧民族鲜卑慕容氏

朱安耐
纽约大学古代世界研究所副研究员

中国北部的自然地貌从肥沃黄土堆积而成的农耕平原，逐渐过渡成鲜有树木生长的草原，从内蒙古延伸至整个欧亚大陆。在这里，中国稳定的农耕文化融合着以放牧为主的混合经济和以游牧为主的草原文化。汉族及少数民族杂居于此，生活在从甘肃和宁夏北部鄂尔多斯高原上的沙漠地带开始经华北、内蒙古东南部到东北地区的广大边缘地带，包括森林、山脉、沙漠和草原[1]（图1）。

图1　草原一角。照片由塞尔吉奥·提塔瑞尼（Sergio Tittarini）提供 (https://www.flicker.com/photos/ 8603336@N05/9758870183/)

尽管在北部边缘建有绵延一千五百多英里（合2413.95千米）的标志性堡垒——长城，但北方游牧民族屡次成功突破这一堡垒。在长城沿线定居的农耕民族和游牧民族之间保持着矛盾的关系，时而敌对，时而友好[2]（参见图录第91号）。在和平时期，双方在边境市场上自由交易，交换牲畜和谷物等农产品，以及玉石、丝绸、皮革和水晶等商品，"骡子、驴子、马和骆驼背着貂、旱獭、狐狸和獾的毛皮，排着长队从边境进入中原"[3]。

除了利润丰厚的贸易，中原农耕民族与周边游牧民族之间复杂的共生关系还包括军事联盟和通婚。

鲜卑是一个由多民族游牧部落或氏族组成的强大联盟。他们建立起历史上第一个游牧民族帝国，一度控制了包括蒙古高原在内的整个中国北部地区。现存文字和考古证据表明，鲜卑族很可能属于突厥化的蒙古人的一支。最新的DNA分析（2023）推测出鲜卑族的蒙古–突厥起源，他们可能源于新石器时代黑龙江流域的盆地和大兴安岭地区[4]。此外，有证据表明鲜卑人曾多次南迁，并在以汉族为主导的农耕社会附近定居。活跃在北方的大多数游牧民族都来自这一地区及内蒙古一带[5]。

在汉代（前206—公元220）典籍中，出现过关于鲜卑族（以及匈奴等少数民族）的零星记载。有学者提出汉语典籍最早提及鲜卑族的时间可能是公元49年，也有人认为是《后汉书》（25—220）中两个较晚的时间——120年和127年[6]。由于鲜卑及其他部分游牧民族没有文字，因此关于其游牧活动、文化习俗、军事活动及其与北方边境和内蒙古地区汉人交往的记录几乎都是通过汉语典籍留存下来的，其中尤以朝代史书为多[7]。

尽管鲜卑人准确的种族起源仍是个谜，但DNA分析初步证实了学术界关于其身份和来源的假设。关于鲜卑族各部落及大多数北方游牧民族的研究一直存在不确定性，部分原因是缺乏该民族自身撰写的记录。此外，当时较小的部落常常为了获取保护或促进经济稳定与提高军事实力，而与较大的部落合并，这种结盟的习俗进一步增加了研究的复杂性。例如，当鲜卑人战胜另一个强大的部落（如北匈奴）时，敌对部落的幸存者会加入胜利者的部落，并改变自己的身份，成为鲜卑人。如今，随着DNA技术应用于北方游牧民族墓地的考古发现，这一情况正逐渐改变。例如，现在我们可以利用新技术来分析金牌上的图像，并借此了解古代金饰工艺[8]。

如前所述，鲜卑族出现在汉代，最早是东胡（东部游牧民族）联盟的一部分。前177年，东胡被匈奴打败，鲜卑人和乌桓人从东胡联盟中分裂出来，分成几支向北方和西方迁徙。 后来在檀石槐（？—181）的有力领导下，分散的鲜卑部落团结起来，占据匈奴故地。由于统治如此广袤的地区是相当大的挑战，檀石槐将领土划分成三个行政军事区域，其中他最重视的是西部的鄂尔多斯高原上的沙漠一带。西部地区从今甘肃敦煌一直延伸到河北北部（怀来一带），由鲜卑拓跋氏（也称"拓跋鲜卑"）治理[9]；中部地区面积较小，位于今河北北部的中部地区（唐山至怀来一带），由鲜卑慕容氏（也称"慕容鲜卑"）控制；东部地区从今河北唐山至辽宁一带，由鲜卑宇文氏（也称"宇文鲜卑"）统治。

然而，几次权力斗争和外部军事的威胁，导致联盟瓦解。 在短暂的团结过后，235年鲜卑联盟再次分裂，各个部落流散。慕容鲜卑在辽宁朝阳一带定居，到342年控制了东北大部分地区，先后建立起四个政权（时间上有部分重叠），国号均为"燕"。慕容鲜卑的文化通常被描述为混合型文化，既保有游牧习俗，又与中原文化紧密相连。四个燕国中三个由慕容氏建立，第四个是汉化政权。

本次展览聚焦于前燕（337—370）、后燕（384—407）和北燕（407—436）的艺术、文化和社会。436年，汉化程度最高的北燕被拓跋鲜卑征服，拓跋鲜卑建立了北魏（386—534），征服并统一了中国北方（439）[10]。 时已汉化的慕容鲜卑与中国北方的汉族和少数民族混居，彻底同化。

本次展览以朝阳市及其周边地区出土的三燕考古发现为主，反映了慕容鲜卑丰富多元的文化，并展示了三条文化线索的交织。慕容鲜卑是马背上的游牧民族，他们在马具上花费大量心思，生产了最早的马镫，并制作出有镂空镀金青铜装饰的马鞍。镂空金饰是慕容鲜卑马具的标志之一，有趣的是，同时期的韩国和日本马具也有同样的特点。

游牧民族艺术的另一个重要特征是大量使用黄金，从鹿等珍奇兽类牌饰到耳环、头饰和胸饰均可见（图2）。在慕容鲜卑金饰中有一种头饰叫"步摇"，形似挂在枝头的细叶，随脚步而摇动（参见图录第61号）。本次展览还展出了铜镜（图3）、砚台、金印、龙纹带具等中原文物及墓葬壁画。 展品中还包括两尊早期佛像、一件罗马产玻璃碗及少数民族或外国人面孔的泥塑头像等，体现了不同民族与国家间跨文化的联系。

图2　新月形牌饰（参见图录第80号）

3a   3b

图 3 "长宜子生"镜（参见图录第 27 号）

注释：

[1] Annette L. Juliano and Judith A. Lerner. *Monks and Merchants, Silk Road Treasures from Northwest China*. New York: Harry N. Abrams, Inc and Asia Society, 2001: 51.

[2] 长城历史悠久，始于东周时期各诸侯国修建的一系列防御性城墙。其目的在于阻止北方游牧部落的入侵，并抵御邻国获取更多领土的企图。见 "Arthur Waldron, *The Great Wall from History to Myth*. Cambridge, England and New York: Cambridge University Press, 1990."。

[3] Ying-shih Yü, *Trade and Expansion in Han China: A Study in the Structure of Sino-Barbarian Economic Relations*. 1967:251. Henry Serruys, "A Note on China's Northern Frontiers," *Monumenta Serica*. 1969: 50.

[4] Cao, D., Zheng, Y., Bao, Q. et al. "Ancient DNA sheds light on the origin and migration patterns of the Xianbei Confederation," *Archaeological and Anthropological Sciences*. November 24, 2023.15: 9–10.

[5] Charles Holcombe, "Foreign Relations," Chapter 13:297. Edited by Albert E. Dien and Keith N. Knapp. *The Cambridge History of China: II: The Six Dynasties 220–589*. Cambridge University Press, London, 2019.

[6] Charles Holcombe，"The Xianbei in Chinese History," *Early Medieval China*, 2019. 范晔：《后汉书》卷九十，中华书局，1965，第2985页。《后汉书》直到五世纪才编纂完成，因此应持保留态度。"鲜卑"一词较早在《楚辞》（前472—前221）中出现过，指的并非一个民族，而是指胡人挂在腰上的带扣。见林幹：《东胡史》，内蒙古人民出版社，2007，第71—72页。

[7] 关于提到鲜卑的其他文字记录见莎拉·劳尔森的论文，但《魏书》是最好的资料来源。见 "'Leaves that Sway: Gold Cup Ornaments from Northeast China,' University of Pennsylvania, 2011: 13–14 (UMI Number 3463014)."。

[8] 同上书，第186—211页。

[9] 宇文氏是游牧民族匈奴的后裔，后被鲜卑族同化。

[10] 北燕灭亡后，439年拓跋鲜卑征服了甘肃，巩固了对华北地区的控制。见 "Juliano and Lerner, *Monks and Merchants*，2001:113."。

A Review of Archaeological Research on Three Yan Culture

Tian Likun

Former Director of Chaoyang County Museum, Liaoning Provincial Museum, and Liaoning Provincial Institute of Cultural Relics and Archaeology

In the early years of the Cao Wei dynasty Mohuba, the leader of a tribe of steppe-nomads known as the Murong Xianbei 慕容鲜卑 settled north of the Great Wall and established a succession of states in Northeast Asia that ruled during the third and fifth centuries CE. Mohuba settled his clan in western Liaoning, traditionally known as the Liaoxi region. Mohuba's grandson, Shegui 涉归, later moved the tribes to the northeast region of modern Liaoning, known as Liaodong. In the tenth year of the Taikang era of the Western Jin dynasty (289 CE), Shegui's son, Murong Wei 慕容廆, relocated the capital to Qingshan in Tuhe, and in the fourth year of the Yuankang era (294 CE), he moved the capital to Jicheng. In the third year of the Xiankang era of the Eastern Jin dynasty (337 CE), Murong Wei's son, Murong Huang 慕荣皝, declared himself prince of Yan in Jicheng, marking the official creation of the Former Yan state. In the seventh year of the Xiankang era (341 CE), Murong Huang built Longcheng ("Dragon City") to the north of Liucheng and the west of Longshan, and relocated his capital to Longcheng the following year. In February of the sixth year of the Yonghe era (350 CE), the Former Yan advanced southward to the Central Plains, and Longcheng became the old capital. In November of the fifth year of the Taihe era (370 CE), the Former Qin attacked the city of Ye, capital of the Former Yan, and the Former Yan fell.

In January of the ninth year of the Taiyuan era (384 CE), Murong Chui established the Later Yan, and in March of the first year of the Long'an era (397 CE), Murong Bao abandoned Zhongshan and retreated to Longcheng. In the third year of the Yixi era (407 CE), Gao Yun (a descendant of the royal house of Goguryeo, who was adopted into the Later Yan imperial house) and [his general] Feng Ba killed Murong Xi in Longcheng, and the Later Yan fell. Gao Yun and Feng Ba established the Northern Yan. In May of the second year of the Taiyan era of the Northern Wei dynasty (436 CE) Longcheng was attacked and the Northern Yan fell.

During the more than two hundred years recounted above, the Liaoxi region of northeastern China was home to a variety of ethnic groups, and the interaction with and integration of the Murong Xianbei and Han cultures were main themes throughout this historical period. "Three Yan [or San Yan] culture" refers to the cultures that formed within this dynamic context, with present-day Chaoyang as the center of cultural diffusion and the Murong Xianbei tribe its principal representative. Three Yan culture was influenced by Han culture, while it also absorbed various elements from the Xiongnu 匈奴, Wuhuan 乌桓, Fuyu 夫余 (or Buyeo), Goguryeo 高句丽, and Tuoba Xianbei 拓跋鲜卑 cultures. Its distinctive features and rich connotations are revealed by the archaeological remains of the Former Yan and Later Yan, the states founded by Murong Xianbei, as well as of the Northern Yan established by Gao Yun and Feng Ba.

Since the discovery of the tombs at Fangshen village in Beipiao county[1] in 1956, which was recognized as a Murong Xianbei burial site of the Jin dynasty, archaeological research on the Wei, Jin, and Sixteen Kingdoms period in the Liaoxi region can be divided into three phases: prior to 1989, 1990–1999, and from 2000 to the present.

Phase I: Prior to 1989

Before 1989, in addition to the analytical comparison with other tombs to deduce the age and nature of the burial site, the academic community also paid close attention to the study of Three Yan culture. Following Su Bai's examination of the Xianbei remains in northeastern China and eastern Inner Mongolia in 1977, he affirmed that the Fanshen tomb in Beipiao county was a Xianbei site related to the Murong tribe and the "gold floral crown ornaments" unearthed there were presumed to be the *buyao*, a type of ornament (fig. 1). Moreover, Su believed that "inlaid rings" found at the site were common in Xiongnu culture and the burial custom of interring daily utensils with the deceased showed significant Han influence, indicating a close relationship between the Murong Xianbei and Han people. The golden jewelry found at the Bao'ansi stone tomb in Yi county, dated earlier than the Fangshen tomb, was considered by Su Bai to be "similar to those of the Murong Xianbei remains, while the pottery and various bead ornaments were similar to those of the Tuoba Xianbei." A gilt repoussé seated Buddha statue from the Feng Sufu tomb is the earliest Buddha statue discovered in Liaoxi, indicating that Northern Yan was an important center for the dissemination of Buddhism in the northern area. The glassware was likely imported from Western countries, "perhaps through the Rouran Khaganate tribe."[2] Further research by An Jiayao revealed that the five pieces of glassware unearthed from the Feng Sufu tomb were products of the Roman Empire.[3]

Fig. 1   Flowering tree—shaped gold *buyao* head ornament. Sixteen Kingdoms—Former Yan (337–70). Unearthed from Xituanshan, Muyingzi, Chaoyang. Photo courtesy of Chaoyang Museum.

In the fall of 1981, at the inaugural meeting of the Liaoning Provincial Archaeological and Museum Society, two research papers, "Preliminary study of Xianbei horse tack in the Chaoyang area" and "Notes on Xianbei *buyao* ornaments,"[4] were presented. These papers disclosed information on some of the horse trappings and *buyao* ornaments unearthed in Chaoyang that had not been previously published and raised questions related to the two subjects.

After the disclosure of two sets of complete horse tack from tomb M154 in Xiaomintun, Anyang[5], and the mural-decorated tomb in Yuantaizi, Chaoyang[6] Yang Hong promptly pointed out that the early fourth century was a critical period for the development of horse tack, for which the complete sets unearthed from the tombs in Xiaomintun and Yuantaizi provide typical specimens. Horse tack found in Goguryeo tombs in Korea shared similarities with those from Xiaomintun and Yuantaizi, suggesting that Goguryeo was influenced by the style represented by the tack found in Xiaomintun tomb M154. The same influence was also observed in the remains of Silla in the southern part of the Korean peninsula and even extended to Japan.[7] In 1987, Qi Dongfang, when examining gilt-bronze tack excavated from the Fujinoki tomb in Nara, Japan, traced the cultural origins of horse tack in the Korean peninsula and Japan to the Chinese horse tack represented by Xiaomintun tomb M154, the mural-decorated tomb in Yuandaizi, and the tomb of Feng Sufu.[8]

In 1986, Xu Ji, who had worked for many years at the regional Chaoyang County Museum, submitted a paper titled "Preliminary Investigation on the Remains of the Xianbei Murong Clan" at the sixth annual meeting of the Chinese Archaeological Society.[9] The paper focused on previously unpublished materials that were found from 1973 to 1979 in the vicinity of Chaoyang city and Fangshi village of Beipiao county, including various gilt-bronze tack unearthed in tomb M8 of Beigou, Beipiao county, the earliest of its kind found in the Chaoyang area. Combined with previous discoveries and studies, the article summarizes the characteristics of Murong Xianbei culture from four aspects: pottery, headwear and ornaments, horse tack and arms, and burial customs. The author believes that the Murong Xianbei remains can be divided into three groups: "the first group reveals the ethnic culture of the Xianbei Murong clan," "the second group of artifacts is imported from the Han, Xiongnu, or other ethnic groups," and "the third group shows the influence of advanced technology and culture of neighboring ethnic groups to the Xianbei Murong clan." The author further divides the Murong Xianbei remains into four groups and six segments in terms of era. The first group, represented by the Shegen tombs in Horqin Left Rear Banner, Inner Mongolia, dates back to the late Eastern Han dynasty or earlier. The second group is mainly represented by early Beigou tombs in Fangshen village, Beipiao county, dated to the Western Jin dynasty. The third group, centered around Chaoyang city, includes late Beigou tombs in Fangshen villages, Beipiao county, and the Yuantaizi and Yaoeryingzi tombs near the ancient Han city of Liucheng, in southern Chaoyang. The tombs of Xiaomintun, Anyang should be classified in this group. The fourth group is represented by the tombs of Cui Yu of the Later Yan and the Feng family of the Northern Yan.

A paper titled "The zoning and classification of Wei, Jin, and Sixteen Kingdoms burials in the Northern Region," published in 1987[10], classified the Wei, Jin, and Sixteen Kingdoms-period tombs in the Daling River basin of Liaoxi as being in the third period of the Northeastern region, i.e. the Sixteen Kingdoms period. The paper also analyzed the historical background and relationship with the Central Plains.

The "Preliminary study of the murals of the Jin tombs in Yuantaizi, Chaoyang" discussed the composition and painting techniques of the Jin tomb murals in Yuantaizi, Chaoyang.[11]

Although the number of published papers and research findings during this period was small, their importance cannot be overstated. For example, the discovery of a golden *buyao* in the Jin tomb in Fangshen village, Beipiao, directly linked the tomb owner to the Murong Xianbei clan mentioned in historical documents. The two stone tablets found in the Yaojingou stone coffin tomb in Chaoyang, engraved with "*Yan Jianxing Shi Nian* [tenth year] *Changli Taishou Qinghe Wucheng Cui Yu*" and "*Yan Jianxing Shi Nian* [tenth year] *Changli Taishou Qinghe Dongwucheng Cui Yu*," provide clear documentation about the tomb's date, as well as the tomb owner's official position, hometown, and name.[12] Based on the four accompanying seals, the stone coffin tomb in Xiguanyingzi, Beipiao, has been identified as belonging to Feng Sufu, the younger brother of Northern Yan king Feng Ba, who died in the seventh year of Taiping (415 CE).[13] These findings provide accurate references and standards for understanding the cultural landscape of archaeological remains of the Wei, Jin, and Sixteen Kingdoms period in the Liaoxi region, thus laying a solid foundation for further research.

The view that the glassware unearthed from Feng Sufu's tomb is an "imported Western product" and that the horse tack found in Goguryeo, Silla, and Japan were influenced by the horse tack in Xiaomintun tomb M154 and the mural-decorated tombs in Yuantaizi is groundbreaking, broadening the perspective for future in-depth research. In particular, Xu Ji's comprehensive analysis of cultural factors and periodization of the Wei, Jin, and Sixteen Kingdoms archaeological remains in Liaoxi, as well as the proposal of the concept of "Murong Xianbei culture," goes beyond the specific dating of tombs or the identification of ethnic groups, marking a major advancement in archaeological nomenclature of the Wei, Jin, and Sixteen Kingdoms period in the Liaoxi region.

Phase II: 1990–1999

The discoveries and studies in the 1990s and earlier laid a solid foundation for advancing research on the Wei, Jin, and Sixteen Kingdoms-period remains in Liaoxi. However, it must be acknowledged that during this period, published articles mostly focused on specific descriptions, dating, or identifying the ethnic affiliations of tombs. Comparisons between sites were limited to dating references. The naming of remains was simply based on location and dating, or the name and ethnic affiliation of the tomb owner, such as the Jin tombs in Fangshen village, Beipiao; the Jin tombs in Xiaomintun, Anyang; the Eastern Jin mural-decorated tombs in Yuantaizi; the Feng Sufu tomb of the Northern Yan; and the Cui Yu tomb of the Later Yan. The lack of comprehensive understanding and systematic research resulted in some tombs being broadly categorized as Xianbei remains, Xianbei horse tack, or Murong Xianbei culture. Such a generalization fails to explain phenomena like the similarity of coffin shapes, with a large front and a small back, in the wooden coffin tomb of Shiertaizi[14], and the Cui Yu tomb, where one coffin belonged to the Murong Xianbei and the other to a prominent family in the Central Plains and were a hundred years apart in time. Additionally, some important remains, such as the Yuantaizi tomb, commonly referred to as the "mural-decorated tomb of the Eastern Jin dynasty," have naturally been excluded from the study of the "Xianbei remains" or "Murong Xianbei culture," impeding a comprehensive and accurate overview of the culturally connected archaeological remains of the Wei, Jin, and the Sixteen Kingdoms period in the Liaoxi region.

In response to this issue, in the "Preliminary study on the Three Yan culture remains," which was submitted to the 1990 Dalian International Academic Conference on Archaeology around the Bohai Sea, the archaeological remains of the Wei, Jin, and Sixteen Kingdoms period in the Liaoxi region were named "Three Yan culture."[15] The study proposed that the tomb groups in Shiertai, Shegen, Xinshengtun, and Fangshen village in Beipiao were the remains of the Murong Xianbei before the establishment of the Yan state and thus the origin of the Three Yan remains. It is also argued that the Three Yan remains were formed under the strong influence of Han culture on the Murong Xianbei, as well as varying degrees of influence from the Xiongnu, Goguryeo, and others. Therefore, the remains had their own distinct cultural characteristics, and should not be simply regarded as Murong Xianbei remains. The proposal of the Three Yan culture categorization was both an inevitable result of the accumulation of research and a requirement for in-depth research, signifying a new stage in archaeological research on the Wei, Jin, and Sixteen Kingdoms period in the Liaoxi region.

Other scholars, such as Xu Yongjie, Tian Likun, Zheng Junlei, and Qiao Liang, as well as Shang Xiaobo and Chen Ping, have also contributed to the identification of Murong Xianbei remains and the discussion of their relationships with other Xianbei remains.

Scholars who participated in the discussion of the classification of the tombs of the Wei, Jin, and

Sixteen Kingdoms period in Liaoxi include Xu Yongjie[16], Tian Likun[17], Zheng Junlei[18], and Qiao Liang[19], as well as Shang Xiaobo[20] and Chen Ping.[21]

The specific case studies are as follows:

Research on the representative artifact of the Murong Xianbei, the gold *buyao*, began with the publication of "*Buyao, buyao* crown, and *buyao* ornament" in 1991.[22] This study compared the gold *buyao* ornament mentioned in the *Xu Han Shu, Yu Fu Zhi* [Sequel of the Book of Han, records of ceremonial attire and carriages] with regalia from ethnic burials. The *buyao* was part of the grand attire worn by Eastern Han empresses when they paid homage at the imperial ancestral temple. The *buyao* unearthed in the Liaoxi region were compared with the gold crown from the tomb of an elite Sarmatian woman in Novocherkassk, dating to the first century CE, and the gold crown unearthed from Tillya-tepe tomb 6 near modern Sheberghan in northern Afghanistan, dating from the early first century BCE to the first century CE. By analyzing these artifacts, the paper argues that *buyao* ornament originated from the West and *buyao* crowns formally appeared around the beginning of the Common Era, later spreading eastward across Eurasia, through China, and on to Japan. The author also points out that the ornaments were popular for more than six hundred years, making them a noteworthy cultural phenomenon. The book *Xianbei, Three Kingdoms, Ancient Tombs—Cultural Exchanges between China, Korea, and Japan in Ancient Times*[23], published in 1996, further supported this view by studying a "wreath made of lapis lazuli and carnelian beads decorated with swaying gold leaves" unearthed at the royal cemetery of Ur in the southern Mesopotamian plain, dating to 2600–2500 BCE. The study regarded the gold *buyao* as an ornament that originated in Western Asia and the Western Regions beyond Dunhuang, then passed into China—where it was adopted especially by the Murong Xianbei—before spreading to the Korean peninsula and Japan.

As for horse tack and its relationship with Goguryeo in the Korean peninsula and during Japan's Kofun period, several scholars, including Wei Cuncheng[24], Qi Dongfang[25], Tian Likun[26], Dong Gao[27], Xu Bingkun[28], Sun Shoudao[29], Zhang Keju[30], and Wang Wei[31], among others, have contributed to the discussion.

In 1985, Shin Kyung Chul of Pusan National University in Korea published "A Study of Ancient Stirrups,"[32] which divided the stirrups unearthed from Bokcheon-dong, Dongnae in Korea into two types, A and B, tracing their origins back to the stirrups unearthed from the Xiaomintun tomb M154 and the Feng Sufu tomb. In 1996, this study was translated into Chinese and published by Yao Yitian, enabling the Chinese academic community to learn from the achievements of Korean scholars.

Through archaeological investigations, combined with analysis of classic literature, the location of Jicheng, the first capital city of Former Yan, was confirmed, constituting another important research result of this period.[33]

In the field of physical anthropology, "Research on human skeletal remains from Xianbei tombs of the Wei and Jin periods in Chaoyang,"[34] published in 1996, concluded that the skull characteristics of the owners of the Shiertai vertical earthen pit tomb fit the characteristics of the "Ancient Mongolian Plateau Type," providing strong anthropological support for the assumption that the Shiertai tomb is a Murong Xianbei remain.

The Japanese academic community also showed great interest in the archaeological discoveries of the Wei, Jin, and Sixteen Kingdoms period in the Liaoxi region. Starting in 1996, the Liaoning Provincial Institute of Cultural Relics and Archaeology and the Nara National Research Institute for Cultural Properties of Japan conducted collaborative research on the theme "Research and conservation of ancient Asian capital remains—excavated iron and other metal artifacts from the Three Yan capital sites."[35]

In 1995, a symposium on Three Yan culture was held in Chaoyang by the Liaoning Provincial Institute of Archaeology. During the event, Dong Gao, Lang Chenggang, Li Xinquan, Zhou Yali, and Shang Xiaobo presented papers on the study of Three Yan culture.[36]

Phase III: 2000 to the Present

During the decade from 1990 to 1999, over forty tombs from the Wei, Jin, and Sixteen Kingdoms period in the Liaoxi region were unveiled to the public, including tombs of various architectural styles, from vertical earthen pit tombs and brick chamber tombs to stone chamber tombs and stone coffin tombs. One ancient tomb discovered during this period in Jinzhou, Liaoning, the tomb of Li Hui, was even clearly dated. Building on these new findings, the paper "Types and phases of the burials of Three Yan culture,"[37] published in 2000, categorized Three Yan culture tombs into three phases and eight types, with fewer architectural styles in the early period, a dramatic increase in the middle phase, and a tendency toward consistency of style in the late phase. Throughout this process, cultural elements indigenous to the Murong Xianbei, represented by trapezoidal vertical earthen pit tombs with wooden coffins, remained dominant. Although the middle period saw the emergence of brick chamber tombs representing Han culture of the Central Plains, stone-slab-covered chamber tombs representing this culture during Han and Wei rule of Liaodong, and rectangular vertical earthen pit tombs with wooden coffins representing Fuyu culture, each with its own origin, were absent or rare in the late period. On the other hand, stone coffin tombs or stone chamber tombs, representing the traditional culture of Liaoxi, developed under the influence of trapezoidal vertical earthen pit tombs with wooden coffins from the beginning, with stone coffin tombs with small fronts and large backs becoming the predominant late-period structure. The evolution of tomb architecture styles aligns with the Murong Xianbei's entry into the Liaoxi region and their interactions, integration, and eventual fusion with Han culture and other neighboring cultures. The classification and periodization of Three Yan culture burials provides a valuable framework for archaeological research of the Wei, Jin, and Sixteen Kingdoms period in the Liaoxi region.

The Lamadong cemetery in Beipiao is the largest and most extensively excavated tomb site from the Wei, Jin, and Sixteen Kingdoms period in Liaoxi. It boasts the highest quantity and variety of excavated artifacts. While there are evident similarities in burial relics of this period with those found in the past, there are significant differences in tomb structures and burial customs that cannot be ignored. In the paper titled "Questions around the Lamadong cemetery of the Three Yan culture,"[38] submitted in the year 2000 to the Conference on Ancient Cultures in Northeast China from the Third to the Tenth Centuries, a comprehensive discussion was conducted regarding the Lamadong cemetery's date, characteristics, and ethnic affiliation. It was suggested that the Lamadong cemetery's dating falls within the range of 289 to 350 CE. Combined with historical records that state that the Murong Xianbei attacked Fuyu twice and captured a large number of its people, the paper proposed that the main population in the Lamadong cemetery consisted of Fuyu people relocated to Jicheng by the Murong Xianbei.

The mural-decorated Yuantaizi tomb in Chaoyang, discovered in 1984, is an important archaeological finding of the Wei, Jin, and Sixteen Kingdoms period, but there is significant disagreement regarding its exact dating. In the paper "Reconsideration of the Yuantaizi tomb,"[39] published in 2002, the researcher reconstructed partially preserved ink inscriptions on the tomb walls as "□□□ [year] second month Ji□ [Su] □ [Wu (or Geng)] Zi..." Combined with the fact that the tomb structure and mural's contents owe their origin to the mural-decorated tombs of the Wei-Jin period in Liaoyang, as well as the major events that took place in the Liaohai region at the time, the remaining inscriptions were further restored to "[Yonghe shi nian] er yue Ji [Maoshuo shi (er shi er) ri Wu (geng)] Zi," (Tenth year of Yonghe, 354 CE), or [Taihe yuan nian] er yue Ji [Sishuo er shi er ri Wu] Zi", (First year of Taihe, 366 CE). This confirms that the tomb belongs to the "prominent Liaodong clans" who were relocated by Murong Huang from Liaodong to Jicheng in the ninth year of Xianhe in the Eastern Jin dynasty (334 CE). This new achievement provides a reliable reference date for the study of tombs from the Wei, Jin, and Sixteen Kingdoms period in the Liaohai region.

"A review of the research on Murong Xianbei and Three Yan culture in the Liaoxi region," a paper published in 2002[40], examines several characteristics of Three Yan archaeological findings: the coherence of Xianbei burials and archaeological sites as seen in palaces, imperial gardens, and cemetery complexes; the significance of dated Three Yan tombs with examples of the Li, Cui, and Feng tombs; the presence of typical metal artifacts from Xianbei and Three Yan culture, in particular, gold buyao ornaments and gilt bronze horse tack; and the distinctiveness of Xianbei burials in the Daling River basin—a result of the eastward spread of the Murong clan's swaying leaves ornaments.

The "1998 Excavation report of the Lamadong cemetery in Beipiao, Liaoning,"[41] published in 2004, concludes that the Three Yan culture tombs in Lamadong primarily belong to the Jin dynasty's Murong Xianbei cultural sphere in the Daling River basin in Liaoxi. To be more precise, these are tombs of the Former Yan and the period shortly before that with a dominance of Murong Xianbei culture, although they exhibit relatively deep Han influence and potential incorporation of cultural elements from other groups such as Fuyu. Their dating falls approximately between the late third century CE and the mid-fourth century CE, corresponding to the period from shortly after Murong Wei led the clan back to the Daling River basin in 289 CE to the rule of the Former Yan (337–70 CE) established by Murong Huang.

In the 2009 "Study of Xianbei burials,"[42] the Shegen and Liujiazi tomb sites in Horqin Left Rear Banner and Left Central Banner, Inner Mongolia, were identified as remains of the Wuhuan culture, dating to the mid- to late Eastern Han period.

A 2013 paper, "Reconsideration of the dating of some remains associated with the Xianbei,"[43] argued that most of the pottery, gold, silver, and gilded bronze artifacts collected from the Liujiazi cemetery in Inner Mongolia were similar to items found in northern Xianbei tombs from the Western Jin to Sixteen Kingdoms period, as well as Jin tombs in the Central Plains and southern regions, rather than resembling artifacts from the Eastern Han dynasty. It was, therefore, suggested that, with the exception of two wreath-bottom pottery jars, the dating of Liujiazi cemetery should fall within the Western Jin to Sixteen Kingdoms period, and not extend back to the late Eastern Han period.

A gilded circular perforated bronze belt ornament and a gilded silver circular perforated bronze ornament unearthed from the Liujiazi cemetery were used to fasten belt buckles to saddles. A similar horse tack component was found in Chaoyang in a cemetery dating to the late Western Jin period, indicating that the dating of the Liujiazi cemetery should not be earlier than or contemporaneous with the Chaoyang tomb site. It also suggests that the Liujiazi cemetery belongs to the Three Yan culture.

Apart from the study of the burials, gold buyao and horse tack remained focal points of interest during this period. "A summary of research on Murong Xianbei and Three Yan culture in the Liaoxi region" used the example of the golden *buyao* ornament found in the Tiancaogou cemetery to discuss its usage and arrangement.

Based on the historic record and the golden *buyao* found in the Liaoxi region, the 2006 publication "A study of *buyao*"[44] categorizes *buyao* in the region south of the Great Wall from the Warring States to the Sixteen Kingdoms into three types: "*chuizhu*" (beaded pendants), "*jueshou*" (birds and beasts), and "*huashu*" (flowers and trees). Among them, *chuizhu* tends to sway easily with movement, hence the name "*buyao*," which literally means swaying with steps or "step and sway." The gold *buyao* ornament that was mentioned in the *Xu Han Shu, Yu Fu Zhi* [Sequel of the Book of Han, records of ceremonial attire and carriages] and which was worn by empresses during temple visits, belongs to the *jueshou* type, while the typical Three Yan culture *buyao* falls under the *huashu* type. Both the *jueshou* and *huashu* types were introduced from the Western regions, but they arrived in China through different routes and at different times. The *jueshou buyao* was introduced to the Central Plains via the Silk Road during the Han dynasty, while the *huashu buyao* was brought to the Liaoxi region by the Murong Xianbei when they migrated southward from the grasslands, shortly after the establishment of the Cao Wei state. These two types of *buyao* both exhibit the swaying feature and were subsequently named "*buyao*" upon their introduction to the East. These three types of *buyao* have distinct materials, structures, and uses, however. It is not, therefore, appropriate to confuse them without differentiating among types. Further research is needed to explore the relationship between the Murong Xianbei clan and *buyao* ornaments.

In the 2012 paper "Discovery and study of gold *buyao* ornaments,"[45] artifacts with swaying metal leaf decorations such as plaques, earrings, belt ornaments, and horse tack were collectively referred to as "gold *buyao* ornaments." The study extensively analyzed all these gold *buyao* ornaments, discussing the current state of research, and highlighting existing issues.

The 2013 paper "*Jindang* and *buyao*—an exploration of crown decorations for Han-Jin nobles"[46] discussed Murong Xianbei's gold *buyao* while exploring crown decorations for noblewomen of the Han and Jin dynasties. "*Buyao* ornaments and the Murong Xianbe clan,"[47] published in 2014, systematically reviewed historical records of *buyao*, *buyao* crowns, and related archaeological findings, providing an extensive examination of the relationship between the Murong Xianbei clan and *buyao* ornaments. The study argued that Mohuba, who settled in Liaoxi during the early Cao Wei period, was the "Grand Murong general" of the middle section of the Xianbei confederation led by Tanshihua during the late Eastern Han period. The paper also suggested that the term "Murong" in the *Jin Shu, Murong Wei Zai Ji* [Book of Jin, records of Murong Wei] could be a misinterpretation of *buyao* due to phonetic similarity.

The study of horse stirrups is a focal point within the field of horse tack research. Published in 2002, "The origin of stirrups"[48] was a comprehensive study of several hundred stirrups using Silk Road artifacts (including some depicted in wall paintings and sculptures) found across the Eurasian continent. The study observed that the single stirrup is not intended for riding and its function is fundamentally different from that of the common stirrup. As such, it should not be confused with the common stirrup in academic research. The 2009 publication "A new discussion on the origin of stirrups and their spread in the medieval period"[49] argued that "currently known single stirrups should not be excluded from the developmental theories of stirrups." The author speculated that the origin of horse stirrups might be related to the Wuhuan people, who were known for their horsemanship during the Han and Jin dynasties. Yang Hong, in his work discussing the stirrups of the Feng Sufu tomb and the development of Chinese horse armor, emphasized the significance and influence of the invention of stirrups and the use of horse armor.[50]

Published in 2013, "A new examination of ancient stirrups"[51] proposed that early stirrups from the third to fourth centuries could be categorized into three lineages based on material selection, crafting techniques, and structure: the *qumu* (bent wood frame) stirrup, the *zhuomu* (chopped wood frame) stirrup, and the *roumu* (circled wood frame) stirrup. The first two types originated in the Liaoxi region, while the last was found in the Yangtze River basin.

Fig. 2   Gilded openwork bronze saddle pommel. Sixteen Kingdoms-Former Yan (337–70). Unearthed in 1988 from Tomb 88M1, Shi'ertai brick factory, Chaoyang. *Photo courtesy of Chaoyang Museum.*

The next area of study is Gaoqiao saddles or saddles with high pommels (fig. 2). Published in 2003, "Research on newly discovered Three Yan horse tack in Beipiao"[52] categorized the pommels of the Gaoqiao saddle found in various East Asian countries into four types: "In terms of the appearance of horse tack, the Murong Xianbei is the earliest, followed by Goguryeo, then the southern countries of the Korean peninsula, and finally Japan. Murong Xianbei's horse tack is a source of influence on the development of saddle pommels in other regions. The earliest Gaoqiao saddle appeared with plain slanted and arched high pommels in the early fourth century, with the near-elliptical form being a later result of its evolution. The upright style also appeared relatively early, as seen in the example of tomb No. 96 in Qixingshan, which dates to the mid-to-early-fourth century. The extended style is a variation of the upright style....This progression can also be observed in the changing patterns of saddle pommels."

The paper "On the horse tack unearthed in the Lamadong cemetery,"[53] presented at the Twelfth Gaya History International Academic Conference in Gimhae, South Korea, in 2006, classified saddle pommels into two types: Type A, an arch shape characterized by a wide upper part, a narrower lower part, and downward slanting sides, and Type B, which lacks arched shoulders, has inward slanting sides, and an overall elliptical shape. Each type is associated with its own set of bridle and stirrup, as well as distinct decorative patterns. These two types represent different cultural factors associated with the Murong Xianbei and Fuyu respectively. Saddle pommels from the Fujinoki tomb in Japan, dating to the fifth or sixth century, belong to Type A, while those from another ancient Japanese tomb, the Kondamaruyama kofun, dating to the same period, belong to Type B. These examples showcase the parallel development of Type A and Type B saddle pommels.

Based on the horse tack from Xiaomintun tomb M154 in Anyang, the 1983 publication "Reconstruction of horse tack from Jin tombs in Anyang"[54] recreated a Gaoqiao saddle composed of front and rear pommels combined with two vertical seat panels. Published in 2002, the book *Ancient*

Chinese Chariots and Horse Equipment[55] presented reconstructions of the saddles from Xiaomintun tomb M154 and the Yuantaizi tomb in painted form, utilizing the outcomes of the 1983 paper. An intact wooden saddle pommel encased in a decorative sheath was found at the Shiertaizi tomb 88M1 in Chaoyang. Based on this find, the 2006 paper "Reconstruction and related issues of Gaoqiao saddles,"[56] reconstructed a Gaoqiao saddle comprising five components: front and rear pommels, left and right seat panels, and a ridge panel. This structure was considered more reasonable in comparison to the previous reconstruction composed of only four components.

Horse trappings of the Goguryeo, Silla, and Gaya kingdoms on the Korean peninsula, as well as those of the Kofun period in Japan, have all been directly or indirectly influenced by Three Yan culture. They have, therefore, received significant attention from the academic community. Particularly noteworthy is the exquisite craftsmanship and decoration of horse tack unearthed from the Fujinoki tomb in Japan. The exact place of origin of these artifacts has been the subject of various theories, including connections to China's Liang dynasty, the Silla Kingdom on the Korean peninsula, and the eastern region of China's Northern Wei dynasty, among others. However, no consensus was reached. In the 2006 paper "Three cases of horse tack from Japan's Kofun period,"[57] a comprehensive analysis of the historical context, decorative patterns, and buckle forms led to the conclusion that the horse tack from Fujinoki tomb most likely originated from the capital city of Pyongyang in Goguryeo. The paper also discussed the influence of horse bridles of Three Yan culture on Japan's Kofun period and explored the naming of *sanlinghuan* (three-bell ring). Furthermore, in the academic literature there are discussions on topics such as horse bits with bells[58], decorative patterns[59], horseshoes[60], and more.

Between 2003 and 2006, excavations in the old city area of Chaoyang revealed the remains of the southern gate of Longcheng, the capital city during the Three Yan period. These excavations not only provided insights into the structure and historical use of the site but also accurately determined the location of the palatial city. This discovery offered crucial clues for studying the overall layout of Longcheng and its connection to the city of Ye of the Cao Wei dynasty.[61] In 2012, the publication *A New Examination of Longcheng* conducted an analytical discussion on the scientific rationale behind the selection of the site for Longcheng, the first city built by the Murong Xianbei.[62]

The discovery of large-scale architectural remains in Jinlingsi, Beipiao[63] is an important archaeological finding of this period. The 2012 essay "The Jinlingsi remains as the Hui Temple"[64] presented the argument that the Jinlingsi site is likely the location of the "Wei Temple" 廆庙 established by Murong Jun to honor his grandfather Murong Wei 慕容廆, the founder of the Former Yan. This conclusion was drawn through a comprehensive analysis of historical records, the site's location, layout characteristics, architectural structures, and the composition of artifacts.

The period also saw new research achievements in the following areas: a study of the composition and technical characteristics of the Yuantaizi tomb murals[65]; research on the preservation and study of metal artifacts[66]; examination of glassware, jade, and ceramics unearthed from the Feng Sufu tomb[67]; research on architectural components from excavations at Chaoyang's old city and the Jinlingsi site[68]; and identification of Western cultural influences on Three Yan culture.[69]

Published in 2012, the "Biological archaeological study of the ethnic affiliation of owners of the Lamadong cemetery"[70] argued that there were significant differences between the owners of the Lamadong cemetery of the Three Yan culture and those of the Shiertai vertical earthen pit tomb. The overall characteristics of the former were more similar to ancient Northeastern and Northern people with high cranial vaults. The study found a substantial genetic difference between the Lamadong owners and the Xianbei people, ruling out the possibility that they belonged to the Xianbei clan. Combined with the study of burial forms and relics as well as relevant literature, the paper concluded that the Shiertai pit tomb was associated with the Murong Xianbei, and the Lamadong cemetery of the Three Yan culture was associated with the Fuyu (Buyeo) people. This research significantly advanced the study of Three Yan culture.

Japanese and Korean scholars have made significant contributions to the study of horse tack and accessories. The Liaoning Provincial Institute of Cultural Relics and Archaeology has collaborated with the Nara National Research Institute for Cultural Properties of Japan on four projects, resulting in the publication of the Northeast Asia Archaeology Series and *Research on the Culture of Eastern Jin and Sixteen Kingdoms Capitals in the Liaoxi Region*.[71]

Over the past sixty years, archaeological research on the Wei, Jin, and Sixteen Kingdoms period in the Liaoxi region has evolved significantly. The research has progressed from the description and analysis of specific archaeological remains to a broader understanding of the overall culture known as Three Yan culture. Further studies have delved into various factors and individual cases that constitute Three Yan culture. In this regard, archaeological research on this period in the Liaoxi region has just begun, and many more issues remain to be discovered and studied.

First, it is essential to broaden the scope of investigation. The study of Three Yan culture should not be confined solely to the central area of the Liaoxi region.

Secondly, there is a need to address the typology of Three Yan culture. The Shiertai, Lamadong, and Beipiao tomb sites have unique characteristics that differentiate them from the others. These differences could potentially lead to the subdivision of Three Yan culture.

The third issue is the influence of Western culture on Three Yan culture. Gold artifacts, particularly the gold *buyao* ornament, were introduced into the Liaoxi region by the Murong Xianbei clan.[72] Glassware found in the tomb of Feng Sufu may have been imported through the Rouran Khaganate tribe.[73] The presence of the seamless pattern seen in Dahuting Han tombs in Mixian[74], coexisting with scenes depicting the Sogdian whirl dance, suggests a close connection with the Sogdian people.[75] According to historical records in the *Wei Shu*, *An Tong Zhuan* [Book of Wei biography of An Tong], "An Tong was of the northern people from Liaodong. His ancestor was An Shigao, who stayed in the Han court as a servant of the prince of Parthia. During the tumultuous years from Wei to Jin, he fled to Liaodong and settled there. His father, An Qu, served Murong Wei as the Commandant of the Palace Guards."[76] An Tong was, in fact, from the Sogdian region of the Parthian Empire. According to the epitaph of Kang Hui from the first year of the Tang Yongtai era, unearthed in Xi'an, the Former Yan dynasty once bestowed Kang Qian the title Marquess of Guiyi, indicating that he also had Sogdian origins.[77] It is undeniable that Sogdian people had joined the Former Yan regime[78], though whether the seamless pattern was introduced through them remains uncertain.

The fourth issue is the identification of the remains of the Di people in the Liaohai region. After the fall of Former Yan, a large number of Di people migrated to the Liaohai region.[79] The Sixteen Kingdoms tomb at Qianshan in Jinzhou, containing terracotta warriors and horses[80], might represent the remains of Di culture.

The fifth issue is the Goguryeo and Fuyu migration. During the reigns of Murong Wei and Murong Huang, a large number of Fuyu and Goguryeo people were relocated to the Liaoxi region. The Lamadong cemetery is believed to represent the remains of the Fuyu people who migrated to Liaoxi during the time of Murong Wei.[81] There are also clues to Goguryeo remains.[82] It is anticipated that further discoveries will lead to new research topics in the archaeology of Goguryeo, Fuyu, and the whole Sixteen Kingdoms period.

The sixth issue concerns research on the ancient capital cities of Jicheng and Longcheng. Current research on Jicheng has mostly focused on its location, while the study of Longcheng is just beginning. Archaeological sites like the Jinlingsi site and the Longteng Garden site[83] are also of significant interest.

The seventh issue is the presence of Three Yan culture artifacts on the Korean peninsula and in Japan. After the downfall of the Northern Yan, Three Yan culture disappeared in the Liaoxi region, while horse tack and gold artifacts with Three Yan cultural traits continued to be prevalent in the Korean peninsula and ancient Japan. Identifying and studying these artifacts to uncover their impact on local society, politics, economy, and culture is a meaningful endeavor.

NOTES

[1]   Chen Dawei, "Liaoning beipiao fangshencun jinmu fajue jianbao" [Briefing on the excavation of Jin tomb in Fanshen Village, Beipiao, Liaoning]. *Kaogu* [Archaeology] 1960.1: 24–26.

[2]   Su Bai, "Dongbei, Neimenggu diqu de xianbei yiji jilu zhiyi" [Remains of Xianbei in the Northeast and Inner Mongolia: A collection of Xianbei remains, vol. 1]. *Wenwu* [Cultural Relics] 1977.5:46.

[3]   An Jiayao, "Zhongguo de zaoqi boli qimin" [Early glassware in China]. *Kaogu xuebao* [Journal of Archaeology] 1984.4: 417.

[4]   Dong Gao, "Chaoyang diqu Xianbei maju de chubu yanjiu" [Preliminary study of Xianbei horse tack in the Chaoyang area] in *Liaoning sheng kaogu bowuguan xuehui chengli dahui huikan* [Proceedings of the inaugural meeting of the Liaoning Provincial Archaeological and Museum Society (1981)], 115–20. Sun Guoping "Xianbei zu de *buyao*" [Notes on Xianbei crown ornaments] in *Liaoning sheng kaogu bowuguan xuehui chengli dahui huikan* [Proceedings of the inaugural meeting of the Liaoning Provincial Archaeological and Museum Society (1981)], 121–22.

[5]   Chinese Academy of Social Sciences, Institute of Archaeology Anyang Task Force, "Anyang xiaomintun jinmu fajue baogao" [Report on the excavation of Jin tombs in Xiaomintun, Anyang]. *Kaogu* [Archaeology] 1983.6: 501–506.

[6]   Liaoning Provincial Museum Bureau of Cultural Relics, Chaoyang Regional Museum Bureau of Cultural Relics, Chaoyang County Museum of Culture, "Chaoyang yuantaizi dongjin bihua mu" [Mural-decorated tomb of the Eastern Jin dynasty in Yuantaizi, Chaoyang]. *Wenwu* [Cultural Relics] 1984.6: 35–38.

[7]   Yang Hong, "Zhonguo gudai maju de fazhan he duiwai yingxiang" [Development and influence of ancient Chinese horse tack]. *Wenwu* [Cultural Relics] 1984.9: 50–54.

[8]   Qi Dongfang, "Guanyu riben tengzhimu gufen chutu maju wenhua yuanyuan de kaocha" [Examination of the cultural origins of horse tack unearthed at Fujinoki ancient tomb in Japan]. *Wenwu* [Cultural Relics] 1987.9: 62–68, 75.

[9]   Xu Ji, "Guanyu Xianbei. Murong bu yiji de chubu kaocha" [Preliminary investigation on the remains of the Xianbei Murong clan] in *Zhongguo kaogu xuehui diliuci nianhui lunwenji* [Anthology of the Sixth Annual Meeting of the Chinese Archaeological Society (1990)], Cultural Relics Publishing House, 160–73.

[10]   Zhang Xiaozhou, "Beifang diqu weijin shiliuguo muzang de fenqu yu fenqi" [The zoning and classification of Wei, Jin, and Sixteen Kingdoms burials in the Northern Region]. *Kaogu xue bao* [Journals of Archaeology]. 1987.1: 19–45.

[11]   Liu Zhongcheng, "Guanyu Chaoyang Yuantaizi jinmu bihua de chubu yanjiu" [Preliminary study on the murals of the Jin tombs in Yuantaizi, Chaoyang]. *Liaohai wenwu xuekan* [Journal of Cultural Relics of Liaohai]. 1987.1: 95–101.

[12]   Chen Dawei, Li Yufeng, "Liaoning Chaoyang houyan cuiyu mu de faxian" [Discovery of Cui Yu tomb of Later Yan in Chaoyang, Liaoning]. *Kaogu* [Archaeology] 1982.3: 270–74.

[13] Li Yaobo, "Liaoning beipiaoxian xiguan yingzi beiyan feng sufu mu" [Feng Sufu tomb of Northern Yan in Beipiao, Liaoning]. *Wenwu* [Cultural Relics] 1973.3: 2–28.

[14] Liaoning Provincial Institute of Cultural Relics and Archaeology, Chaoyang Municipal Museum, "Chaoyang Wangzifenshan muqun 1987 1990 niandu kaogu fajue de zhuya shouhuo" [Main achievements of archaeological excavations in 1987 and 1990 in the cemetery complex of Wangzifenshan, Chaoyang]. *Wenwu* [Cultural Relics] 1997.11: 1–18.

[15] The title was changed to "Sanyan wenhua yicun de chubu yanjiu" [Preliminary study of the Three Yan culture remains] when published in *Liaohai wenwu xuekan* [Journal of Cultural Relics of Liaohai] 1991.1: 90–97.

[16] Xu Yongjie, "Xianbei yicun de kaoguxue kaocha" [Archaeological examination of Xianbei remains]. *Beifang wenwu* [Northern Cultural Relics] 1993.3: 3–17.

[17] Tian Likun, "Xianbei wenhua yuanliu de kaoguxue kaocha" [Archaeological examination of the origin of Xianbei culture] in *Qingguoji—Jilin daxue kaogu zhuanye chengli ershi zhounian kaogu lunwenji* [Archaeological procedings of the twentieth anniversary of the establishment of the Archaeology Program of Jilin University], Knowledge Publishing House, 1993. 361–67. Tian Likun, "Lun Liaoxi hanweimu de Wuhan wenhua yinsu [On Wuhuan cultural influence in the Han-Wei tombs of Liaoxi]" in *Zhongguo kaoguxue guashiji de huigu yu qianzhan—1999 nian xiling guoji xueshu yantaohui wenji* [Retrospect and prospects of Chinese archaeology across the century-proceedings of the 1999 Xiling international symposium], Science Publishing House, (2000) 317–26.

[18] Zheng Junlei, "Zaoqi dongbu xianbei yu zaoqi Tuoba Xianbei zuyuan gailun" [Overview of the origins of the early Eastern Xianbei and early Tuoba Xianbei] in *Qingguoji—Jilin daxue kaogu zhuanye chengli ershi zhounian kaogu lunwenji* [Anthology of the tenth anniversary of the establishment of the archaeology program of Jilin University], Knowledge Publishing House (1998) 309–18.

[19] Qiao Liang, "Xianbei yicun de rending yu yanjiu" [Identification and study of Xianbei remains] in *Zhongguo kaoguxue de kuashiji fansi* [Cross-century reflections on Chinese archaeology], Hong Kong: The Commercial Press (1999). 483–508.

[20] Shang Xiaobo, "Chaoyang diqu liangji shiqi muzang leixing fenxi [Analysis of tomb types of the Jin dynasty in the Chaoyang Area]" in *Qingguoji—Jilin daxue kaogu zhuanye chengli ershi zhounian kaogu lunwenji* [Anthology of the tenth anniversary of the establishment of the archaeology program of Jilin University], Knowledge Publishing House (1998). 351–54.

[21] Chen Ping, "Liaoxi sanyan muzang lunshu" [Discussion of Three Yan burials in Liaoxi]. *Neimenggu wenwu* [Cultural Relics of Inner Mongolia] 1998.2: 52–61.

[22] Sun Ji, "Fuyu Buyaoguan yu yaoye shipian" [*Buyao*, *buyao* crown, and *buyao* ornament]. *Wenwu* [Cultural Relics] 1991.11: 55–65.

[23] Xu Bingkun, *Xianbei sanguo gufen—Zhongguo chaoxian Riben Gudai de wenhua jiaoliu* [Xianbei, Three Kingdoms, ancient tombs-cultural exchanges between China, Korea, and Japan in ancient times], Liaoning Classics Publishing House (1996). 153–60.

[24] Wei Cuncheng, "Gaogouli maju de faxian yu yanjiu" [Discovery and research on Goguryeo horse tack]. *Beifang wenwu* [Northern Cultural Relics] 1991.4: 18–27.

[25] Qi Dongfang, "Zhongguo zaoqi madeng de youguan wenti" [Issues regarding early Chinese stirrups]. *Wenwu* [Cultural Relics] 1993.4: 89.

[26] Tian Likun and Li Zhi, "Chaoyang faxian de Sanyan wenwu ji xiangguan wenti" [Three Yan culture remains found in Chaoyang and related issues]. *Wenwu* [Cultural Relics] 1994.11: 20–32. Tian Likun, "Sanyan wenhua yu gaogouli kaogu yicun zhi bijiao [Comparison of Three Yan culture and Goguryeo archaeological remains]" in *Qingguoji—Jilin daxue kaogu zhuanye chengli ershi zhounian kaogu lunwenji* [Anthology of the tenth anniversary of the establishment of the

archaeology program of Jilin University], Knowledge Publishing House (1998). 328–41.

[27]   Dong Gao, "San zhi liu shiji Murong Xianbei Gaogouli, Chaoxian, Riben maju zhi bijiao yanjiu" [Comparative study of horse tack in Murong Xianbei, Goguryeo, Korea, and Japan in the third to sixth centuries CE]. *Wenwu* [Cultural Relics] 1995.10: 34–42.

[28]   Xu Bingkun, *Xianbei Sanguo gufen—zhongguo chaoxian riben gudai de wenhua jiaoliu* [Xianbei, Three Kingdoms, ancient tombs-cultural exchanges between China, Korea, and Japan in ancient times], Liaoning Classics Publishing House (1996). 140–53.

[29]   Sun Shoudao, "Zhongguo Sanyan shiqi yu Riben gufen qima wenhua de bijiao yanjiu" [Comparative study of the horse-riding cultures of the Three Yan period in China and the Kofun period in Japan] in *Dongbeiya kaoguxue yanjiu* [Northeast Asian Archaeological Research], Cultural Relics Publishing House 1997: 312–20.

[30]   Tian Likun and Zhang Keju, "Qianyan de jiaqijuzhuang" [Horse armor of Former Yan], *Wenwu* [Cultural Relics] 1997.11: 72–75.

[31]   Wang Wei, "Cong chutu maju kan san zhi liu shiji dongya zhuguo de jiaoliu" [Exchanges among East Asian countries from the third to the sixth centuries as seen from unearthed horse tack]. *Kaogu* [Archaeology] 1997.12: 66–85.

[32]   Shin Kyung Chul's (申敬澈) [A study of ancient stirrups] was published in *Busan Historical Review*, 1985.9. It was later translated by Teishin Hideo (定申秀夫) and published in *Kodai Bunka* 1986: 38–6. Yao Yitian translated the Japanese publication into Chinese and published it as "Madeng kao" in *Liaohai wenwu xuekan* [Journal of Cultural Relics of Liaohai] 1996.1: 141–59.

[33]   Tian Likun, "Jicheng xinkao" [New examination of Jicheng]. *Liaohai wenwu xuekan* [Journal of Cultural Relics of Liaohai] 1996.2: 117–22.

[34]   Zhu Hong, "Chaoyang weijin shiqi Xianbei muzang rengu yanjiu" [Research on human skeletal remains from Xianbei tombs of the Wei and Jin periods in Chaoyang]. *Liaohai wenwu xuekan* [Journal of Cultural Relics of Liaohai] 1996.2: 80–91.

[35]   Liaoning Provincial Institute of Cultural Relics, Archaeology, and the Nara National Research Institute for Cultural Properties of Japan, "Liaoning beipiaoshi Lamadong Xianbei guizu mudi chutu tieqi de baohu chuli ji chubu yanjiu" [Conservation and preliminary study of ironware excavated from the Xianbei noble cemetery in Lamadong, Beipiao, Liaoning]. *Kaogu* [Archaeology] 1998.12: 38–45, 103.

[36]   Dong Gao, "Sanyan fojiao luekao" [A brief study of Buddhism in the Three Yan period]. *Liaohai wenwu xuekan* [Journal of Cultural Relics of Liaohai] 1996: 1–7, 55. Li Xinquan, "Sanyan wadang kao" [Examination of eave tile of the Three Yan period], *Liaohai wenwu xuekan* [Journal of Cultural Relics of Liaohai] 1996.1:12–15. Lang Chenggang, "Chaoyang beita sanyan chushi kao" [Examination of plinth of Chaoyang north tower]. *Liaohai wenwu xuekan* [Journal of Cultural Relics of Liaohai] 1996.1: 8–11, 15. Zhou Yali, "Chaoyang Sanyan Beiwei yicun zhong fanying chude Han wenhua yinsu" [Han influence found in remains of the Three Yan period and Northern Wei dynasty in Chaoyang]. *Liaohai wenwu xuekan* [Journal of Cultural Relics of Liaohai] 1996.1: 16–25. Shang Xiaobo, "Daling he liuyu xianbei wenhua shuanger loukong quanzu fu ji xiangguan wenti kao" [Examination of Xianbei double-eared cauldron with foot ring found in Daling River basin and related problems]. *Liaohai wenwu xuekan* [Journal of Cultural Relics of Liaohai] 1996.1: 26–33.

[37]   The eight types of tombs are trapezoidal vertical earthen pit tombs, rectangular vertical earthen pit tombs, brick chamber tombs, stone slab-covered chamber tombs, stone-built stone coffin tombs, stone slab-covered stone coffin tombs, stone-built stone chamber tombs, and stone-built vaulted stone chamber tombs. The early period refers to the rule of Mohuba, Muyan, and Shegui, between the first year of Cao Wei and 289 CE when Murong Wei relocated the tribes from the northern region of Liaodong to Qingshan in Tuhe; the middle period falls between 289 CE to the fall of Former Yan in 370 CE; the late period is from Later Yan to Northern Yan (384–436 CE). See Tian Likun, "Sanyan wenhua muzang de leixing yu fenqi" [Types and phases of the burials of Three Yan culturet] in *Hantang zhijian wenhua yishu de hudong yu*

jiaoliu [The interaction and integration of culture and art between Han and Tang], Cultural Relics Publishing House (2001). 215–22.

[38] Tian Likun, "Guanyu beipiao Lamadong sanyan wenhua mudi de jige wenti" [Questions around the Lamadong cemetery of the Three Yan culture]. *Liaoning kaogu wenji* [Liaoning Archaeological Anthology], Liaoning Ethnic Publishing House 2003: 263–67.

[39] Tian Likun, "Yuantaizi bihuamu de zairenshi" [Reconsideration of the Yuantaizi tomb]. *Wenwu* [Cultural Relics] 2002.9: 41–48.

[40] Wan Xin, "Liaoning diqu murong xianbei yu sanyan wenhua yanjiu zongshu" [A review of research on the Murong Xianbei, and Three Yan culture in the Liaoxi region]. *Sanyan wenwu jingcui* [Highlights of cultural heritage of Three Yan culture], Liaoning People's Publishing House(2002). Wan Xin, "Xianbei muzang sanyan shiji yu jinbuyao de faxian yu yanjiu" [Xianbei burials, Three Yan culture archaeological sites, and the discovery and study of gold *buyao* ornaments]. *Liaoning kaogu wenju* [Liaoning Archaeological Anthology], Liaoning Ethnic Publishing House 2003: 268–81.

[41] Liaoning Provincial Institute of Cultural Relics and Archaeology, Chaoyang Museum, Beipiao Administration of Cultural Relics, "Liaoning beipiao lamadong mudi 1998 nian fajue baogao" [1998 Excavation report of the Lamadong cemetery in Beipiao, Liaoning], *Kaogu xuebao* [Journal of Archaeology] 2004.2: 235.

[42] Wei Zheng, "Xianbei muzang yanjiu" [Study of Xianbei burials], *Kaogu xuebao* [Journal of Archaeology] 2009.3: 349–78.

[43] Pan Ling, "Dui bufen yu xianbei xiangguan yicun niandai de zaitantao" [Reconsideration of the dating of some remains associated with the Xianbei], *Bianjiang kaogu yanjiu* [Archaeological research on the frontier] (vol. 13), Science Publishing House 2013: 215.

[44] Tian Likun, "*Buyao* kao" [A study of *buyao*], *4–6 shiji de Beizhongguo yu Ouya dalu* [Northern China and Eurasia in the fourth-sixth centuries], Science Publishing House (2006). 47–67.

[45] Jiang Nan, "Jinbuyao shipin de faxian yu yanjiu" [Discovery and study of gold *buyao* ornaments], *Caoyuan wenwu* [Prairie Cultural Relics] 2012, 2:74–83.

[46] Wei Zheng, "Jindang yu *buyao*— Hanjin mingfu guanshi shitan" [An exploration of crown decorations for Han and Jin noblewomen], *Wenwu* [Cultural Relics] 2013.5: 60–69.

[47] Xu Bingkun, "Buyao yu murong xianbei" [*Buyao* ornaments and the Murong Xianbe clan]," *Wenshi* [Literary and History] 2014.4, 5–35. Also in Beiyan fengsufu mu [Feng Sufu tomb of Northern Yan], Cultural Relics Publishing House (2015). 284–313.

[48] Wang Tieying, "Madeng de qiyuan" [The origin of stirrups], *Ouya xuekan* [Eurasia Studies] (vol. 3), Zhonghua Book Company, 2002: 78–79.

[49] Chen Ling, "Madeng qiyuan jiqi zai zhonggu shiqi de chuanbo xinlun" [A new discussion on the origin of stirrups and their spread in the medieval period], *Ouya xuekan* [Eurasia Studies] (vol. 9), Zhonghua Book Company, 2009: 181, 202.

[50] Yang Hong, "Fengsufu mu madeng he zhongguo zhuangjia de fazhan" [Stirrups of the Feng Sufu tomb and development of Chinese horse armor], *Liaoningsheng bowuguan guankan* [Journal of Liaoning Provincial Museum], Liaohai Publishing House, 2010. 1–6.

[51] Tian Likun, "Gudeng xinkao" [A new examination of ancient stirrups], *Wenwu* [Cultural Relics] 2013.11: 53–60.

[52] Chen Shan, "Beipiao xinfaxian de sanyan maju yanjiu" [Research on newly discovered Three Yan horse tack in Beipiao], *Wenwu* [Cultural Relics] 2003.3: 64–65.

[53] Tian Likun, "Lun lamadong mudi chutu de maju" [On the horse tack unearthed in the Lamadong cemetery], *Wenwu* [Cultural Relics] 2010.2: 69–76.

[54] Chinese Academy of Social Sciences Institute of Archaeology Technical Department, "Anyang jinmu maju fuyuan" [Reconstruction of horse tack from Jin tombs in Anyang], *Kaogu* [Archaeology] 1983.6: 554–59.

[55] Liu Yonghua, *Zhongguo gudai che yu maju* [Ancient Chinese chariots and horse equipment], Shanghai Lexicographical Publishing House (2002). 205–206.

[56] Tian Likun, Gaoqiaoan de fuyuan ji youguan wenti [Reconstruction and related issues of Gaoqiao saddles], *Dongbeiya kaoguxue luncong* [Northeast Asia Archaeology Series], Science Publishing House (2010). (The Japanese version was published in 2006 by Nara National Research Institute for Cultural Properties). 93–98.

[57] Tian Likun and Lü Xueming, Riben gufen shidai maju sanze [Three cases of horse tack from Japan's Kofun period], *Dongbeiya kaoguxue luncong* [Northeast Asia Archaeology Series], Science Publishing House 2010: 105–16.

[58] Tian Likun, "Luanbiao kao" [A study of a horse bit with bells], *Liaoning sheng bowuguan guankan* [Journal of Liaoning Provincial Museum]. Liaohai Publishing House. 2011: 38–46.

[59] Tian Likun, "Sanyan wenhua maju zhuangshi wenyang yanjiu" [A study of the decorative patterns of Three Yan culture horse tack], *Liaoning sheng bowuguan guankan* [Journal of Liaoning Provincial Museum]. Liaohai Publishing House 2012: 103–22.

[60] Tian Likun, "Mazhang xiaokao" [A study of horseshoes] in *Kaogu yishu yu lishi—Yanghong xiansheng bazhi huadan jinian wenji* [Archaeology, Art, and History—Anthology in Honor of Yang Hong's 80th Birthday], Cultural Relics Publishing House (2018). 374–84.

[61] Tian Likun, Wan Xiongfei, and Bai Baoyu, "Chaoyang gucheng kaogu jilue" [Archaeology of Chaoyang Old City], *Bianjiang kaogu yanjiu* [Archaeological research on the frontier] (vol. 6), Science Publishing House. (2007). Wan Xiongfei, "Sanyan longcheng gongcheng nanmen yizhi jiqi jianzhu tedian" [Remains of the South Gate of Longcheng of the Three Yan culture and its architectural characteristics], in *Liaoxi diqu weijin shiliuguo shiqi ducheng wenhua yanjiu* [Research on the Culture of Eastern Jin and Sixteen Kingdoms Capitals in the Liaoxi Region], Liaoning People's Publishing House (2017).

[62] Tian Likun, "Longcheng xinkao" [A new examination of Longcheng], *Bianjiang kaogu yanjiu* [Archaeological Research on the Frontier] (vol. 12), Science Publishing House, 2012: 315–25.

[63] Xin Yan, Mu Qiwen, and Fu Xingsheng, "Liaoning beipiao jinlingsi weijin jianzhu yizhi fajue baogao" [Report on the excavation of the Wei-Jin architectural site of Jinlingsi in Beipiao], *Liaoning kaogu wenji* [Liaoning Archaeology Anthology] (vol. 2), Science Publishing House 2010: 198–224.

[64] Tian Likun, "Jinlingsi jianzhuzhi wei huimiao shuo" [The Jinlingsi remains as the Hui temple] in *Qingzhu Zhangzhongpei xiansheng bashisui lunwenji* [A collection of essays in celebration of Zhang Zhongpei's 80th birthday], Science Publishing House (2014). 461–77.

[65] Zheng Yan, *Weijin nanbeichao bihuamu yanjiu* [A study of mural tomb painting in the Wei, Jin, and Northern and Southern dynasties], Cultural Relics Publishing House (2002). 40–41.

[66] Wan Xin, "Lamadong tiegong chulun—Jianyi Zhongguo Murong Xianbei Chaoxian Sanguo shiqi he Riben gufen shidai tieqi zangsu de yizhixing yu chayixing" [A preliminary study of ironwork in Lamadong cemetery: consistency and differences in ironwork in burial practices in the Murong Xianbei of China, the Three Kingdoms of Korea, and the Kofun period of Japan], *Dongbeiya kaoguxue luncong* [Northeast Asia Archaeology Series], Science Publishing House, 2010: 67–84. Beijing Scientific University Institute of Metallurgy and Materials History, Liaoning Provincial Institute of Cultural Relics and Archaeology, "Beipiao Lamadong mudi chutu tieqi de jinxiang shiyan yanjiu" [Experimental metallographic study of ironware excavated from Beipiao Lamadong cemetery], *Wenwu* [Cultural Relics] 2001.12: 71–79. Han Rubin, "Beipiao Fengsufu mu chutu jinshuqi de jianding yu yanjiu" [Identification and research on metalware unearthed from Beipiao Feng Sufu tomb], *Liaoning sheng bowuguan guankan* [Journal of Liaoning Provincial Museum], Liaohai Publishing House, 2010: 7–19. Liu Ning and Liu Bo, "Fengsufu mu chutu de tiejing" [Iron mirror unearthed from the Feng Sufu tomb]. *Liaoning sheng bowuguan guankan* [Journal of Liaoning Provincial Museum], Liaohai Publishing House, 2011: 9–13. Shen Guiyun, Wang Yiwei, and Liu Bo, "Fengsufu mu chutu jinqi de fenxi yu yanjiu" [Analysis and study of

gold artifacts unearthed from the Feng Sufu tomb], *Beiyan fengsufu mu* [Feng Sufu tomb of Northern Yan], Cultural Relics Publishing House (2015). 204–10.

[67] An Jiayao, "Fengsufu mu chutu de boliqi" [Glassware unearthed from the Feng Sufu tomb] in *Taolichengxi ji— Qingzhu anzhimin xiansheng bashi shouchen* [Anthology in celebration of An Zhimin's 80th Birthday], The Chinese University of Hong Kong Center of Chinese Archaeology and Art (2004). 377–87. Zhou Xiaojing, "Fengsufu mu chutu de yuwan yu yuqian" [Jade bowl and jade sword unearthed from the Feng Sufu tomb]. *Liaoning sheng bowuguan guankan* [Journal of Liaoning Provincial Museum], Liaohai Publishing House, 2011: 14–19. Liu Ning, "Beiyan rouran yu caoyuan sichou zhilu—cong fengsufu mu chutu de boliqi tanqi" [Northern Yan, the Rouran khaganate and the Steppe Road—from glassware unearthed in the Feng Sufu tomb], *Beiyan fengsufu mu* [Feng Sufu Tomb of Northern Yan], Cultural Relics Publishing House (2015). 238–45. Tao Liang and Lu Yeping, "Fengsufu mu taoqi zonghe kaocha" [A comprehensive examination of pottery from the Feng Sufu tomb]. *Beiyan fengsufu mu* [Feng Sufu Tomb of Northern Yan], Cultural Relics Publishing House (2015). 278–83.

[68] Wan Xiongfei and Bai Baoyu, "Chaoyang laocheng beidajie chutu de 3–6 shiji lianhua wadang chutan" [A preliminary study of the third-to sixth-century lotus flower eave tiles unearthed in North Street of Chaoyang Old City], *Dongbeiya kaogu luncong* [Northeast Asia archaeology series], Science Publishing House, 2010: 61–66. Wang Feifeng, "Sanyan wadang yanjiu" [Examination of eave tile of the Three Yan], *Bianjiang kaogu yanjiu* [Archaeological research on the frontier] (vol. 12), Science Publishing House, 2012: 295–313. Li Xinquan, "Sanyan wenhua jiege tu'an wadang yuanliu kao" [A study of the origin of the grid pattern of Three Yan culture eave tiles], *Liaoxi diqu weijin shiliuguo shiqi ducheng wenhua yanjiu* [Research on the culture of Eastern Jin and Sixteen Kingdoms capitals in the Liaoxi region], Liaoning People's Publishing House, (2017). 118–31. Wang Feifeng, "Sanyan gaoguoli lianhuawen wadang de chuxian jiqi guanxi" [The appearance of lotus-pattern eave tiles in Three Yan and Goguryeo and their relationships], *Liaoxi diqu weijin shiliuguo shiqi ducheng wenhua yanjiu* [Research on the culture of Eastern Jin and Sixteen Kingdoms capitals in the Liaoxi region], Liaoning People's Publishing House(2017). 132–53.

[69] Tian Likun, "Liufang lianxu wenhyang kao" [An examination of the seamless pattern] in *Xinguoji—Qingzhu linyun xiansheng qishi huadan lunwenji* [Anthology in celebration of Lin Yun's 70th birthday], Science Publishing House, (2009). Tian Likun, "Qianyan de liangge lite jiazu" [Two Sogdian families of Former Yan], in *Literen zai zhongguo—kaogu faxian yu chutu wenxian de xin yinzheng* [Sogdians in China, new corroboration of archaeological discoveries and excavated documents], Science Publishing House, (2016). 532–41.

[70] Zhu Hong, Zeng Wen, Zhang Quanchao, Chen Shan, and Zhou Hui, "Lamadong sanhyan wenhua jumin zushu wenti de shegnwu kaoguxue kaocha" [Biological archaeological study of the ethnic affiliation of owners of the Lamadong cemetery], *Jilin daxue shehui kexue xuebao* [Journal of Social Sciences of Jilin University] 2012.1: 44–51, 159.

[71] Liaoning Provincial Institute of Cultural Relics and Archaeology and the Nara National Research Institute for Cultural Properties of Japan, *Dongbeiya kaoguxue luncong* [Northeast Asia Archaeology Series], Science Publishing House, 2010. Liaoning Provincial Institute of Cultural Relics and Archaeology and the Nara National Research Institute for Cultural Properties of Japan, *Liaoxi diqu dongjin shiliuguo shiqi ducheng wenhua yanjiu* [Research on the culture of Eastern Jin and Sixteen Kingdoms capitals in the Liaoxi region], Liaoning People's Publishing House, 2017.

[72] Tian Likun, "Buyao kao" [A study of *buyao*], in *4–6 shiji de Beizhongguo yu Ouya dalu* [Northern China and Eurasia in the fourth to sixth centuries], Science Publishing House, 2006: 53–57.

[73] Su Bai, "Dongbei neimenggu diqu de xianbei yiji—xianbei yiji jilu zhiyi" [Remains of Xianbei in the Northeast and Inner Mongolia: a collection of Xianbei remains], *Wenwu* [Cultural Relics] 1977.5: 46.

[74] Henan Provincial Institute of Cultural Relics, *Mixian dahuting hanmu* [Dahuting Han tombs in Mixian], Cultural Relics Publishing House (1993). 238–39.

[75] Tian Likun, "Liufang lianxu wenhyang kao" [An examination of the seamless pattern] in *Xinguoji—Qingzhu linyun*

xiansheng qishi huadan lunwenji [Anthology in celebration of Lin Yun's 70th birthday], Science Publishing House (2009). 474–78.

[76] *Wei shu* [Book of Wei] (vol. 30), *Antong zhuan* [Biography of An Tong], Zhonghua Book Company (1974). 712.

[77] Edited by Shaanxi Provincial Classics Management Office, (Wu Gang, editor-in-chief), *Quantangwen buyi* [Addendum on complete literary works of Tang dynasty] (vol. 5), *Kanghui muzhi* [Epitaph of Kang Hui], San Qin Publishing House, 1998. 408.

[78] Tian Likun, "Qianyan de liangge lite jiazu" [Two Sogdian families of Former Yan], *Literen zai zhongguo—kaogu faxian yu chutu wenxian de xin yinzheng* [Sogdians in China: new corroboration of archaeological discoveries and excavated documents], Science Publishing House, (2016). 533, 536.

[79] Archaeological discoveries have been made of the epitaphs of Lü Xian, a Liaodong official, and Lü Ta, an official of Youzhou. See Lu Yao, Houqin <Lüta mubiao> yu <Lüxian mubiao> [Epitaphs of Lü Ta and Lü Xian of Later Qin], *Wenbo* [Relics and Museology] 2001.5: 62–65.

[80] Jinzhou Municipal Cultural Relics and Archaeology Team, "Liaoning jinzhoushi qianshan shiliuguo shiqi muzang de qingli" [Tidying up the Qianshan Sixteen Kingdoms tomb in Jinzhou, Liaoning]. *Kaogu* [Archaeology] 1998.1: 92–94.

[81] Tian Likun, "Sishiji Fuyu shiji gouchen" [Fourth century Fuyu historical sites], paper presented at the International Symposium on Culture and Cultural Diversity in Medieval China (4th to 7th Centuries), Ludwig Maximillian University of Munich, 2017. Published in English and Chinese as "Exploring the forgotten history of the *buyao* of the fourth century: an archaeological and textual survey" in *Early Medieval North China: Archaeological and Textual Evidence* (Asiatische Forschungen, 159), eds. Shing Müller, Thomas O. Höllmann, and Sonja Filip. Wiesbaden: 2019. 39–56.

[82] Liaoning Provincial Institute of Cultural Relics and Archaeology, Chaoyang Regional Bureau of Cultural Relics, "Liaoning sheng chaoyang xian tuchengzi liangzuo qianyanmu" [Two Former Yan tombs in Tuchengzi, Chaoyang county, Liaoning province], *Beifang wenwu* [Northern Cultural Relics] 2015.2: 19.

[83] Zhu Zhifang, Ji houyan longtengyuan yizhi de faxian [Discovery of the Longteng Garden archaeological site of Later Yan], *Dongbei difangshi yanjiu* [Study of Northeast Regional History] 1984.1: 7–8.

三燕文化研究回顾

田立坤
朝阳博物馆原馆长、辽宁省博物馆原馆长、
辽宁省文物考古研究所原所长

曹魏初年，鲜卑慕容部首领莫护跋率其诸部入居辽西。其孙涉归时，再迁辽东北。西晋太康十年
（289）涉归之子慕容廆又迁回徒河之青山（今辽宁朝阳至义县之间），元康四年（294）移居棘城。
东晋咸康三年（337）慕容廆之子慕容皝在棘城自称燕王，史称"前燕"。咸康七年（341），慕容
皝于柳城（治今辽宁朝阳南）之北、龙山之西筑龙城（今辽宁朝阳），第二年迁都龙城。永和六年
（350）二月，前燕南下中原，龙城为留都。太和五年（370）十一月，前秦攻陷邺城，前燕亡。太元
九年（384）正月，慕容垂建后燕，隆安元年（397）三月慕容宝弃中山（治今河北定州）退守龙城。
义熙三年（407），高云、冯跋杀慕容熙于龙城，后燕亡。高云、冯跋建北燕。北魏太延二年（436）
五月，占领龙城，北燕亡。

上述二百多年间，辽西地区多民族错居杂处，其中慕容鲜卑与汉文化的交流与融合，是贯穿这一历史
时期的主线。"三燕文化"即指在此背景下形成的，以今朝阳为分布中心，以慕容鲜卑为主体，在汉
文化影响下，同时也吸收了匈奴、乌桓、夫余、高句丽、拓跋鲜卑等多种文化因素，特征鲜明、内涵
丰富的慕容鲜卑及所建前燕、后燕、鲜卑化高云和冯跋所建北燕的魏晋十六国时期考古遗存。
自1956年发现北票房身墓地[1]，确认为晋代慕容鲜卑墓葬以来，辽西地区魏晋十六国时期考古研究可
以分为1989年以前、1990—1999年、2000年至今三个阶段。

第一阶段 1989年以前

1989年以前的研究，除资料报告者通过与文献和其他遗存进行分析比较，以推定墓葬年代、性质之外，学术界也给予了密切的关注。1977年，宿白先生在对东北、内蒙古东部的鲜卑遗迹进行考察时，肯定了北票房身墓地为慕容鲜卑遗存，以及"金花冠饰"为金步摇的推测（图1）；认为"镶嵌饰物的指环"为匈奴文化中所常见，随葬的日用器物、葬俗都受到汉族的影响，表明慕容鲜卑与汉族关系密切。义县保安寺石椁墓的"金饰品与慕容相类，陶器和各种珠饰则与拓跋相近"，时代早于北票房身墓地。冯素弗墓出土的锤鍱坐佛像，是辽西发现的最早的佛像，表明北燕是北方佛教传播的重要地区之一。其玻璃器很可能是西方输入品，"或许是经由柔然辗转传来的"[2]。安家瑶先生的进一步研究成果表明，冯素弗墓出土的五件玻璃器皿为罗马帝国的产品[3]。

图1 十六国前燕 花树状金步摇
　　　朝阳木营子西团山出土
　　　朝阳博物馆藏

1981年秋，董高、孙国平在辽宁省考古、博物馆学会成立大会上提交的《朝阳地区鲜卑马具的初步研究》《试论鲜卑族的步摇冠饰》[4]，披露了一部分朝阳出土但没有发表的马具、步摇资料的信息，提出马具与步摇问题。

安阳孝民屯M154[5]、朝阳袁台子壁画墓[6]出土的两套完整马具资料发表后，杨泓先生随即发文指出：公元4世纪初是马具发展的关键时期，安阳孝民屯和朝阳袁台子壁画墓出土的成套马具，提供了马具发展关键时期的典型实物标本。高句丽墓葬出土的马具与安阳孝民屯、朝阳袁台子壁画墓出土的马具具有相同的特点，形制几乎是相同的，明显受到以安阳孝民屯M154为代表的马具的影响。在朝鲜半岛南部的新罗遗物中，也可以看到同样的影响，这种影响也波及到日本[7]。1987年，齐东方先生在对日本奈良藤之木古坟出土铜鎏金马具考察时，即将朝鲜半岛、日本马具文化渊源追溯至以安阳孝民屯M154、朝阳袁台子壁画墓、冯素弗墓为代表的中国马具[8]。

1986年，曾供职朝阳地区博物馆（今朝阳博物馆）多年的徐基先生，在中国考古学会第六次年会上提交的《关于鲜卑慕容部遗迹的初步考察》[9]，重点介绍了1973—1979年间，在朝阳周边及北票房身村等地调查清理的尚未发表的有关资料，包括朝阳目前所见年代最早的北票北沟M8出土的成套铜鎏金马具，内容极为丰富。该文结合以往的相关发现与研究成果，从陶器组合，头戴和装饰品，成套的马具、具装、兵器，墓葬制度、习俗四个方面，总结出"慕容鲜卑文化"特征，认为慕容鲜卑遗存明显地可以分成三组："第一组可视为鲜卑族慕容部的民族文化"，"第二组器物，为汉族、匈奴族或其他民族传入的部分"，"第三组器物，系指鲜卑慕容部在周边民族先进技术、文化影响下，学习仿造的部分"。在年代上将慕容鲜卑遗存分成四组六段：第一组以舍根墓群为代表，早至东汉中晚期或略早；第二组主要以大凌河中游的北票房身村北沟墓地早期墓为代表，时代定在西晋为宜；第三组以朝阳市为中心，包括北票房身村北沟墓地后期墓和朝阳南汉代"柳城"附近的袁台子、腰而营子墓，安阳孝民屯的几座墓亦应划在此组；第四组以后燕崔遹墓和北燕冯氏墓为代表。

1987年发表的《北方地区魏晋十六国墓葬的分区与分期》[10]，将辽西大凌河流域魏晋十六国时期墓葬归入东北地区的第三期，即十六国时期，同时分析了其历史背景及与中原地区的关系。《关于朝阳袁台子晋墓壁画的初步研究》[11]则对朝阳袁台子壁画墓中壁画的构图、绘画技法等进行了讨论。

这一时期发表的资料和研究成果数量虽然不多，但是其重要性不言而喻。如北票房身墓地出土的金步摇，将墓主人与文献中的慕容鲜卑直接联系在一起。朝阳姚金沟石椁墓出土的两方分别刻有"燕建兴十年昌黎太守清河武城崔遹"十五字、"燕建兴十年昌黎太守清河东武城崔遹"十六字墓表，墓葬年代，墓主人官职、籍贯、姓名一目了然[12]；北票西官营子石椁墓亦可通过随葬的四枚印章考定墓主人为卒于北燕太平七年（415）的北燕王冯跋之弟冯素弗[13]。这些发现为认识魏晋十六国时期辽西地区考古遗存文化面貌、判断其年代提供了准确的参考样本和标尺，由此奠定了深入研究的坚实基础。

关于冯素弗墓出土的玻璃器为"西方输入品"，高句丽、新罗、日本成套马具是受到安阳孝民屯M154、朝阳袁台子壁画墓马具影响的产物的观点，都具有开创性，为以后的深入研究拓宽了视野。特别是徐基先生对辽西地区魏晋十六国时期考古遗存进行的综合文化因素分析、分期研究，提出"慕容鲜卑文化"概念，不再停留在对墓葬具体年代的考定或族属辨识上，可谓是辽西地区魏晋十六国时期考古研究的一大进步。

第二阶段 1990—1999 年

20世纪80年代及以前，辽西地区魏晋十六国时期考古遗存的发现与研究成果，为推动三燕文化考古研究的深入奠定了坚实的基础。但是，毋庸讳言，这一时期发表的报告多是对遗存的具体描述、年代推定、墓主族属考证，各遗存之间的相互比较也仅限于年代方面的参证。遗存的命名则是发现地点与年代或墓主名、族名的简单相加，如"北票房身村晋墓""安阳孝民屯晋墓""朝阳袁台子东晋壁画墓""北燕冯素弗墓""后燕崔遹墓"等，缺少整体上的认识与系统的综合研究，或者笼统地称之为"鲜卑遗存""鲜卑马具""慕容鲜卑文化"。如此笼而统之，则无法解释如十二台乡砖厂土坑竖穴木棺墓[14]与后燕崔遹墓墓主人，前者是慕容鲜卑，后者是中原世家大族，而且时代前后相距一百多年，但是二者都使用形制独特的前大后小木棺这一现象；有些重要遗存如袁台子壁画墓被命名为"东晋壁画墓"，自然被排除在"鲜卑遗存""慕容鲜卑文化"之外，显然都失之片面，没能从整体上全面、准确地概括辽西地区魏晋十六国时期考古遗存丰富的文化内涵及它们之间的密切关系。基于此，提交1990年大连环渤海考古国际学术讨论会的《三燕遗存的初步研究》[15]，将辽西地区魏晋十六国时期考古遗存命名为"三燕文化"，认为十二台乡砖厂墓群、舍根墓群、新胜屯墓群、北票房身村晋墓为慕容鲜卑建国前的遗存，即三燕遗存之源，"三燕遗存是慕容鲜卑在汉文化的强烈影响下，同时也受到匈奴、高句丽等不同程度的影响而形成的一种具有自身特点的文化遗存，不能简单视为慕容鲜卑遗存"。"三燕文化"的提出，既是材料积累之必然，亦为深入研究之必需，标志辽西地区魏晋十六国时期考古研究进入一个新的阶段。

这一时期参与慕容鲜卑遗存的认定及与其他各鲜卑遗存关系讨论的还有许永杰[16]、田立坤[17]、郑君雷[18]、乔梁[19]等，尚晓波[20]、陈平[21]则对辽西地区魏晋十六国时期墓葬的分类等进行了研究。

具体的个案研究有以下几方面。

其一，慕容鲜卑的代表性器物金步摇的研究。发其端者为孙机在1991年发表的《步摇、步摇冠与摇叶饰片》[22]，通过《续汉书·舆服志》中所记东汉皇后盛装谒庙时戴的首饰"金步摇"、辽西地区出土的金步摇实物，与1864年在顿河下游新切尔卡斯克萨尔马泰女王墓中出土的公元前2世纪金冠、1979年在阿富汗北部席巴尔干金丘6号大月氏墓出土的公元1世纪前期金冠的比较，提出"步摇装饰起源于西方，步摇冠约在公元前后正式形成，然后向东传播，横跨欧亚大陆经我国到达日本，流行时间长达600多年，是一个值得注意的文化现象"。1996年出版的《鲜卑·三国·古坟——中国朝鲜日本古代的文化交流》[23]踵其后，根据前2600—前2500年的美索不达米亚平原南部的乌尔王朝皇家墓园出土的"用琉璃、红玉髓珠串缀金摇叶而制成的饰圈"，认为金步摇叶是"发源于西亚和西域，经过中国，尤其是经过鲜卑慕容部传到朝鲜半岛和日本的一项服饰品"。

其二，马具及其与高句丽和朝鲜半岛、日本古坟的关系。先后有魏存成[24]、齐东方[25]、田立坤[26]、董高[27]、徐秉琨[28]、孙守道[29]、张克举[30]、王巍[31]等撰文参与讨论。

1985年，韩国釜山大学申敬澈先生发表《古镫考》[32]，将韩国东莱福泉洞出土的马镫划分为A、B两型，溯其源头分别至安阳孝民屯M154出土马镫与冯素弗墓出土马镫。1996年，《古镫考》被姚义田先生译为中文发表，使中国学界得以了解、借鉴韩国学者关于马镫研究取得的成果。

此外，通过考古调查，结合相关文献分析论证，确认前燕第一个都城——棘城遗址之所在，也是这一时期的一项重要研究成果[33]。

体质人类学方面，1996年发表的《朝阳魏晋时期鲜卑墓葬人骨研究》[34]，结论为朝阳十二台乡砖厂土坑竖穴墓地居民基本种系特征属于低颅性质的古蒙古高原类型，为推断十二台乡砖厂土坑竖穴墓地为慕容鲜卑遗存提供了体质人类学上的有力支持。

日本学界对辽西地区魏晋十六国时期的考古发现也十分关注。1996年起，辽宁省文物考古研究所（今辽宁省文物考古研究院）与日本奈良文化财研究所以"亚洲古代都城遗迹研究与保护——三燕都城等出土铁器及其他金属器的保护与研究"为主题开展合作研究[35]。

1995年在朝阳召开的辽宁省考古学会第四届年会暨三燕文化研讨会上，董高、李新全、郎成刚、周亚利、尚晓波分别提交了关于三燕文化研究的论文[36]。

第三阶段 2000 年至今

1990—1999年这十年间，又有四十多座辽西地区魏晋十六国时期墓葬资料公开发布，含土坑竖穴墓、砖室墓、石室墓、石椁墓等多种形制，李廆墓还有明确的纪年。在这些新资料的基础上，2000年发表的《三燕文化墓葬的类型与分期》将三燕文化墓葬分为三期八类[37]，早期墓葬形制种类较少，中期种类剧增，晚期形制趋于一致。在这一过程中，以梯形土坑竖穴木棺墓为代表的属慕容鲜卑固有的文化因素始终处于主导地位，尽管中期出现了代表中原汉文化因素的砖室墓、代表辽东汉魏时期文化因素的石板搭盖石室墓、代表夫余文化因素的矩形土坑竖穴木椁墓，且都具有各自的渊源，但是到晚期都不见或少见；而代表辽西传统文化因素的石椁墓或石室墓一出现就接受梯形土坑竖穴木棺墓的影响而发展起来，尤其是前大后小的石椁墓成为晚期的主要形制。墓葬形制发展演变过程，与慕容鲜卑进入辽西之后，与汉文化及周边其他文化接触、共处、吸收、最后融为一体的经历正相吻合。三燕文化墓葬的分类与分期，为辽西地区魏晋十六国时期考古研究提供了一个可资参考的时空框架。

北票喇嘛洞墓地是辽西地区经科学发掘规模最大、出土遗物数量最多、种类最丰富的魏晋十六国时期墓地，与以往发现的这一时期墓葬在随葬遗物上虽然有明显的共性，但是在墓葬形制和葬俗上却有不容忽视的差别。提交2000年东北地区三至十世纪古代文化学术讨论会的《关于北票喇嘛洞三燕文化墓地的几个问题》[38]，就喇嘛洞墓地的年代、特征、族属进行了系统的讨论，推定喇嘛洞墓地的年代在289年至350年之间，结合文献所记慕容鲜卑曾前后两次攻打夫余，并迁徙大批夫余人的史实，提出喇嘛洞墓地的主体人群应是被慕容鲜卑迁到棘城的夫余人的观点。

1984年发现的朝阳袁台子壁画墓，是魏晋十六国时期考古的一个重要发现，但是不同的研究者对其具体年代的判断差距较大。2002年发表的《袁台子壁画墓的再认识》[39]，通过对墓壁上残存的"……二月己……[丿]子……"墨书纪年题记研究，将它复原为"□□□[年]二月己□[朔] □[戊（庚）]子……"，再结合墓葬形制、壁画内容都与辽阳魏晋壁画墓有直接渊源关系，以及当时辽海地区发生的重大事件，将残存的纪年题记进一步复原为"[永和十年]二月己[卯朔十（廿二）日戊（庚）]子"（354），或者"[太和元年]二月己[巳朔廿日戊]子"（366），确认此墓为东晋咸和九年（334）被慕容皝从辽东迁徙到棘城的"辽东大姓"遗存。这一新成果为辽海地区魏晋十六国时期墓葬研究提供了一个有绝对年代可考的标本。

2002发表的《辽西地区慕容鲜卑与三燕文化研究综述》，总结出"宫城、皇苑与墓群——关于辽西地区鲜卑墓葬与三燕史迹的整体性""李氏、崔氏和冯氏墓——三燕时期纪年墓葬的重要性""金步摇饰和铜鎏金马具——关于辽西地区鲜卑与三燕金属文物的典型性""慕容氏摇叶文化的东传——大凌河流域鲜卑墓葬的特殊性"[40]。

2004年发表的《辽宁北票喇嘛洞墓地1998年发掘报告》，结论是"喇嘛洞三燕文化墓葬……仍主要属于辽西地区大凌河流域两晋时期慕容鲜卑文化的范畴。确切些说，它们是汉化程度较深且可能吸收了夫余等族的某些文化因素的，以慕容鲜卑文化成分为主的前燕及前燕以前不久的墓葬，其相对年代约当公元3世纪末至4世纪中叶，亦即慕容廆率部回迁至大凌河流域（289）以后至慕容皝建立的前燕时期（337—370）的遗存"[41]。

2009年发表的《鲜卑墓葬研究》[42]，将内蒙古科左后旗舍根、科左中旗六家子墓地比定为乌桓遗存，年代为东汉中晚期。

2013年发表的《对部分与鲜卑相关遗存年代的再探讨》，认为内蒙古科左中旗"六家子墓地征集的大多数陶器、金银器及铜鎏金的器物都与西晋至十六国时期北方鲜卑的或者中原和南方晋墓所出的同类器物相似，而不见与东汉时期相似的器物，因此，六家子墓地（除了两件圜底陶罐）的年代应在西晋至十六国时期，不会早到东汉晚期"[43]。

六家子墓地出土的"鎏金圆形镂孔铜带饰"和"鎏银圆形镂孔铜饰件"，是将连接攀胸、后鞧带的带扣固定在高桥鞍鞍桥上的底座，这种马具部件在朝阳出现的时间为西晋末年，既表明六家子墓地的年代不会早于或同于朝阳出土同样器物墓葬的年代，同时也说明六家子墓地亦属于三燕文化系统。

除对墓葬研究之外，步摇与马具仍然是这一时期颇受关注的重点。

《辽西地区慕容鲜卑与三燕文化研究综述》以田草沟墓地出土的金步摇为例，讨论了其用法与配置组合。

2006年发表的《步摇考》[44]，根据文献中所记之金步摇与辽西地区发现的金步摇实物资料，将长城以南地区战国至十六国时期的步摇分为垂珠、爵兽、花树三型，其中垂珠步摇是一种具有"步则摇动"特征的首饰，故以"步摇"名之。《续汉书·舆服志》中所记皇后谒庙时戴的金步摇为爵兽步摇，三燕文化的典型遗物金步摇则属花树步摇。爵兽步摇与花树步摇皆源自西方，但是二者传入中国的时间与路线不同，前者是汉代通过丝绸之路传入中原地区，后者则是曹魏初年随着慕容鲜卑从草原南下传入辽西地区。这两种首饰同样具有"步则摇动"的特征，东传之后也被冠以"步摇"之名。三者的质地、结构、用法不尽相同，因此，不宜不加区别，混为一谈。慕容鲜卑与"步摇"的关系也还有进一步研究的必要。

2012年发表的《金步摇饰品的发现与研究》[45]，将具有金属摇叶装饰的牌饰、耳坠、带饰、马具遗物统称为"金步摇饰品"，与金步摇一起进行了详细统计，同时对金步摇饰品的研究现状进行评述，指出存在的问题。

2013年发表的《金珰与步摇——汉晋命妇冠饰试探》[46]，在探讨汉晋命妇的冠饰时，也对慕容鲜卑金步摇进行了讨论。

2014年发表的《步摇与慕容鲜卑》[47]，对文献记载的步摇、步摇冠与考古发现的金步摇及相关实物资料进行了系统梳理，从多方面论证了慕容与步摇之间的关系，认为曹魏初年入居辽西的莫护跋，就是东汉后期檀石槐鲜卑部落大联盟中部的"慕容大帅"，力主《晋书·慕容廆载记》中的"慕容"为"步摇"音讹说。

马镫是马具研究的重点。2002年发表的《马镫的起源》[48]，对欧亚大陆目前发现的几百件马镫实物（包括部分壁画和雕塑所表现的马镫）进行综合研究，认为单镫并非骑行使用，它和马镫的功用是截然不同的，不是真正意义上的马镫，不能"和马镫混为一谈"。这与学界通用的马镫概念截然不同。

2009年发表的《马镫起源及其在中古时期的传播新论》，"主张不能把目前已知的单镫排除在马镫的发展系列之外"，推测"马镫的产生可能与汉晋时代号为天下名骑的乌桓有关"。[49]杨泓先生以冯素弗墓马镫与中国马具装铠的发展为题，讨论了马镫发明和马具装铠使用的重大意义及其影响。[50]2013年发表的《古镫新考》，认为目前所见3—4世纪的早期马镫因选材和制作工艺、结构不同，分属"屈木为镫""揉木为镫""斫木为镫"三个谱系，"屈木为镫""斫木为镫"都发生于辽西地区，"揉木为镫"发生于长江流域。[51]

其次是高桥鞍研究。2003年发表的《北票新发现的三燕马具研究》，将东亚诸国的高桥鞍鞍桥分为四种类型，"从马具出现的年代看，以慕容鲜卑为最早，高句丽次之，朝鲜半岛南部诸国再次，日本最晚。慕容鲜卑的马具是影响其他地区鞍桥发展变化的源头，素面斜收式拱形高鞍桥出现的时间最早，在4世纪初叶，近椭圆式是其发展变化的结果，出现时间相对较晚。直立式出现的时间也比较早，以七星山96号墓为例，其年代可能在4世纪中叶，上限可早到4世纪的初期。外侈式是直立式的一种变异……这种时间上的早晚从鞍桥图案的变化中亦可见反映"。[52]提交2006年韩国金海市第十二届伽耶史国际学术会议的《论喇嘛洞墓地出土的马具》[53]，将喇嘛洞墓地出土的鞍桥分为"上宽下窄、两翼向下斜收的拱形"的A型和"没有拱肩、两翼内收、整体呈椭圆形"的B型两类，并提出其各自配套的马镳和马镫，以及装饰纹样也存在较大差异，形成A、B两套不同的组合，分别代表慕容鲜卑和夫余两种不同的文化因素。晚至5、6世纪的日本藤之木古坟出土的鞍桥属于A型，誉田丸山古坟出土的2号鞍桥属于B型，是A型与B型鞍桥并列发展的例证。

1983年发表的《安阳晋墓马具复原》[54]，据安阳孝民屯M154马具，复原一件由前后鞍桥和左右鞍座板四个部件组合而成的高桥鞍。2002年出版的《中国古代车舆马具》，以绘画形式复原的安阳孝民屯M154和袁台子壁画墓高桥鞍完全采用了《安阳晋墓马具复原》的成果[55]。朝阳十二台乡砖厂88M1与鞍桥包片共存的木质鞍桥完整无损，提供了鞍桥与鞍座结合的可靠信息（图2）。2006年发表的《高桥鞍的复原及有关问题》，据此复原出一件由前后鞍桥、左右鞍座板、鞍座脊板五个部件组合而成的高桥鞍，与由前后鞍桥、左右鞍座板四个部件组合而成的复原相比，结构更加合理。[56]

图2　十六国前燕　鎏金镂空铜鞍桥包片
　　　1988年朝阳十二台乡砖厂88M1出土
　　　朝阳博物馆藏

高句丽和朝鲜半岛新罗、伽耶及日本古坟时代马具，都直接或间接受到三燕文化的影响，因此也受到学术界的格外关注。尤其是日本藤之木古坟出土的马具，制作工艺之精美，装饰之华丽，十分罕见。其原产地众说纷纭，有中国南朝萧梁、朝鲜半岛新罗、中国北魏东部多种说法，莫衷一是。2006年发表的《日本古坟时代马具三则》，从时代背景、装饰纹样、带扣形制综合分析后认为，藤之木古坟马具原产地为高句丽都城平壤的可能性最大。同时对三燕文化马镳对日本古坟时代的影响、三铃环的命名也做了讨论。[57]

此外还有关于鸾镳[58]、装饰纹样[59]、马掌[60]等问题的讨论。

2003—2006年对朝阳老城区的发掘，发现了三燕龙城宫城南门遗址，不仅了解到其结构和使用沿革，而且确定了龙城宫城的准确位置，为研究龙城的整体布局和所受曹魏邺城的影响提供了重要的线索[61]。2012年发表的《龙城新考》，对慕容鲜卑所建的第一座城——龙城的选址的科学性进行了分析讨论。[62]

北票金岭寺大型建筑址[63]，是这一时期考古的重要发现。2012年发表的《金岭寺建筑址为"庿庙"说》[64]，根据文献记载与遗址所在位置、布局特征、建筑结构、遗物组合等因素综合推断，金岭寺建筑址很可能就是慕容儁为其祖父前燕奠基者慕容廆所建的"庿庙"。

袁台子壁画墓构图、技法特点研究[65]，金属器保护与研究[66]，冯素弗墓出土玻璃器、玉器、陶器研究[67]，朝阳老城、金岭寺建筑址出土建筑构件研究[68]，三燕文化中的西方文化因素辨认[69]，也是这一时期新的研究成果。

2012年发表的《喇嘛洞三燕文化居民族属问题的生物考古学考察》[70]，认为喇嘛洞三燕文化墓地居民与十二台乡砖厂土坑竖穴墓地居民差异显著，总体特征比较接近高颅性质的古东北类型和古华北类型；喇嘛洞居民和鲜卑人之间存在着很大的遗传学距离，直接排除了喇嘛洞三燕文化居民为鲜卑人的可能性，间接支持运用考古类型学对墓葬形制、随葬遗物研究，结合相关文献得出十二台乡砖厂土坑竖穴墓地为慕容鲜卑遗存、喇嘛洞三燕文化墓地为夫余遗存的结论。这一研究成果对促进三燕文化研究起到重要的推动作用。

日本、韩国学者在马具、装身具的研究方面取得了很多成果。

至2020年，辽宁省文物考古研究所与日本奈良文化财研究所已合作完成四个项目，形成《东北亚考古学论丛》《辽西地区东晋十六国时期都城文化研究》两部与辽西地区魏晋十六国考古相关的成果[71]。

回顾六十多年来辽西地区魏晋十六国时期考古研究，从对具体遗存的描述、考证，到整体上作为一种考古学文化——三燕文化，再对构成三燕文化的各种因素及个案进行研究，认识不断深化。辽西地区魏晋十六国时期考古研究才刚刚破题，还有很多问题需要去发现、研究。

一是要拓宽视野，三燕文化研究不能仅局限于辽西中心分布区。

二是三燕文化的类型问题。朝阳十二台乡砖厂墓地、喇嘛洞三燕文化墓地、北票大板营子墓地都各有区别于其他两墓地的特点，可进一步划分为不同的类型。

三是西方文化因素问题。以金步摇为主的黄金制品是随慕容鲜卑传入辽西的[72]，冯素弗墓的玻璃器可能是经柔然传入的[73]，六方连续纹样在密县打虎亭汉墓中与胡旋舞共存[74]，可见与粟特人有密切关系[75]。据《魏书·安同传》："安同，辽东胡人也。其先祖曰世高，汉时以安息王侍子入洛。历魏至晋，避乱辽东，遂家焉。父屈，仕慕容晭，为殿中郎将。"[76]被称为辽东胡人的安同，实际应是粟特地区的安国人。另据出土于西安的唐永泰元年（765）《康晖墓志》可知，前燕还曾封康迁为归义侯，康氏也是粟特人[77]。毫无疑问，已有粟特人加入前燕政权中[78]，六方连续纹样是否通过他们传入的暂不得而知。

四是辨认辽海地区的氐人遗存。前秦灭前燕后，曾有大批氐人来到辽海地区[79]。随葬陶鞍马与武士俑的锦州前山十六国墓[80]，或许即为氐人遗存。

五是高句丽与夫余移民。慕容廆、慕容皝时期，曾经将大批的夫余、高句丽人迁到辽西，喇嘛洞三燕文化墓地即为慕容廆时迁到辽西的夫余人遗存[81]，高句丽遗存也有线索可寻[82]。相信以后会有更多新的发现，为高句丽、夫余历史考古，乃至十六国历史考古研究提出更多更新的课题。

六是棘城、龙城问题。目前对棘城还仅仅是停留在位置的考定上，龙城研究也刚刚起步。相关的金岭寺建筑址、龙腾苑遗址[83]都值得高度关注。

七是朝鲜半岛和日本古坟时代的三燕文化遗物问题。北燕灭亡后，三燕文化在辽西地区成为绝响，具有三燕文化特征的马具、黄金制品在朝鲜半岛和日本继续流行，辨识、研究这些遗物，揭示其流传过程及对当地社会政治、经济、文化的影响，也是一项很有意义的工作。

注释：

[1] 陈大为：《辽宁北票房身村晋墓发掘简报》，《考古》1960年第1期，第24—26页。

[2] 宿白：《东北、内蒙古地区的鲜卑遗迹——鲜卑遗迹辑录之一》，《文物》1977年第5期，第46页。

[3] 安家瑶：《中国的早期玻璃器皿》，《考古学报》1984年第4期，第417页。

[4] 董高：《朝阳地区鲜卑马具的初步研究》，载辽宁省考古、博物馆学会编《辽宁省考古、博物馆学会成立大会会刊》，1982，第115—120页；孙国平：《试论鲜卑族的步摇冠饰》，载辽宁省考古、博物馆学会编《辽宁省考古、博物馆学会成立大会会刊》，1982，第121—122页。

[5] 孙秉根：《安阳孝民屯晋墓发掘报告》，《考古》1983年第6期，第501—506页。

[6] 李庆发：《朝阳袁台子东晋壁画墓》，《文物》1984年第6期，第35—38页。

[7] 杨泓：《中国古代马具的发展和对外影响》，《文物》1984年第9期，第50—54页。

[8] 齐东方：《关于日本藤之木古坟出土马具文化渊源的考察》，《文物》1987年第9期，第62—68页、第75页。

[9] 徐基：《关于鲜卑慕容部遗迹的初步考察》，载中国考古学会编《中国考古学会第六次年会论文集》，文物出版社，1990，第160—173页。

[10] 张小舟：《北方地区魏晋十六国墓葬的分区与分期》，《考古学报》1987年第1期，第19—45页。

[11] 刘中澄：《关于朝阳袁台子晋墓壁画的初步研究》，《辽海文物学刊》1987年第1期，第95—101页。

[12] 陈大为、李宇峰：《辽宁朝阳后燕崔遹墓的发现》，《考古》1982年第3期，第270—274页。

[13] 黎瑶渤：《辽宁北票县西官营子北燕冯素弗墓》，《文物》1973年第3期，第2—28页。

[14] 尚晓波：《朝阳王子坟山墓群1987、1990年度考古发掘的主要收获》，《文物》1997年第11期，第1—18页。

[15] 该文于《辽海文物学刊》1991年第1期刊出时，题目改为《三燕文化遗存的初步研究》，第90—97页。

[16] 许永杰：《鲜卑遗存的考古学考察》，《北方文物》1993年第3期，第3—17页。

[17] 田立坤：《鲜卑文化源流的考古学考察》，载吉林大学考古学系编《青果集——吉林大学考古专业成立二十周年考古论文集》，知识出版社，1993，第361—367页；田立坤：《论辽西汉魏墓的乌桓文化因素》，载张忠培、许倬云主编《中国考古学跨世纪的回顾与前瞻——1999年西陵国际学术研讨会文集》，科学出版社，2000，第317—326页。

[18] 郑君雷：《早期东部鲜卑与早期拓跋鲜卑族源概论》，《青果集——吉林大学考古学系建系十周年纪念文集》，知识出版社，1998，第309—318页。

[19] 乔梁：《鲜卑遗存的认定与研究》，载许倬云、张忠培主编《中国考古学的跨世纪反思》，商务印书馆（香港），1999，第483—508页。

[20] 尚晓波：《朝阳地区两晋时期墓葬类型分析》，载吉林大学考古学系编《青果集——吉林大学考古学系建系

十周年纪念文集》，知识出版社，1998，第351—354页。

[21] 陈平：《辽西三燕墓葬论述》，《内蒙古文物考古》1998年第2期，第52—61页。

[22] 孙机：《步摇、步摇冠与摇叶饰片》，《文物》1991年第11期，第55—65页。

[23] 徐秉琨：《鲜卑·三国·古坟——中国朝鲜日本古代的文化交流》，辽宁古籍出版社，1996，153—160页。

[24] 魏存成：《高句丽马具的发现与研究》，《北方文物》1991年第4期，第18—27页。

[25] 齐东方：《中国早期马镫的有关问题》，《文物》1993年第4期，第71—78页、第89页。

[26] 田立坤、李智：《朝阳发现的三燕文化遗物及相关问题》，《文物》1994年第11期，第20—32页；田立坤：《三燕文化与高句丽考古遗存之比较》，载吉林大学考古学系编《青果集——吉林大学考古学系建系十周年纪念文集》，知识出版社，1998，第328—341页。

[27] 董高：《公元3至6世纪慕容鲜卑、高句丽、朝鲜、日本马具之比较研究》，《文物》1995年第10期，第34—42页。

[28] 徐秉琨：《鲜卑·三国·古坟——中国朝鲜日本古代的文化交流》，辽宁古籍出版社，1996，第140—153页。

[29] 孙守道：《中国三燕时期与日本古坟骑马文化的比较研究》，载郭大顺、秋山进午主编《东北亚考古学研究——中日合作研究报告书》，文物出版社，1997，第312—320页。

[30] 田立坤、张克举：《前燕的甲骑具装》，《文物》1997年第11期，第72—75页。

[31] 王巍：《从出土马具看三至六世纪东亚诸国的交流》，《考古》1997年第12期，第66—85页。

[32] 申敬澈先生的《古镫考》发表在《釜山史学》第9辑（1985年），定申秀夫译为日文刊于《古代文化》38卷6期（1986年）。姚义田从日文转译为《马镫考》，刊于《辽海文物学刊》1996年第1期，第141—159页。

[33] 田立坤：《棘城新考》，《辽海文物学刊》1996年第2期，第117—122页。

[34] 朱泓：《朝阳魏晋时期鲜卑墓葬人骨研究》，《辽海文物学刊》1996年第2期，第80—91页。

[35] 万欣、张国林、张克举等：《辽宁北票市喇嘛洞鲜卑贵族墓地出土铁器的保护处理及初步研究》，《考古》1998年第12期，第38—45页、第103页。

[36] 董高：《三燕佛教略考》，《辽海文物学刊》1996年第1期，第1—7页、第55页；李新全：《三燕瓦当考》，《辽海文物学刊》1996年第1期，第12—15页；郎成刚：《朝阳北塔三燕础石考》，《辽海文物学刊》1996年第1期，第8—11页、第15页；周亚利：《朝阳三燕、北魏遗存中反映出的汉文化因素》，《辽海文物学刊》1996年第1期，第16—25页；尚晓波：《大凌河流域鲜卑文化双耳镂孔圈足釜及相关问题考》，《辽海文物学刊》1996年第1期，第26—33页。

[37] 八类墓葬分别是梯形土坑竖穴木棺墓、矩形土坑竖穴木椁墓、砖室墓、石板搭盖石室墓、石块垒砌石椁墓、石板搭盖石椁墓、石块垒砌石室墓、石块垒砌券顶石室墓。早期为莫护跋、木延、涉归时期，上限为曹魏初年，下限到西晋太康十年（289）慕容廆从辽东北迁回"徒河之青山"；中期始于慕容廆迁回"徒河之青山"，至前燕灭亡，即东晋太和五年（前燕建熙十一年，370年）；晚期为后、北燕时期（384—436）。见田立坤：《三燕文化墓葬的类型与分期》，载巫鸿主编《汉唐之间文化艺术的互动与交融》，文物出版社，2001，第215—222页。

[38] 田立坤：《关于北票喇嘛洞三燕文化墓地的几个问题》，载辽宁省文物考古研究所编《辽宁考古文集》，辽宁民族出版社，2003，第263—267页。

[39] 田立坤：《袁台子壁画墓的再认识》，《文物》2002年第9期，第41—48页。

[40] 万欣：《辽西地区慕容鲜卑与三燕文化研究综述》，载辽宁省文物考古研究所编《三燕文物精粹》，辽宁人民出版社，2002，第3—12页；万欣：《鲜卑墓葬、三燕史迹与金步摇饰的发现与研究》，载辽宁省文物考古研究所编《辽宁考古文集》，辽宁民族出版社，2003，第268—281页。

[41] 辽宁省文物考古研究所、朝阳市博物馆、北票市文物管理所：《辽宁北票喇嘛洞墓地1998年发掘报告》，《考古学报》2004年第2期，第235页。

[42] 韦正：《鲜卑墓葬研究》，《考古学报》2009年第3期，第349—378页。

[43] 潘玲：《对部分与鲜卑相关遗存年代的再探讨》，载教育部人文社会科学重点研究基地吉林大学边疆考古研究中心编《边疆考古研究》第13辑，科学出版社，2013，第215页。

[44] 田立坤：《步摇考》，载张庆捷、李书吉、李钢主编《4～6世纪的北中国与欧亚大陆》，科学出版社，

2006，第47—67页。

[45] 江楠：《金步摇饰品的发现与研究》，《草原文物》2012年第 2 期，第74—83页。

[46] 韦正：《金珰与步摇——汉晋命妇冠饰试探》，《文物》2013 年第5期，第60—69页。

[47] 徐秉琨：《步摇与慕容鲜卑》，《文史》2014年第4期，第5—35页；收入《北燕冯素弗墓》，文物出版社，2015，第284—313页。

[48] 王铁英：《马镫的起源》，载余太山主编《欧亚学刊》第3辑，中华书局，2002，第76—100页。

[49] 陈凌：《马镫起源及其在中古时期的传播新论》，载余太山、李锦绣主编《欧亚学刊》第9辑，中华书局，2009，第181、202页。

[50] 杨泓：《冯素弗墓马镫和中国马具装铠的发展》，载辽宁省博物馆编《辽宁省博物馆刊（2010）》，辽海出版社，2010，第1—6页。

[51] 田立坤：《古镫新考》，《文物》2013年第11期，第53—60页。

[52] 陈山：《北票新发现的三燕马具研究》，《文物》2003年第3期，第64—65页。

[53] 田立坤：《论喇嘛洞墓地出土的马具》，《文物》2010年第2期，第69—76页。

[54] 王振江：《安阳晋墓马具复原》，《考古》1983年第6期，第554—559页。

[55] 刘永华：《中国古代车舆马具》，上海辞书出版社，2002，第205—206页。

[56] 田立坤：《高桥鞍的复原及有关问题》，载辽宁省文物考古研究所、日本奈良文化财研究所编《东北亚考古学论丛》，科学出版社，2010，第93—98页。

[57] 田立坤、吕学明：《日本古坟时代马具三则》，载辽宁省文物考古研究所、日本奈良文化财研究所编《东北亚考古学论丛》，科学出版社，2010，第105—116页。

[58] 田立坤：《鸾镳考》，载辽宁省博物馆编《辽宁省博物馆馆刊（2011）》，辽海出版社，2011，第38—46页。

[59] 田立坤：《三燕文化马具装饰纹样研究》，载辽宁省博物馆编《辽宁省博物馆馆刊（2012）》，辽海出版社，2013，第103—122页。

[60] 田立坤：《马掌小考》，载杨泓先生八秩华诞纪念文集编委会编《考古、艺术与历史——杨泓先生八秩华诞纪念文集》，文物出版社，2018，第374—384页。

[61] 田立坤、万雄飞、白宝玉：《朝阳古城考古纪略》，载教育部人文社会科学重点研究基地、吉林大学边疆考古研究中心编《边疆考古研究》第6辑，科学出版社，2007，第301—311页；万雄飞：《三燕龙城宫城南门遗址及其建筑特点》，载辽宁省文物考古研究所、日本奈良文化财研究所编《辽西地区东晋十六国时期都城文化研究》，辽宁人民出版社，2017，第75—77页。

[62] 田立坤：《龙城新考》，载教育部人文社会科学重点研究基地、吉林大学边疆考古研究中心编《边疆考古研究》第12辑，科学出版社，2012，第315—325页。

[63] 辛岩、穆启文、付兴盛：载辽宁省文物考古研究所编《辽宁北票金岭寺魏晋建筑遗址发掘报告》，《辽宁考古文集》2，科学出版社，2010，第198—224页。

[64] 田立坤：《金岭寺建筑址为“庑庙”说》，载吉林大学边疆考古研究中心编《庆祝张忠培先生八十岁论文集》，科学出版社，2014，第461—477页。

[65] 郑岩：《魏晋南北朝壁画墓研究》，文物出版社，2002，第40—41页。

[66] 万欣：《喇嘛洞铁工初论——兼议中国慕容鲜卑、朝鲜三国时期和日本古坟时代铁器葬俗的一致性与差异性》，载辽宁省文物考古研究所、日本奈良文化财研究所编《东北亚考古学论丛》，科学出版社，2010，第67—84页；陈建立、韩汝玢、万欣等：《北票喇嘛洞墓地出土铁器的金相实验研究》，《文物》2001年第12期，第71—79页；韩汝玢：《北票冯素弗墓出土金属器的鉴定与研究》，载辽宁省博物馆编《辽宁省博物馆馆刊（2010）》，辽海出版社，2010，第7—19页；刘宁、刘博：《冯素弗墓出土的铁镜》，载辽宁省博物馆编《辽宁省博物馆馆刊（2011）》，辽海出版社，2011，第9—13页；申桂云、王怡威、刘博：《冯素弗墓出土金器的分析与研究》，载辽宁省博物馆编著《北燕冯素弗墓》，文物出版社，2015，第204—210页。

[67] 安家瑶：《冯素弗墓出土的玻璃器》，载邓聪、陈星灿主编《桃李成蹊集——庆祝安志敏先生八十寿辰》，

香港中文大学中国考古艺术研究中心，2004，第377—387页；周晓晶：《冯素弗墓出土的玉碗与玉剑首》，载辽宁省博物馆编《辽宁省博物馆馆刊（2011）》，辽海出版社，2011，第14—19页；刘宁：《北燕、柔然与草原丝绸之路——从冯素弗墓出土的玻璃器谈起》，载辽宁省博物馆编《北燕冯素弗墓》，文物出版社，2015，第238—245页；陶亮、卢治萍：《冯素弗墓陶器综合考察》，载辽宁省博物馆编《北燕冯素弗墓》，文物出版社，2015，第278—283页。

[68] 万雄飞、白宝玉：《朝阳老城北大街出土的3—6世纪莲花瓦当初探》，载辽宁省文物考古研究所、日本奈良文化财研究所编《东北亚考古学论丛》，科学出版社，2010，第61—66页；王飞峰：《三燕瓦当研究》，载教育部人文社会科学重点研究基地吉林大学边疆考古研究中心边疆考古与中国文化认同协同创新中心编《边疆考古研究》第12辑，科学出版社，2012，第295—313页；李新全：《三燕文化界格图案瓦当源流考》，载辽宁省文物考古研究所、日本奈良文化财研究所编《辽西地区东晋十六国时期都城文化研究》，辽宁人民出版社，2017，第118—131页；王飞峰：《三燕、高句丽莲花纹瓦当的出现及其关系》，载辽宁省文物考古研究所、日本奈良文化财研究所编《辽西地区东晋十六国时期都城文化研究》，辽宁人民出版社，2017，第132—153页。

[69] 田立坤：《六方连续纹样考》，载吉林大学边疆考古研究中心编《新果集——庆祝林沄先生七十华诞论文集》，科学出版社，2009，第466—481页；田立坤：《前燕的两个粟特家族》，载荣新江、罗丰主编，宁夏文物考古研究所、北京大学中国古代史研究中心编《粟特人在中国——考古发现与出土文献的新印证》下册，科学出版社，2016，第532—541页。

[70] 朱泓、曾雯、张全超等：《喇嘛洞三燕文化居民族属问题的生物考古学考察》，《吉林大学社会科学学报》2012年第1期，第44—51页、第159页。

[71] 辽宁省文物考古研究所、日本奈良文化财研究所编《东北亚考古学论丛》，科学出版社，2010；辽宁省文物考古研究所、日本奈良文化财研究所编著《辽西地区东晋十六国时期都城文化研究》，辽宁人民出版社，2017。

[72] 田立坤：《步摇考》，载张庆捷、李书吉、李钢主编《4—6世纪的北中国与欧亚大陆》，科学出版社，2006，第53—57页。

[73] 宿白：《东北、内蒙古地区的鲜卑遗迹——鲜卑遗迹辑录之一》，《文物》1977年第5期，第46页。

[74] 河南省文物研究所编《密县打虎亭汉墓》，文物出版社，1993，第238—239页。

[75] 田立坤：《六方连续纹样考》，载吉林大学边疆考古研究中心编《新果集——庆祝林沄先生七十华诞论文集》，科学出版社，2009，第474—478页。

[76] 魏收：《魏书》卷三十《安同传》，中华书局，1974，第712页。

[77] 陕西省古籍整理办公室编《全唐文补遗》第五辑《康晖墓志》，吴钢主编，王京阳本辑副主编，王京阳、李慧、吴敏霞等点校，三秦出版社，1998，第408页。

[78] 田立坤：《前燕的两个粟特家族》，载荣新江、罗丰主编，宁夏文物考古研究所、北京大学中国古代史研究中心编《粟特人在中国——考古发现与出土文献的新印证》下册，科学出版社，2016，第533页、第535—536页。

[79] 考古发现已有辽东太守《吕宪墓表》、幽州刺史《吕他墓表》。见路远：《后秦〈吕他墓表〉与〈吕宪墓表〉》，《文博》2001年第5期，第62—65页。

[80] 鲁宝林、辛发：《辽宁锦州市前山十六国时期墓葬的清理》，《考古》1998年第1期，第92—94页。

[81] 田立坤：《四世纪夫余史迹钩沉》，中国中古时期（4—7世纪）的文化与文化多样性国际学术研讨会会议论文，慕尼黑，2017。收入《从考古与文献看中古早期的中国北方》（德国），2019年，第39—56页。

[82] 张桂霞、杜晓红、杜守昌等：《辽宁省朝阳县土城子两座前燕墓》，《北方文物》2015年第2期，第19页。

[83] 朱子方：《记后燕龙腾苑遗址的发现》，《东北地方史研究》1984年第1期，第7—8页。

Northern Yan and the Steppe-Silk Road

Liu Ning

Deputy Director, Liaoning Provincial Museum; Second Level
Researcher; Exhibition Curator, *Gold from Dragon City:
Masterpieces of Three Yan from Liaoning, 337–436*

In 1965, an important Northern Yan (407–36 CE) tomb was discovered in Beipiao, Liaoning Province, which opened doors to the study of Northern Yan and the Steppe-Silk Road, an ancient network of overland routes through the Eurasian steppe. The tomb belonged to Feng Sufu of Northern Yan and is a rare example from the Sixteen Kingdoms period with a specific date (415 CE) and known identity of the owner. According to the *Jin Shu Feng Ba Zai Ji* [Book of Jin], Feng Sufu was the younger brother of Feng Ba, the emperor of Northern Yan, who assisted his elder brother in establishing the Northern Yan regime. Feng Sufu was titled Duke of Fanyang and later Duke of Liaoxi. He achieved remarkable success in attaining various important posts such as chief minister, general of the cavalry, minister of record, and grand marshal. He was in charge of local affairs of the southwestern part of present-day Liaoning and the northeastern part of Hebei. Feng Sufu died in the seventh year of the Taiping era of Northern Yan (415 CE) and was buried in the same year. His brother, Emperor Feng Ba, is said to have visited his grave seven times, crying mournfully.

Fig. 1   Duck-shaped glassware. Sixteen Kingdoms-Northern Yan (407–436). Unearthed in 1965 from the tomb of Feng Sufu in Xiguanyingzi, Beipiao. *Photo courtesy of Liaoning Provincial Museum.*

Among the many artifacts unearthed in Feng's tomb are five pieces of glassware, including a duck-shaped vessel (fig. 1) , a bowl, a cup, a pot, and a partially broken vessel. These are some of the earliest and largest groups of glassware unearthed in China.[1] Never before has such a large quantity of glassware been found in a single tomb of the same period in mainland China, the Korean peninsula, and the Japanese archipelago. Therefore, they are critical for the study of ancient glass craftsmanship and the Steppe-Silk Road.

An Jiayao, a Chinese scholar specializing in the study of glassware, believes that all the glassware in this set was made with the glassblowing technique commonly used in the Roman imperial period; the craftsmanship is of a high level, and the bowl and the cup, in particular, contain few air bubbles or impurities and are highly translucent. The duck-shaped vessel is the most exquisite piece in the group, with a distinctive shape and decoration. No other piece of glassware with exactly the same shape has been found in China or abroad. All five pieces are made of soda-lime glass, and are likely produced in the northeastern province of the Roman Empire. [2]

In her paper, An Jiayao compared this set of glassware, including an emerald green cup, with the Roman glassware found outside China. She points out that Roman craftsmen had made glassware of a similar color in the third century. But glassware similar in shape to this cup did not appear until the end of the fourth century.

No example earlier than 375 CE has been found. Therefore, these pieces are likely produced in the late Roman imperial period. Considering that Feng Sufu died in 415 CE, this set of glassware would have been made and transported to Northern Yan between 375 and 415 CE. This period corresponds to the Eastern Jin in China, when glass was a symbol of status and wealth. The Roman glassware unearthed in Feng's tomb was probably brought to Northern Yan via the Rouran Khaganate.

The Rouran was one of the northern minorities of ancient China, mainly active from the late fourth century to the mid-sixth century. In the fifth year of Tianxing in Northern Wei (402 CE), the Rouran ruler Shelun united the clan and declared himself khagan. The Rouran regime began to grow in strength. Its territory "expanded to Yanqi in the west and to Korea in the east, across the desert and the sea in the north, and reached the Gobi desert in the south. The imperial court was built north of Dunhuang and Zhangye."[3] Ruoran became a nomadic empire comparable to Northern Wei. The relationship between the two countries was complicated by incessant fighting during the period of 402–87.[4] Thus, when the Rouran khagan traveled to Northern Yan, he would have taken a route bypassing the Northern Wei capital of Pingcheng (in modern Datong, Shanxi province) which means that besides the academically recognized northern route connecting the Western Regions to Pingcheng, there was another route on the steppe.

Regarding the relationship between Rouran and Northern Yan, according to historical documents, Rouran had many dealings with the Western Regions during the Northern Yan period. At that time, transportation between central China and Central and Western Asia was mainly through the Western Regions. Located in the northern steppe, Rouran was geographically convenient since it was connected to the Western Regions in the west and Northern Yan in the east. Rouran and Northern Yan had close exchanges. Moreover, the Rouran khagan had lived in Northern Yan territory for a long time, suggesting why it is likely that this group of glassware was found there.

Hulü Khagan, who reigned Rouran from 410 to 414, had a kinship with the Northern Yan emperor Feng Ba. In the year 411, soon after his accession to power, Hulü offered a tribute to Northern Yan with a request to marry Feng Ba's daughter, Princess Lelang. Feng Ba agreed. His brother Feng Sufu had suggested refusing the request and sending another woman of the imperial family instead because Rouran was "not of our race." So when Hulü later visited Northern Yan with his family, he tried to foster good relations with Feng Sufu by offering extraordinary gifts.

In 414, Hulü was, in turn, about to marry his daughter to Feng Ba. Hulü's elder brother, Buluzhen, conspired with his minister Shuli to expel Hulü and claimed the title of khagan himself. Hulü took his whole family to Northern Yan, but later asked Feng Ba to send troops to escort them back to their country. However, Hulü was killed on the way by the general who escorted them. In the same year, not long after Buluzhen succeeded to the throne, there was infighting in the imperial family. Buluzhen, who had held the throne for a little longer than a year, was hanged by Datan, the son of Shelun's youngest uncle, Pu Hun. Datan became the tenth khagan of Rouran and reigned from 414 to 429. Under his rule, the Rouran Khanate reached its peak and continued its alliance with Northern Yan. Datan sent three thousand horses and ten thousand sheep to Northern Yan. While making amends with Northern Yan through marriage and tribute, Hulü and Datan also established kinship with the Later Qin—another state in the Sixteen Kingdoms period (384–417)—in the south, and maintained close relations with Song of the Southern dynasty. Their aim was to keep the Northern Wei in check so they could expand southward and obtain more food and resources. Therefore, Datan would have sent horses and sheep to Northern Yan shortly after he ascended the throne.

The Rouran regime (402–552 CE) existed for roughly the same number of years as the Northern Wei dynasty (386–534 CE). Among the minorities in the north of China during this period, only Rouran had the ability to fight Northern Wei. The two countries were alternately at war and at peace. At that time, if travellers followed the traditional Silk Road from the Hexi Corridor to the Northern Yan capital of Longcheng, they had to pass through Northern Wei, Later Qin, and several Liang states in the northwest. As mentioned above, Rouran established its imperial court north of Dunhuang and Zhangye, which means the territory controlled by Rouran would have been north of the Hexi Corridor. There would, therefore, have been a passage from Ruonan to Northern Yan north of the Silk Road and Northern Wei's Pingcheng.

After Hulü arrived at Northern Yan, Feng Ba made him the Marquis of Shanggu and married his daughter as a concubine. But Hulü wanted to return to his country. He told Feng Ba that if he could make it to Chi-le, the Rouran people would welcome him there. So Feng Ba sent Wanling, a general of Northern Yan, with three hundred cavalry to escort Hulü back to Rouran. Wanling was worried about the long journey, however, and well before they reached Chi-le, he killed Hulü at Heishan, or Black Mountain, located not far from Northern Yan and outside Northern Wei territory.

The name Heishan appeared in the historical records of the Tang dynasty. According to documents, in the third year of Xianqing of the Tang dynasty (660 CE), General Xue Rengui, Xin Wenling, and others led the Tang army to attack the Khitan. The army entered the steppe and fought in Heishan. They captured the Khitan leader Abugu and brought him to Luoyang.[5] It is also recorded in *Zizhi Tongjian* [Comprehensive mirror for aid in government], vol. 200,] *Tang Ji 16* [Tang record 16], that in the fifth year of Xianqing, Emperor Gaozong of Tang sent Ashide Shubin and others to lead an army to crush the rebellious Xi people, who then sent an envoy to surrender. Ashide Shubin then joined Xue Rengui in his crusade against the Khitan. The army defeated the Khitan at Heishan. They captured Abugu and transferred him to the eastern capital, where the emperor was at that time. There are also many references in Liao dynasty historical documents to Heishan, which may have been a necessary stop on one of the traditional routes to the north of the Gobi desert. The *Liao Shi Yingwei Zhi* [History of Liao] recorded: "Heishan is thirteen miles north of Qingzhou, where there is a pool in which there are lotus flowers." Qingzhou is in present-day Balin, north of the Xilamulun River. According to archaeological excavations and relevant evidence, Heishan should be present-day Hanshan in Balin Right Banner, where sites of Liao dynasty rituals are found.[6] Balin Right Banner is under the administration of Chifeng, Inner Mongolia. Its jurisdiction extends from Chifeng city to the north and across the Xilamulun River via the Balin Bridge. During the Northern Yan period, the Chifeng area was the territory of the Kumo Xi people, whose regime was not yet strong enough to fight against Northern Yan. Therefore, when Hulü tried to return to Rouran and avoid the territory of Northern Wei, going north from Longcheng (present-day Chaoyang) was the safest route. On the other hand, Hulü's belief that he would be welcomed in Chi-le and would be able to reach Rouran safely via Chi-le suggests that the two countries had a close relationship at that time.

Chi-le is also known as Gaoche, Dili, Tiele, and Dingling. After the Han dynasty crushed the Northern Xiongnu, the Chi-le people began to move southward and interact with the Han people in the Central Plains. From the end of the fourth century to the middle of the sixth century, following the Xiongnu and Xianbei, the Chi-le and Rouran people were active in a vast area of northwestern China.

Chi-le and Rouran fought and tolerated each other, with Rouran dominating for a prolonged time. According to *Wei Shu* [Book of Wei], Chiluohou, a high-ranking official of Chi-le, defected to Rouran and helped its leader Shelun to defeat the Chi-le tribes. With its main force severely damaged, Chi-le submitted to Rouran, laying the cornerstone of Rouran's hegemony north of the Gobi desert. Shelun declared himself khagan and established the Rouran state (402 CE). He rewarded Chiluohou and made him a lord. Shelun's successor Hulü also treated Chiluohou with honor. But after Hulü had been expelled to Northern Yan,

Buluzhen committed adultery with Chiluohou's young wife. The wife revealed to Buluzhen that Chiluohou would support Datan against Buluzhen, and he had given Datan a golden bridle as a sign of fidelity. In response, Buluzhen sent eight thousand cavalry to surround Chiluohou and burned all his treasures. Chiluohou slit his own throat and died. Buluzhen then attacked Datan, but Datan was victorious and hanged Buluzhen and his accomplice, Sheba, son of Shelun, before declaring himself khagan.[7]

Where did Chiluohou's treasures, including the golden bridle, come from? Treasures were rare on the desert steppe. Chiluohou's treasures most likely came via the Silk Road, which means there was a route on the steppe that could lead to Chi-le. Since Chi-le was subordinate to Rouran, the Steppe-Silk Road must also have been able to connect to Rouran. At that time, Western merchants who traveled along the Silk Road were called "*shanghu*," and these treasures would likely have been acquired through them.

According to *Wei Shu* [Book of Wei], after Shelun's invasion, Chi-le had to pay tribute to Rouran and also participate in the wars waged by Rouran. Unwilling to endure the oppression, the Chi-le people revolted many times. In 487 CE, Afuzhiluo, a Chi-le leader, and his brother Qiongqi fled from Rouran and established the Gaoche state. To defeat Rouran, Afuzhiluo decided to ally with the Northern Wei (at this time Northern Yan had fallen.) In 490, Afuzhiluo sent *shanghu* to the Northern Wei capital and offered two arrows to the imperial court as a sign of friendship and alliance.[8] *Shanghu* played an important role during this period. In order to do business along the Silk Road, they had to deal with various countries and could therefore act as intermediaries. They had been traveling on the Silk Road long before 490 and must have visited Rouran and Chi-le territories. Therefore, it is likely that the glassware in Feng Sufu's tomb was brought to Rouran by *shanghu*.

The fact that Gaoche (Chi-le) sent *shanghu* to Northern Wei suggests that the route Western merchants frequented could lead both to Pingcheng in Northern Wei and to the Chi-le and Rouran territories in the north of the Gobi desert. Feng Sufu was buried in 415 CE. Two of the three recorded exchanges between Rouran and Northern Yan occurred before that year (in 411 and 414). In addition, as mentioned earlier, the emerald green Roman glass cup unearthed in Feng's tomb was fabricated later than 375 CE. Therefore, it can be assumed that the glassware from Feng's tomb would have been brought to Northern Yan from Rouran by Hulü between 411–14.

So, what journey did the glassware undergo to reach Rouran? We have to take into account the relationship between Rouran and other countries along the Silk Road. When Rouran was powerful, the small countries in Western regions all suffered from looting and were forced to submit to the stronger state.[9] During the reign of Hulü, Rouran's influence reached the states of Yiwu and Gaochang (both in present-day Xinjiang). Allied with the Yueban tribe, Rouran defeated the Wusun state and divided its land. The Wusun people were forced to migrate westward to the Pamir Mountains.[10] With these victories, Rouran controlled a vast area stretching from Korea in the east to Lake Balkhash in the west.[11] However, from the beginning of the fifth century, Northern Wei had been competing with Rouran for control of the Western Region, with both sides winning and losing. Therefore, the traditional Silk Road, which passes through the Hexi Corridor and Yiwu, across northern and southern Xinjiang, and over the Pamir Mountains, would have been unsafe in the period of frequent wars between Rouran and Northern Wei or other countries in the Western Region.

On the southeast coast of the Caspian Sea, a city named Qumis 和犊城 (present-day Damghan, Iran) served as an important stop on the Silk Road. From here to the east, via Samarkand and across the Pamir Mountains, there were three routes connecting to the Hexi Corridor: the North Road via Suyab (in present-day Kyrgyzstan); Gaochang, and Hami (in present-day Xinjiang); the Middle Road across the Kunlun Mountains and Tianshan Mountains, through Shule, Kucha, and Yanqi (all in present-day Xinjiang); and the South Road through the kingdoms of Khotan and Qiemo (both in present-day Xinjiang). All three routes led to Dunhuang, from where one can reach Chang'an via the Hexi Corridor, an important passage on the Silk Road first traversed by Zhang Qian (?–114 BCE) in the Han dynasty (fig. 2).

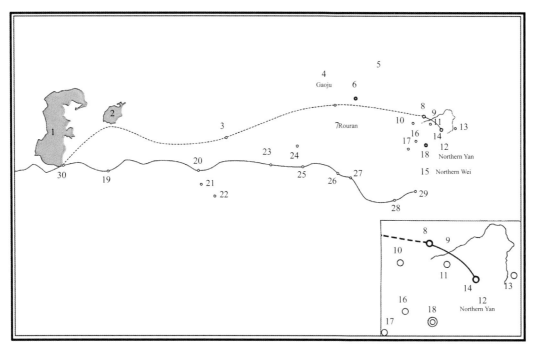

Fig.2   Map of the Steppe-Silk Road (Rouran-Northern Yan)

1. Caspian Sea 2. Aral Sea 3. Gongyuecheng 4. Gaoche (Chi-le) 5. Eastern Gaoche 6. Ulaanbaatar 7. Rouran Khaganate 8. Heishan (present-day Hanshan) 9. Xilamulun River 10. Weichang 11. Chifeng 12. Northern Yan 13. Liaoyang 14. Longcheng (present-day Chaoyang) 15. Northern Wei 16. Zhangjiakou 17. Pingcheng (present-day Datong) 18. Youzhou (present-day Beijing) 19. Samarkand 20. Kingdom of Shule 21. Kingdom of Shache 22. Kingdom of Khotan 23. Kingdom of Loulan (Shanshan) 24. Kingdom of Yiwu (present-day Hami) 25. Dunhuang 26. Zhangye 27. Wuwei 28. Chang'an (present-day Xi'an) 29. Luoyang 30. Damghan

The *Sui Shu·Tie Le Zhuan* [Book of Sui] describes the Tiele (Chi-le) as follows: "Tiele's ancestors were the descendants of the Xiongnu and were the most diverse. [Their land] stretches from the West Sea in the east, across the valleys."[12] The West Sea refers to the present-day Caspian Sea. For *shanghu* to reach Chi-le or Rouran from the city of Qumis, besides the Silk Road over the Pamir Mountains and through the Xinjiang region, there would have to have been another route going northeast. Therefore, the Roman glassware in Feng's tomb may have traveled from Qumis along the east coast of the Caspian Sea all the way to the northeast, through the Steppe-Silk Road to the territory of Chi-le (present-day Kazakhstan, which belonged to the Great Yuezhi in the Han dynasty) and Rouran. The glassware was either brought to Chi-le by *shanghu* before it was offered as tribute to Ruoran, or it was brought directly to Ruoran by *shanghu*.

Thus, from Qumis, the Silk Road was divided into two routes: one heading east over the Pamir Mountains, through Xinjiang and via the Hexi Corridor, known as the traditional Desert Silk Road; and the other northeastward along the eastern shore of the Caspian Sea, stretching into the territories of Chi-le and Rouran, namely the Steppe-Silk Road.

In addition, there were at least two eastward routes on the steppe. One route passed through the Northern Wei capital of Pingcheng, which was used by the *shanghu* sent as envoys by Gaoche to Northern Wei to show goodwill in 490. This was the Steppe-Silk Road centered on Pingcheng and connected to Iwu in the west in the fifth century. Regarding the route that the glassware of Feng's tomb traveled, it is generally believed that it was transported to Chinese territory via Qumis, and passed through present-day Datong (Pingcheng), Zhangjiakou, Chifeng, before turning southeast to reach Chaoyang (Longcheng). The Roman glassware imported to East Asia along the Steppe-Silk Road would have been products of the eastern provinces in the late Roman period. Analyzed from the manufacturing process, the glass vessels from Feng's tomb are similar to Roman glassware unearthed in Gyeongju, South Korea and in Jingxian, Hebei province.[13] Jingxian is located southeast of Datong in Shanxi province, close to the seaport in the Shandong peninsula. The discovery of Roman glassware here suggests that the Roman glassware found on the Korean peninsula was possibly imported by sea via the Shandong peninsula, which was connected to the Steppe-Silk Road via Pingcheng. But this would have been the case after the Northern Wei dynasty unified the north. Before that, during the period of Northern Yan, the communication between Rouran and Northern Yan was obviously along a different route.

This other route ran north of Northern Wei territory. This was the route taken by the Rouran khagan Hulü, when he brought his family to Northern Yan. From the fact that he was killed in Heshan (in present-day Balin Right Banner) when he tried to return home, it can be inferred that this route went northward from present-day Chaoyang, crossing the Xilamulun River and passing via Heshan to enter the territory of Chi-le, before arriving at Rouran. (Or one could take the Chifeng-Zhangjiakou route, which passed through present-day Weichang county in Hebei instead of the Xilamulun River). This route, which bypassed the capital of the Northern Wei dynasty, also led to present-day northeastern China. Therefore, it is also possible that the Roman glassware found on the Korean peninsula was imported via this northern steppe route, that is, northward along the Caspian Sea, through Chi-le and Rouran territories before entering into Northern Yan, and then transported to the northern part of the Korean peninsula. This route could be verified through various historical documents, but it seems to have received little academic attention. I hope that this paper will contribute to further study of the Steppe-Silk Road.

NOTES

[1] Li Yaobo, "Liaoning beipiaoxian xiguan yingzi beiyan feng susu mu" [Feng Sufu tomb of Northern Yan in Beipiao, Liaoning], *Wenwu* [Cultural Relics] 1973.3: 2–28.

[2] An Jiayao, "Fengsufu mu chutu de boliqi" [Glassware unearthed from the Feng Sufu tomb] in *Taolichengxi ji— Qingzhu anzhimin xiansheng bashi shouchen* [Anthology in celebration of An Zhimin's 80th birthday], The Chinese University of Hong Kong Center of Chinese Archaeology and Art (2004): 377–87.

[3] *Wei shu* [Book of Wei] (vol. 103), *Ruru, xiongnu yuwen mohuai, tuhe duanjiuliuyu, gaoche zhuan* [Biography of Rouran, Yuwen Mohuai of Xiongnu, Duanjiuliuyu of Tuhe, and Gaoche], Zhonghua Book Company. (1974): 2291.

[4] Tian Jianping, "Luelun rouran yu beiwei de guanxi" [A brief discussion of the relationship between Rouran and Northern Wei], *Journal of Inner Mongolia University* 1986.3: 110.

[5] *Jiu tang shu* [Old book of Tang] (vol. 83), *Xuerengui liezhuan* [Biography of Xue Rengui], Zhonghua Book Company. (1975): 2781. Also in *Xin tang shu* [New book of Tang] (vol. 3), *Xuerengui liezhuan* [Biography of Xue Rengui], Zhonghua Book Company. (1975): 4140–41.

[6] Inner Mongolia Autonomous Region Cultural Relics Task Force, Balin Right Banner Museum, "Neimenggu balinyouqi hanshan liaodai jisu yizhi fajue baogao" [Report on the excavation of the Liao dynasty ritual site at Hanshan, Balin Right Banner, Inner Mongolia]. *Kaogu* [Archeology] 1988.11: 1002–14.

[7] *Wei shu* [Book of Wei] (vol. 103): 2292.

[8] *Wei shu* [Book of Wei] (vol. 103): 2310.

[9] *Bei shi* [History of the Northern Dynasties] (vol. 98), "Ruru zhuan, xiongnu yuwen mohuai, tuhe duanjiuliuyu, gaoche" [Biography of Rouran, Yuwen Mohuai of Xiongnu, Duanjiuliuyu of Tuhe, and Gaoche], Zhonghua Book Company (1974): 3251.

[10] *Wei shu* [Book of Wei] (vol. 102), *Xiyu wusun guo* [Wusun of the Western Regions], Zhonghua Book Company (1974): 2267.

[11] Wang Jing, *Rouran han guo yanjiu* [Study of the Rouran Khaganate], Master's Thesis, School of History and Culture, Shanxi University (2013).

[12] *Sui shu* [Book of Sui] (vol. 84), "Beidi tiele zhuan" [Biography of Beidi and Tiele], Zhonghua Book Company (1974): 1879.

[13] An Jiayao, "Fengsufu mu chutu de boliqi" [Glassware unearthed from the Feng Sufu tomb] in *Taolichengxi ji— Qingzhu anzhimin xiansheng bashi shouchen* [Anthology in celebration of An Zhimin's 80th Birthday], The Chinese University of Hong Kong Center of Chinese Archaeology and Art (2004): 377–87.

北燕与草原丝绸之路

刘宁
辽宁省博物馆副馆长、二级研究员、
"龙城之金：辽宁三燕文物选萃，
337—436"特展策展人

1965年考古发现了一座很重要的北燕（407—436）墓葬，从而引起了对北燕与草原丝绸之路的研究。那就是辽宁北票发现的北燕冯素弗墓，一座十六国时期有确切纪年（415）及墓主人的墓葬。据《晋书·冯跋载记》冯素弗是北燕皇帝冯跋之弟，助兄建立北燕政权，封范阳公，拜侍中、车骑大将军、录尚书事，后改封辽西公，任大司马职，治理北燕，居功厥伟，即统辖着今辽宁西南部及河北东北部，是一个地方主管。一说卒于北燕太平七年（415），及葬，燕王冯跋七临之，哭之哀恸。

图1　十六国北燕　鸭形玻璃器　1965年北票西官营子冯素弗墓出土　辽宁省博物馆藏

冯墓中众多的出土文物中有五件玻璃器，计有鸭形器（图1）、碗、杯、钵和一件残器，是中国出土的年代较早而数量又最多的一批玻璃器[1]。这些珍贵的玻璃器，数量较多且成一组出现，非常少见，在中国或朝鲜半岛、日本列岛同一时期的同一个墓葬里未曾出现数量这么多的玻璃器，是研究古代玻璃工艺和草原丝绸之路的重要实物。

安家瑶先生认为这批玻璃器皿的工艺相似，都是罗马时期常用的无模吹制成型的玻璃工艺，玻璃的熔制水平较高，尤其是碗和杯，气泡和杂质都很少，透明度好。鸭形器是工艺最复杂、器形和装饰最有特点的一件，全中国唯此一件，国外也无完全一样的造型。这几件均为普通的钠钙玻璃，可以归类到罗马玻璃中，很可能是罗马帝国东北行省的产品[2]。

安家瑶文章中提到冯墓五件玻璃器与域外罗马玻璃器的比较时指出，其中一件深翠绿色的玻璃杯的研究结果表明，公元3世纪，罗马工匠制造有类似颜色的彩色玻璃器，在年代可考的罗马玻璃器中，与此杯器形相似的玻璃器出现于公元4世纪末，没有发现早于375年的，可以说是罗马晚期的器皿。一说冯素弗死于415年，距此中间只有几十年的差距，因此375—415年是这批玻璃器制造和输入的最宽泛的年代。此时中国正处于历史上的东晋时期，玻璃器是这一时期身份地位，尤其是财富的重要象征。具体到冯素弗墓出土的这五件罗马玻璃器的来源，应是从草原汗国柔然带入北燕的。

柔然是中国古代北方少数民族之一，主要活动于公元4世纪末到公元6世纪中叶。北魏天兴五年（402），柔然君主社仑自称"丘豆伐可汗"，进入政权的强盛时期，其控地"西则焉耆之地，东则朝鲜之地，北则渡沙漠、穷瀚海，南则临大碛，其常所会庭则敦煌、张掖之北[3]"，它是可以与北魏相互敌对的草原游牧王国，且与北魏的关系非常复杂，402—487年间二者战斗居多，和好居少[4]。因此柔然王往来草原丝绸之路是可以不走经过北魏都城平城（治今山西大同市东北）的路线的，所走的草原丝路应与学术界公认的从西域到平城的北方草原路线有所不同。

关于北燕和柔然的关系，一方面，据文献记载，北燕时期与草原及西域诸国有较多往来的有柔然；另一方面，当时中国和中西亚的交通主要是通过西域，柔然地处北方草原，西连西域，东接三燕，彼此往来，有地理上的方便。柔然与北燕的往来是很密切的，柔然王又曾长期客居北燕，这应当是这批玻璃器的由来。

410—414年在位的柔然斛律可汗，与北燕主冯跋曾有姻亲关系。斛律即位不久，411年便派人到北燕求婚，北燕将乐浪公主嫁给了斛律。当时北燕的辽西公冯素弗认为柔然是"非我族类"，应依照前代的惯例以宗室女嫁之，反对以公主远嫁。因此，当后来斛律举家来北燕时，势必要与冯素弗这个北燕的重臣搞好关系，所呈献的礼物应该非同一般。

414年斛律将嫁女与北燕冯跋和亲时，斛律兄子步鹿真与大臣树黎共谋，将斛律父女逐往北燕，步鹿真立为可汗。斛律举家来北燕，后请还其国，在回归时半途被杀。也是在同一年，步鹿真继可汗位不久，王族内讧，为社仑季父仆浑之子大檀绞杀，步鹿真在位并未超过一年。大檀是继步鹿真之后柔然的第十位可汗，大檀于414—429年在位，也是柔然汗国的极盛期，继续与北燕冯跋联盟，送马三千匹、羊万口给北燕。无论是斛律还是大檀在与北燕和亲、赠送马匹的同时，还与地处其南方的后秦和亲，与南朝的宋等通好，目的都是为了牵制北魏，以便向南进攻，获取更多的粮食等物资。因此送马羊与北燕的时间亦应在大檀即位后不久。

柔然政权存在时间（402—552）与北魏王朝存在时间（386—534）大体相当。这个时期内，我国北方诸少数民族中，只有柔然能与北魏相抗衡，故二者既时相攻战，又时相和好。从上述文献记载柔然与北燕往来的时间段分析，从柔然到北燕，如果走传统的丝绸之路，从河西走廊到龙城，其间隔着北魏、后秦及西北的几个凉国，且柔然"其常所会庭则敦煌、张掖之北"，也就是说柔然控制的地域在沙漠丝绸之路河西走廊之北，因此柔然王到北燕走的应是比丝绸之路北魏平城更北的一条路线。

柔然斛律到北燕后，燕王冯跋封他为上谷侯，并娶其女为昭仪，后斛律固请回国，并称如果能到达敕勒，柔然的国人必然会欣喜而来迎接。于是冯跋派遣北燕的部将单于前辅万陵率三百骑送斛律回柔然，但万陵畏惧此行路远，送至黑山杀了斛律。这个"黑山"，应在北燕与敕勒之间，离北燕不远，同时，也不应是北魏管辖的地区。

据史料记载，唐显庆五年（660）大将薛仁贵、辛文陵等，率军攻伐契丹，大军进入草原，战于黑山，俘契丹首领阿卜固，解至洛阳[5]。《资治通鉴·卷二〇〇·唐纪十六》亦记，高宗显庆五年，唐高宗以阿史德枢宾、延陁梯真、李合珠并为冷岍道行军总管讨叛奚，奚族遣使来降；再以阿史德枢宾等为沙砖道行军总管，会同营州辽东经略薛仁贵，以讨伐契丹。薛仁贵与辛文陵于黑山大破契丹，擒阿卜固献于当时皇帝所在的东都。辽代史料中多次提到"黑山"，它可能是通往漠北的某条传统路线的一个必经之地。《辽史·营卫志》记载："黑山在庆州北十三里，上有池，池中有金莲。"辽庆州在今西拉木伦河北的巴林右旗。根据考古调查、发掘及有关考证，黑山就在巴林右旗的罕山，当地有辽代祭祀的遗址[6]。巴林右旗今属赤峰市，由赤峰向北经巴林桥跨过西拉木伦河即为右旗辖境。北燕时期，赤峰一带是库莫奚的活动地区，此时尚未强盛，不足与北燕抗衡，因此，斛律归国时，要避开北魏的管辖区域，从龙城（朝阳）出发，向北走是最安全的路线。另一方面，斛律称入敕勒境不仅可安全到达柔然，而且会受到其国人的欢迎，说明其时柔然与敕勒交好，关系密切。

敕勒，又称赤勒、高车、狄历、铁勒、丁零（丁灵）。汉朝击溃北匈奴之后，敕勒的地域开始南移，与中原的汉人交往。公元4世纪末至公元6世纪中叶，继匈奴、鲜卑之后，敕勒人和柔然人活动于中国大漠南北和西北广大地区。

敕勒与柔然互打互包容，柔然曾长期驱使敕勒。据《魏书》记载，高车（敕勒）的叱洛侯叛其渠帅投柔然，引导柔然主社仑破高车诸部落，特别重创高车主力与核心，高车臣服于柔然，奠定了柔然漠北霸权的基石；社仑称汗建国，基于叱洛侯的功绩，社仑德之，封为大人。社仑之后的斛律仍待之如故。步鹿真趁斛律与北燕和亲，将其父女逐往北燕继汗位后，与社仑子社拔共至叱洛侯家，"淫其少妻，妻告步鹿真，叱洛侯欲举大檀为主，遗大檀金马勒为信。步鹿真闻之，归发八千骑往围叱洛侯，叱洛侯焚其珍宝，自刎而死。步鹿真遂掩大檀，大檀发军执步鹿真及社拔，绞杀之，乃自立"[7]。

叱洛侯曾给大檀"金马勒"为信，事发后又"焚其珍宝，自刎而死"，其珍宝从何而来？荒漠草原上很难生产出珍宝，叱洛侯的珍宝应来自丝绸之路，即草原丝路可通高车。敕勒既从属且紧依于柔然，丝绸之路应该也能通连柔然。当时来往于丝绸之路上的西方商人，被称作"商胡"，这些珍宝应与"商胡"有关。

据《魏书》记载，社仑侵入高车后，高车要向柔然纳贡还要参加柔然发动的战争，高车不堪压迫，多次反抗。487年被柔然所役属的高车副伏罗部阿伏至罗及其弟穷奇逃离柔然，建立了高车国，阿伏至罗为了能打败柔然，采取了联合北魏的策略。北魏太和十四年（490）"阿伏至罗遣商胡越者至京师（北魏京师平城，今大同），以二箭奉贡"[8]。这是高车立国后，想脱离柔然，投向北魏（此时北燕已亡），其首领利用"商胡"作为使者，向北魏示好送礼，且有盟誓之意。商胡的记载很重要，他们想顺利地来往于丝路做生意，必然会与沿路的各国打交道，因而可以代行使者之职。出现在490年记载里的商胡，在丝路上往来必然已有很长的一段历史，之前必然也到过柔然和高车控制的地域。所以这几件玻璃器可能来自商胡。

高车遣商胡到北魏示好，说明商胡走的路线既可通到平城，也可通连漠北的敕勒与柔然。冯素弗葬于415年，柔然与北燕的三次往来，特别是前两次都在415年之前，冯墓出土的深绿色罗马玻璃杯的最早产生年代不超过375年，因此推测冯素弗墓出土的这几件玻璃器应该是411—414年之间由斛律带到北燕的。

那么，这批玻璃器是如何到柔然的？再看柔然与丝绸之路诸国之间的关系。当柔然强盛时，西域"小国皆苦其寇抄，羁縻附之"[9]。斛律统治时期，柔然的势力已进入伊吾、高昌之地，并联合悦般国夹击乌孙，瓜分其地，乌孙"其国数为蠕蠕所侵，西徙葱岭山中"[10]。远征西域的胜利，使得柔然号称占有东到朝鲜，西至巴尔喀什湖的广大地区[11]。但北魏与柔然对西域的争夺从公元5世纪初柔然建国起就从未间断，双方争夺的结果，互有胜负。因此，通过河西走廊，经伊吾，横贯南北疆，越葱岭与域外建立联系的丝绸之路，在柔然与北魏争夺西域或柔然征战西域时期，因西域诸国的叛附无常，战乱频仍，应是比较混乱、没有保障的。

里海东南岸有一个重要城市，也是丝路上的一个重要地点"和椟城"（即里海东南的达姆甘），在今伊朗。以里海边上的这个丝路站点为出发点，一路向东，经撒马尔罕，越葱岭，有三条线路通河西走廊，北路走碎叶、高昌、哈密到敦煌，中路沿昆仑山、天山，经疏勒、龟兹、焉耆，还有南路经于阗、且末均至敦煌，沿汉时张骞开辟的河西走廊道路，可直到长安（图2）。

另外，《隋书·铁勒传》提到铁勒（高车）的疆域范围："铁勒之先，匈奴之苗裔也，种类最多。自西海之东，依据山谷，往往不绝。"[12]西海即今里海。商胡要到达高车或柔然，除越葱岭，经新疆地区的丝绸路线外，从和椟城出发还应有一路向东北，即可到高车、柔然的路线。所以冯素弗墓出土的这批罗马玻璃器是从草原丝路可能在里海东南岸和椟城这个点上，沿里海东岸，又一路向东北，到高车、柔然的地域。因此，这批玻璃器或是由商胡带到高车，然后高车向柔然纳贡的，或是由商胡直接带到柔然的。

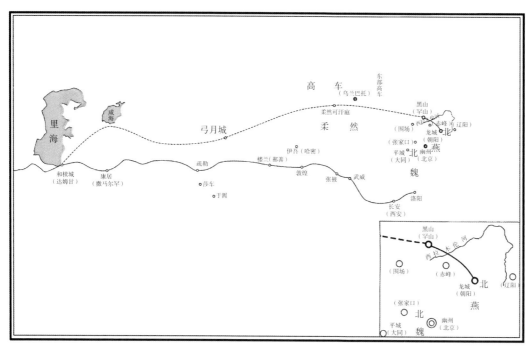

图 2 草原丝绸之路（柔然—北燕）示意图

这样丝路就从和椟城这个点分开，一是越葱岭，穿新疆，经河西走廊向东，是传统的沙漠丝路；二是向东北走里海东岸到高车，经"敦煌、张掖之北"柔然控制地区的草原丝绸之路。

草原丝绸之路也至少有两条路通向东方，一条是传统意义上通向北魏平城的，这是用商胡向北魏通使示好走的路线，也就是公元5世纪北魏时期以平城为中心，西接伊吾的草原丝绸之路。自冯素弗墓出现这组玻璃器之后，对其所经过的草原丝路的走向，学界一般认为是经和椟城进入中国境内后，走大同（平城）、张家口、赤峰而后东南折向朝阳（龙城）。通过草原路线输入东亚的罗马玻璃应属于罗马晚期偏东部行省的产品，从制造工艺方面分析，冯素弗墓出土的罗马玻璃与朝鲜半岛庆州和我国河北景县出土的罗马玻璃比较相近[13]。景县在山西大同的东南，紧邻山东德州，也是离山东半岛出海口较近的、发现罗马玻璃器的一个地点，暗示着在朝鲜半岛发现的罗马玻璃有可能是通过平城这条路线，经山东半岛从海路输入。但这或是北魏统一北方之后的情况。在此之前的北燕时期，柔然和北燕的往来，走的显然是另外一条路线。

这另一条路线就是柔然王斛律举家来北燕时，避过北魏管辖区域的更北的路线。从斛律还家被杀黑山事件，可推知这条路线是由朝阳北上，跨过西拉木伦河走黑山进入高车（东部高车）领域，到达柔然（如果走赤峰—张家口一线，则需经今河北围场，而无须穿过西拉木伦河），这是不用经过平城而可到达中国东北的一条路线。因此，北燕玻璃器及朝鲜半岛发现的玻璃器亦有可能是经里海、高车，通过柔然，经巴林右旗的黑山进入北燕，进而向辽东、向朝鲜半岛北部进入的这条北方草原路线输入的。这是一条可考证于文献记载的切实存在的路线，学界对此似还罕有注意。希望本文的论证对草原丝路的研究有所裨益。

注释：

[1] 黎瑶渤：《辽宁北票县西官营子北燕冯素弗墓》，《文物》1973年第3期，第2—28页。

[2] 安家瑶：《冯素弗墓出土的玻璃器》，载邓聪、陈星灿主编《桃李成蹊集——庆祝安志敏先生八十寿辰》，

香港中文大学中国考古艺术研究中心，2004，第377—387页。

[3] 魏收：《魏书》卷一〇三《蠕蠕、匈奴宇文莫槐、徒何段就六眷、高车传》，中华书局，1974，第2291页。

[4] 田建平：《略论柔然与北魏的关系》，《内蒙古大学学报（哲学社会科学版）》1986年第3期，第110页。

[5] "俄又与辛文陵破契丹于黑山，擒契丹王阿卜固及诸首领赴东都。"文见《旧唐书》卷八十三《薛仁贵列传》，中华书局，1975，第2781页。中华书局1975年2月出版《新唐书》卷一一一《薛仁贵列传》第4140—4141页亦有相同的记载。

[6] 内蒙古自治区文物工作队、巴林右旗文物馆：《内蒙古巴林右旗罕山辽代祭祀遗址发掘报告》，《考古》1988年第11期，第1002—1014页。

[7] 魏收：《魏书》卷一〇三《蠕蠕、匈奴宇文莫槐、徒何段就六眷、高车传》，中华书局，1974，第2292页。

[8] 同上书，第2310页。

[9] 李延寿：《北史》卷九十八《蠕蠕、匈奴宇文莫槐、徒何段就六眷、高车传》，中华书局，1974，第3251页。

[10] 魏收：《魏书》卷一〇二《西域乌孙国》，中华书局，1974，第2267页。

[11] 王静：《柔然汗国研究》，硕士学位论文，山西大学历史学系，2013。

[12] 魏徵、令狐德棻：《隋书》卷八十四《北狄·铁勒》，中华书局，1974，第1879页。

[13] 同[2]。

Gold from
Dragon City

龙城
之金

Masterpieces of
Three Yan from Liaoning
337–436

辽宁三燕文物选萃

337—436

Catalogue 图录

Diversified
Three Yan Culture

I

第一部分
多元的三燕文化

I

After settling in the Liaoxi region, the nomadic Murong Xianbei actively implemented sinicization policies. They transitioned from a nomadic life of migrating from place to place to a settled life based on agriculture. Since the establishment of Chaoyang by Murong Huang, the founder of the Former Yan state, in 341 CE, the city successively served as the capital of the Three Yan states under the name Longcheng ("Dragon City"). Its historical site has been preserved through various dynasties. From Tang dynasty figurines unearthed in the old city, it is possible to glimpse the appearance of the Longcheng people who inhabited the region for generations. Among the burial objects from the Three Yan period, not only are there items like open-mouthed pots, pottery jars with handles, and bronze cauldrons (*fu*) with distinctive Xianbei cultural features, but there are also artifacts such as bronze tripod cauldrons with a handle, bronze irons, bronze vessels (*zun*), and bronze bells with Central Plains cultural characteristics. Most of these bronze artifacts come from the Feng Sufu tomb of the Northern Yan. They reveal the refined lifestyle of this Duke of Liaoxi and demonstrate the integration of Confucian teachings with Xianbei culture. The Murong Xianbei did not have their own written language but adopted the Chinese characters prevalent in Liaoxi during that time. The existing textual materials from this period are all obtained through archaeological discoveries and include seals, pottery inscriptions, bronze engravings, and tomb inscriptions on bricks and stones. From these findings, it is evident that during the Three Yan period, various script styles such as seal script, clerical script, regular script, and cursive script coexisted in the Liaoxi region. Moreover, the new style of regular script was already popular in the region no later than the early Eastern Jin dynasty.

With the influx of a large number of Han Chinese migrants during the Western and Eastern Jin dynasties, Buddhism spread from central China to the Liaoxi region. The Yan states extensively built Buddhist temples in their capital cities and other areas. Buddhism gradually spread throughout the northeastern region. Pottery statues of Buddha and lotus-patterned roof tiles unearthed from the Jinlingsi (Golden Hill Temple) archeological site exemplify the popularity of Buddhism in this region in the fourth century. Glassware discovered in Feng Sufu's tomb is among the earliest and most abundant excavated in China to date. These glass vessels have been identified as originating from the eastern Roman Empire, most likely produced in the northeastern provinces using soda-lime glass. They provide rare tangible evidence for studying the Silk Road and hold significant historical and artistic value.

游牧民族慕容鲜卑自入辽西后，积极融入汉文化，从逐水草迁徙转为农耕定居生活。朝阳自341年前燕慕容皝建城以来，先后作为三燕的都城——龙城，其城址经历朝沿用，直至现代。世代居住此地的龙城人的面貌或可借助老城出土的唐代陶俑略见一瞥。三燕时期的随葬品中，不仅有颇具鲜卑文化特点的侈口壶、有系陶罐、铜鍑等物，还有融合中原文化特征的铜鐎斗、铜熨斗、铜尊、铜钟等器。其中大多青铜器都出自北燕冯素弗墓中，再现了这位"辽西公"精致的生活方式，更显示出他对"儒学之道"的践行及与鲜卑文化的融会贯通。慕容鲜卑没有本民族的文字，而是使用了当时辽西地区通行的汉字。目前掌握的这一时期文字资料均为考古所得，有印章、陶瓦文、铜器铭刻、砖石墓表等，可见三燕时期辽西地区也是篆、隶、楷、行诸体并行，而且不晚于东晋初年，新体的楷书就已经在辽西地区流行了。

两晋时期，随着大批汉族流民的到来，佛教也从内陆地区传入辽西地区，慕容诸燕国在都城和统治区内广泛兴建佛寺。佛教由此在东北地区逐渐传播开来。陶佛像和出土于金岭寺遗址的莲花瓦当，就体现了佛教在4世纪于此地的流行。出土于北燕冯素弗墓中的玻璃器，是中国出土的年代较早而数量又最多的一批玻璃器。经考证它们来自东罗马，很可能是罗马帝国东北行省生产的钠钙玻璃。这些玻璃器是研究丝绸之路难得的实物资料，具有重要的历史和艺术价值。

1 (I–1)

Head of a man

Tang Dynasty (618–907)
Grey stone; H. 4 cm, W. 3.4 cm
Excavated in 2003 from Chaoyang
Liaoning Provincial Institute of
Cultural Relics and Archaeology

男人头像

唐
石质　高4厘米、宽3.4厘米
2003年朝阳老城出土
辽宁省文物考古研究院藏

The facial features in this portrait appear slender. The man has a high brow ridge, eyes with an upward slant, a straight nose bridge, with a sharp gaze looking straight ahead. The man has a mustache and beard. There are round piercings at the earlobes, indicating the presence of earrings. This portrait is small in size, and the depiction of the facial features and expressions is vivid and detailed, displaying distinctive characteristics of a person from a foreign land.

这件人头像面部刻画略显瘦削。高眉骨、凤形眼、鼻梁笔直、双眼炯炯有神地注视前方，有八字须和络腮胡；双耳垂处有圆形戳洞，可见应戴有耳饰。此像小巧，人物五官神态刻画生动、细致，具有异域人的特点。

2 (I–2)

Head of a foreigner

Tang Dynasty (618–907)
Grey pottery; H. 11 cm, W. 7.8 cm
Excavated in 2003 from old city ruins
of Chaoyang
Liaoning Provincial Institute of
Cultural Relics and Archaeology

胡人头像

唐

灰陶   高11厘米、宽7.8厘米
2003年朝阳老城XQ⑤出土
辽宁省文物考古研究院藏

This portrait of a foreign figure features a high bun hairstyle, with hair covering the ears. He wears a headscarf decorated with triangular and diagonal patterns. The man has deep-set eyes, a high nose bridge, lively eyes, prominent cheekbones, full cheeks, a mouth slightly open as if about to speak, and a bearded chin. The facial features and hair ornamentation exhibit distinct characteristics of people from Central Asia.

此胡人头像发髻高梳，留倭发罩住耳朵，头戴以三角纹和斜线纹为饰的巾帻。深目高鼻，双眼有神，颧骨高凸，双颊丰满，嘴微张似欲语，下颌留须。五官及发饰具有鲜明的西域人特点。

3 (I–3)

Tile with a human face

Sixteen Kingdoms, Former Yan (337–70)
Grey pottery; H. 15 cm, W. 30 cm
Excavated in 2004 from Chaoyang,
Liaoning Provincial Institute of Cultural
Relics and Archaeology

人面纹半瓦当

十六国前燕

灰陶　高15厘米、宽30厘米

2004年朝阳老城三号地点04CLIVH19出土

辽宁省文物考古研究院藏

This clay tile is semi-circular in shape, with a raised relief of a human face on it. The face features delicate eyebrows, prominent eyes, a pointed nose, an open mouth revealing teeth, and a beard delineated using lines. The clay tile is the front cover of the cylindrical tiles used to roof the eaves in ancient Chinese architecture. This particular clay tile, adorned with a human face motif, dates back to the Former Yan period of the Sixteen Kingdoms era and was used as a decorative architectural component.

此件瓦当呈半圆形，其上浮雕人的面部，细眉、凸目、悬胆鼻、张口露齿，下颌以线条表示胡须。瓦当是古代中国建筑中覆盖屋檐的筒瓦的前端遮挡，此件人面纹瓦当，为十六国前燕时期的建筑构件。

4 (I–4)

Tripod pot

Wei-Jin period (220–420)
Grey pottery; H. 22.5 cm, Diam. (mouth)
13.5 cm, Diam. (bottom) 11 cm,
Excavated in 2003 from Shi'ertaixiang,
Chaoyang
Chaoyang County Museum

三足壶

魏晋
灰陶　高22.5厘米、口径13.5厘米、底径11厘米
2003年朝阳十二台乡腰而营子村一砖厂出土
朝阳县博物馆藏

This ceramic pot has a slightly curved neck, with a round belly and a circular base. It has three feet at the bottom, with one foot damaged and one missing. There are multiple "string pattern" decorations running from the mouth to the belly. According to the ancient text *Zhou Li* [Rites of Zhou] pots like these were commonly used as wine vessels in ancient times.

此件陶壶直口束颈，圆腹圈底，底置三足，其中一足残，一足缺失。从口沿到腹部有多道弦纹。据《周礼》所载，壶为古代常用酒器。

5 (I–5)

Cups

Sixteen Kingdoms, Former Yan (337–70)
Glazed pottery; H. 2.8 cm, Diam.
(mouth) 7.6 cm, Diam. (bottom) 4.5 cm
Excavated in 2003 from tomb No. 4 at
Wangzifenshan, Shi'ertaixiang brick
factory, Chaoyang
Chaoyang County Museum

杯一组

十六国前燕
酱釉夹砂褐陶　高2.8厘米、口径7.6厘米、底径
4.5厘米
2003年朝阳十二台乡砖厂王子坟山M4出土
朝阳县博物馆藏

This set of flat-based cups has thin walls. They were made on a wheel and later refined, featuring three "string pattern" decorations on the outer wall. There are traces of support nails on the bottom. Judging by their craftsmanship, these glazed ceramics were produced in southern kilns and represent a typical Eastern Jin style. They may serve as evidence of the political and cultural exchanges between the Murong clan of Xianbei and the Eastern Jin dynasty during that period.

这组敛口平底杯，器壁较薄。为轮制，后经修整。外壁饰三道弦纹。底部有支钉痕迹。从其制作工艺来看，是南方窑口烧造的釉陶器，为典型的东晋样式，或可作为当时慕容鲜卑与东晋王朝之间政治、文化交流的实物例证。

6 (I–6)

Jar

Sixteen Kingdoms, Former Yan (337–70)
Glazed pottery; H. 20.5 cm, Diam. (mouth) 12.5 cm, Diam. (rim) 20.5 cm, Diam. (bottom) 10 cm
Excavated in 2003 from tomb No. 6 at Wangzifenshan, Shi'ertaixiang brick factory, Chaoyang
Chaoyang County Museum

罐

十六国前燕

灰陶酱釉 高20.5厘米、口径12.5 厘米、腹径 20.5 厘米、底径10厘米
2003年朝阳十二台乡砖厂王子坟山M6出土
朝阳县博物馆藏

This unadorned, glazed ceramic jar features a wide mouth, flared rim, round lip, short neck, sloping shoulders, and a flat, bulging bottom. Jars like these have been widely used as everyday vessels since ancient times, primarily for storing either liquid or solid food ingredients.

器表施酱釉的素面陶罐，形状似壶，侈口，侈沿，圆唇，短颈斜肩，平底鼓腹。罐是自古以来应用广泛的一类实用器，主要用于贮藏或是液体或是固体的食材。

7 (I–7)

Steamer

Sixteen Kingdoms, Northern Yan (407–36)
Grey pottery; H. 10.5 cm, Diam. (mouth) 22.5 cm, Diam. (bottom) 8 cm
Excavated in 1976 from a tomb at Dapingfang, Chaoyang
Chaoyang County Museum

甑

十六国北燕
灰陶　高10.5厘米、口径22.5厘米、底径8厘米
1976年朝阳大平房公社大平房村北燕墓出土
朝阳县博物馆藏

This unadorned ceramic steamer has a wide mouth, with a rolled rim, a slanting straight belly, and a flat bottom with seven evenly spaced perforations. As a type of multifunctional cooking vessel, the steamer needed to be used in combination with other cooking utensils like pots and tripods, akin to today's steamer. During the Wei, Jin, and Sixteen Kingdoms period, these steamers were often used in conjunction with pots, and some bear traces of ashes, indicating their utility.

素面陶甑，侈口卷沿，斜直腹平底，底部有七个穿孔，孔距相等。作为一种复合炊具，它需要与釜、鬲等炊具组合起来才能使用，相当于现在的蒸锅。魏晋十六国时期的甑多与釜组合，有的留下了灰烬痕迹，应为实用器。

8 (I–8)

Stove

Sixteen Kingdoms, Northern Yan (407–36)

Grey pottery; H. 11.5 cm, W. 7.5–13.4 cm, L. 23.5 cm

Excavated in 1976 from a tomb at Dapingfang, Chaoyang

Chaoyang County Museum

单孔灶

十六国北燕

灰陶　通高11.5厘米、宽7.5～13.4厘米、长23.5厘米

1976年朝阳大平房公社大平房村北燕墓出土

朝阳县博物馆藏

This stove is rectangular in shape, wide at the front and narrow at the back, and resembles a boat. It has a single fire hole, and when it was unearthed, it was found with a pot and a steamer placed on top of it. At the rear, there is a slanting chimney, and the fire door is square and extends all the way to the ground. The front edge of the stove is divided into three sections. Since the Han dynasty stoves of this type were diverse in both functionality and form. There were both immobile masonry stoves for daily use and small metal stoves for warming food and military use. There were single-firehole stoves as well as multi-firehole stoves for cooking various foods simultaneously. The utensils used on the stove were primarily pots and steamers. This clay stove is a model intended for burial with the deceased, representing the concept of "[treating] the deceased like the living."

长方形，前宽后窄如船形，单火眼，出土时上置一釜一甑，后部斜出一烟筒，火门方形通地。灶面前端刻划三格。魏晋十六国时期的灶，功能和形态多样化，既有日常的不可移动的垒砌灶，也有专供温食、行军使用的小型金属灶；既有单火孔灶，也有适合多种烹饪同时进行的多火孔灶。灶上的炊具则以釜、甑为主。此件陶灶是一种陶制模型，即为墓主随葬所用的明器，以表现"逝者如生"的观念。

9 (I–9)

Ladle

Sixteen Kingdoms, Northern Yan (407–36)

Grey pottery; Diam. (mouth) 6.2 cm, L.19 cm

Excavated in 1976 from a tomb at Dapingfang, Chaoyang

Chaoyang County Museum

曲柄匕

十六国北燕

灰陶　勺径6.2厘米、通长19厘米

1976年朝阳大平房公社大平房村北燕墓出土

朝阳县博物馆藏

The ladle is round in shape and slightly deep, with a raised back on the handle. The lower end of the handle bends down to form a bird's-head shape. Ladles are utensils used for scooping food, and this ladle is relatively large in size. It possibly reflects the dining practice of the time, where such large ladles were used to transfer food to diners' bowls, cups, or wine vessels.

长勺呈圆形，略深，柄背隆起，柄端下弯折呈鸟首形。勺为取食之器，此勺较大，或与当时的就餐方式"分餐"有密切关系，即用此类大勺将食物取至食客的碗、盏或耳杯之中。

10 (I–10)

Mortar

Sixteen Kingdoms, Northern Yan (407–36)

Grey pottery; H. 5.5 cm, Diam. (mouth) 8 cm, L. 7.5 cm; Support frame: H. 14 cm, L. 24.5 cm

Excavated in 1976 from a tomb at Dapingfang, Chaoyang

Chaoyang County Museum

踏碓

十六国北燕

灰陶　臼高5.5厘米、口径8厘米、底座边长7.5厘米、支架高14厘米、踏杆长24.5厘米

1976年朝阳大平房公社大平房村北燕墓出土

朝阳县博物馆藏

The pestle consists of a pestle rod, a support frame, and a mortar. In the middle of the support frame, there are opposite holes for placing the pestle. The mortar has a slightly tapered mouth, a round lip, a straight body, and a square flat base. The pestle is a tool used for grinding grains, where one end of the pestle rod is stepped on to make the pestle head pound rice. This is a model and was used for burial.

此胎质较细的踏碓由杵杆、支架、臼组成，支架中间各有一相对孔以置杵，臼微敛口、圆唇、直腹、方形平底座。踏碓是粉碎谷物的工具，即踩踏杵杆一端使杵头起落舂米。此为模型，为随葬用的明器。

11 (I–11)

Cauldron

Sixteen Kingdoms, Former Yan (337–70)
Bronze; H. (total) 19.3cm, Diam. (mouth)
10 cm, Diam. (foot) 8.2 cm
Excavated in 1976 from tomb No. 3 at
Shi'ertai, Shi'ertaixiang, Chaoyang
Chaoyang County Museum

双耳镂空圈足鍑

十六国前燕

铜　通高19.3厘米、口径10厘米、圈足径8.2厘米
1976年朝阳十二台乡十二台M3出土
朝阳县博物馆藏

This vessel has a straight mouth and a deep belly, with bridge-shaped double handles placed on the rim, one of which is damaged. One side of the belly is flat, and there are three trapezoidal perforations in the flaring trumpet-shaped high foot, most commonly made of bronze or iron. The *fu* (鍑) is a type of cooking utensil that was popular in northern China from the Western Zhou period to the Northern Dynasties period. It has distinctive regional characteristics and differs from the bronze vessels found in the Central Plains. The bronze *fu* of the Three Yan culture originated in the northern grasslands, and it exists in two forms: high-footed and flat-bottomed, reflecting the characteristics of inheritance and innovation in the development of utensils.

直口深腹，口沿置桥状双耳，一耳残缺；腹壁一面平直，喇叭状高圈足有三个梯形镂孔，多为铜铁质地。鍑为一种炊具，在西周到北朝时期流行于中国北方地区，具有鲜明的地方特色，有别于中原青铜器。三燕文化的铜鍑源于北方草原地区，有高圈足及平底两种形式，体现了继承、创新的器物发展特征。

12 (I–12)

Cauldron inscribed with " 周 " (*zhou*)

Sixteen Kingdoms, Former Yan (337–70)
Bronze; H. 13.5 cm , Diam. (mouth)
12.8 cm, Diam. (bottom) 12.5 cm,
Excavated in 1980 from tomb No. 2 at
Yaojingou, Yaoeryingzi brick factory,
Shi'ertaixiang, Chaoyang
Chaoyang County Museum

刻 "周" 字款釜

十六国前燕

铜　高13.5厘米、口径12.8厘米、底径12.5厘米
1980年朝阳十二台乡腰而营子砖厂姚金沟M2出土
朝阳县博物馆藏

With a converging mouth, round belly, and a ring foot, this bronze cauldron features a wide flat rim around its belly, and there are traces of soot on the bottom. On one side of the shoulder, the character "*zhou*" (周) is engraved on the shoulder. Chinese cauldrons originated in the middle Neolithic period and were mostly made of pottery with rounded bottoms. After the Qin and Han dynasties, iron cauldrons with both round and flat bottoms appeared. During the Wei and Jin period, bronze cauldrons also emerged. When used alone, a cauldron needed to be set up with a fire burning beneath it. However, in most cases, cauldrons were placed on stoves for cooking. The idiom "*fu di chou xin* (釜底抽薪)" (lit. "drawing firewood from under the cauldron") is derived from the way cauldrons were used.

敛口圆腹圈足，该铜釜腹部有一周宽平沿，底部有烟垢痕迹。肩部一侧錾刻"周"字。釜产生于新石器时代中期，多是圜底、陶制。秦汉以后出现了铁釜，有圜底和平底两种；魏晋时期还出现了铜釜。釜单独使用时需架起来，底下烧火。而大多数情况下，釜是放在灶上使用的。"釜底抽薪"这一成语就是由釜的使用方式而来的。

13 (I–13)

Small pot with handle

Sixteen Kingdoms, Northern Yan
(407–36)
Gilded bronze; H. (total) 13 cm, H.
(pot) 8.5 cm, Diam. (mouth) 5.3 cm
Excavated in 1965 from the tomb of
Feng Sufu (d. 415), Xiguanyingzi,
Beipiao
Liaoning Provincial Museum

Although covered in rust, this small gilded pot with a handle still
displays gilt patterns on its outer surface, with remnants of gilding
above the neck on the inner surface. The pot has a wide mouth, a
narrow neck, a round body, and a circular base. On both sides of the
pot's shoulders, symmetrical slanted ears emerge, connected by an
arched handle with dragon heads at each end; the mouth and eyes of
the dragons are all finely detailed, with a long horn raised on their
foreheads. Small round holes are pierced through the cheeks of the
dragons, linked by three chain rings, connecting to the pot's double
ears. At the center of the handle is a small round hole riveted and
threaded by a wire twisted into a rotatable loop for suspension. It
may have been used as a hanging container for burning herbs.

提梁小铜壶

十六国北燕
鎏金铜　通高约13厘米、壶高8.5厘米、口径
5.3厘米
1965年北票西官营子北燕冯素弗墓出土
辽宁省博物馆藏

这件鎏金提梁小壶，虽已布满铜锈，仍可见外壁鎏金及内壁颈部以上残存
鎏金。壶形为侈口束颈，圆腹，圈底。壶肩两侧对称出双斜耳，上系弓背
提梁，两端出龙首，口目皆具，额上翘起一长角。龙颊透穿小圆孔，系三
节链环，以连于壶的双耳。提梁中心铆一小圆孔，穿一铜丝拧成可以转动
的系柄以供悬挂，当作为悬垂熏爇之用。

14 (I–14)

Pot with handle

Sixteen Kingdoms, Northern Yan (407
–36)
Gilded bronze; H. (pot) 8.5 cm, H.
(total) 13 cm, Diam. (mouth) 5.3 cm
Excavated in 1965 from the tomb of
Feng Sufu (d. 415), Xiguanyingzi,
Beipiao
Liaoning Provincial Museum

This pot with a flat bottom and slightly folded shoulder has double small ears on the shoulders and is fastened with wire coiled into chain links. It has a bow-shaped bronze beam threaded through the mouth of a mythical beast, with a movable vertical handle in the center of the beam. There are three sets of "string pattern" decorations from the mouth to the shoulders and one set on the belly. Cookware, dining vessels, and washing utensils found in the Feng Sufu tomb all largely follow the forms of burial goods from the Han dynasty (206 BCE–220 CE) through the Wei (220–265) and Jin (265–420). This set of combinations stands in stark contrast to the jar and pot combinations representing the Donghu-Xianbei tradition. The coexistence of these two entirely different sets of vessels in a single tomb indicates the significance of Han Chinese culture in Northern Yan or, in other words, the strong influence of Han Chinese funerary tradition among the Xianbei elite.

提梁罐

十六国北燕
铜　通高19.5厘米、罐高9.1厘米、口径9.2厘
米、底径6.5厘米
1965年北票西官营子北燕冯素弗墓出土
辽宁省博物馆藏

平底、折肩、肩上双小耳的敛口罐，系以铜丝盘曲做成的链环，上穿螭首口部以连弓形铜梁，梁中腰有可活动的立式系柄。由口至肩饰有三组弦纹，腹部一组弦纹。从冯素弗墓中出土的炊具、饮食器具与盥洗器具等，基本都继承了汉魏晋墓葬中随葬器物群的形制，即沿用了汉式随葬器物组合。这套组合与代表鲜卑的壶罐组合形成鲜明的对比。两套完全不同的器物群体同时出现在一座墓中，说明北燕对汉式礼制的重视，或者可以说，汉式丧仪在鲜卑族的高层中具有强烈的影响。

15 (I–15)

Cauldron with handle

Sixteen Kingdoms, Northern Yan
(407–36)
Bronze and iron; H. (total) 26.9 cm, H.
(pot) 16.9 cm
Excavated in 1965 from the tomb of
Feng Sufu (d. 415), Xiguanyingzi,
Beipiao
Liaoning Provincial Museum

提梁盖锅

十六国北燕
铜　通高26.9厘米、锅高16.9厘米
1965年北票西官营子北燕冯素弗墓出土
辽宁省博物馆藏

This bronze and iron composite cast bronze pot features an interlocking lid and body called a *zi mu kou*, attached ears, and a tall foot ring with three large trapezoidal cutout openings. On one side of the vessel's body, there is a hook hinged to the iron lid, and a loop handle is attached to the top of the lid as a knob. An iron handle is connected to the double attached ears, and at both ends of the handle are stylized chimeric heads. This type of deep bronze vessel with cutout openings and a tall ring foot represents a cooking utensil form commonly associated with Xianbei and other Northern tribes. However, this type of vessel typically has upright handles, making the presence of attached ears connecting a handle relatively uncommon. Additionally, as the chimeric head motifs around the handle originated in Han culture, the vessel thus suggests a fusion between Xianbei heritage and Central Plains culture.

这件铜、铁复合铸造的铜锅，为子母口加附耳和三个梯形大镂孔的高圈足造型。器腹一侧出一夹鼻，连接可启合的铁盖，盖顶附一游环为钮。双附耳上系铁提梁，提梁两端呈螭首形。这类镂孔高圈足的圜底深腹铜器，为北方鲜卑等民族的炊具形制，但一般为立耳、无提梁。此件铜锅附耳提梁，比较少见，且提梁饰螭首形，带有汉文化色彩，是一件属于鲜卑族而带有中原与鲜卑文化融合痕迹的文物。

16 (I–16)

Ironing pan

Sixteen Kingdoms, Northern Yan (407
–36)
Bronze; H. 4.3 cm, L. 30.2 cm, Diam.
(mouth) 13 cm
Excavated in 1965 from the tomb of
Feng Sufu (d. 415), Xiguanyingzi,
Beipiao
Liaoning Provincial Museum

熨斗

十六国北燕
铜　盘高4.3厘米、通长30.2厘米、盘外沿口
径13厘米
1965年北票西官营子北燕冯素弗墓出土
辽宁省博物馆藏

The iron, known as a *yundou*, is a long-handled, round pan, and it is quite heavy. The long handle extends upwards at a slight angle, making it easy to hold for ironing clothes. The pan's walls and base are both thick, which allows for a slow increase in the temperature of the charcoal fire, preventing the clothes from scorching. The pan is deep enough to hold charcoal and prevent charcoal ash from flying out.

In the Feng Sufu tomb, a similar object resembling an iron was also excavated. When unearthed, there were traces of black oil stains and remnants of fuel inside the pan. The base of that pan is extremely thin, only one millimeter. If charcoal is burned inside the pan, it would conduct heat very quickly, causing clothing to scorch. Therefore, this implement is not suitable for ironing clothes, and it is speculated that it may be a type of portable lamp.

长柄圆斗，较为厚重。长柄斜直向上且微高出斗口，方便执以熨衣。斗壁、底皆厚，可使炭火的温度缓慢升高，不致熨衣致焦。斗深，得容炭火，又免炭灰外飞。

冯素弗墓还出土一件类似器物，形近熨斗，出土时盘内有黑色油垢及线缕等燃料残迹。盘底薄仅1毫米，如盘内爇炭则导热甚快，着衣易焦，不适于熨衣，推测应为行灯。

17 (I–17)

Tripod vessel

Sixteen Kingdoms, Former Yan (337–70)
Bronze; H. (total)7 cm, H., (foot) 5 cm, L.
(handle) 16.5 cm, Diam. 22.2 cm
Excavated in 1980 from a tomb at
Xiasanjiaxiang, Chaoyang
Chaoyang County Museum

This *jiaodou* tripod has a converging mouth with an extravagant rim that folds inward. It has a deep belly and a flat bottom, supported by three animal-shaped feet. There is a dragon-shaped handle on one side of the belly. There are traces of repairs on the other side of the belly. The bottom of the belly is adorned with three sets of "string pattern" decorations, while the lower part of the belly and the upper part of the base have nine sets of "string pattern" decorations. The *jiaodou* is a type of cooking vessel from the Han and Jin periods. Both the bronze cauldron and the bronze *jiaodou* excavated from the tomb of Yuantaizi in Chaoyang have soot marks on their exteriors, indicating that they were once practical cooking vessels before being buried with the deceased.

龙首弦纹鐎斗

十六国前燕
铜　斗高7厘米、足高5厘米、柄长16.5厘米、
斗直径22.2厘米
1980年朝阳县三家乡被下三角乡花墓葬出土
朝阳县博物馆藏

鐎斗敛口侈沿，沿下内折，深腹平底，底置三兽形足，腹部置一龙首柄。腹部另一侧有修补痕迹。腹底部各饰弦纹三道，腹下部、底上部饰弦纹九道。鐎斗是汉晋时期的一种炊器。朝阳袁台子壁画墓中出土的铜釜及铜鐎斗的外底部均有烟炱痕，说明铜釜及铜鐎斗均曾为实用炊器而用作随葬品。

18 (I–18)

Ladle

Sixteen Kingdoms, Northern Yan (407–36)

Bronze; H. 15.3 cm, L. 33 cm, Diam. (mouth) 24.8 cm, Diam. (bottom) 13.9 cm

Excavated in 1965 from the tomb of Feng Sufu (d. 415), Xiguanyingzi, Beipiao

Liaoning Provincial Museum

This large, round ladle, known as a *kui*, has a curved handle, a short ring foot, and a flat inner base. There are three sets of "string pattern" decorations below the mouth and on the belly. The ladle handle is cast on the exterior of the ladle body, and at the end of the handle, there is a long dragon-head-shaped ornament. The dragon's head has a long, single horn that curves backward and points upward. The dragon has two long eyes on each side, and its long snout extends forward, revealing two rows of large teeth. Bronze ladles are a relatively common type of serving vessel, used for dishes such as meat broth and sauces. According to the ancient text *Yi Dong Lin*, the *kui* is a food-serving vessel that has been in use since the Han dynasty. The bronze *kui* and bowls excavated from the tomb of Yuantaizi in Chaoyang both contained sheep vertebrae, while the bronze *kui* excavated from the tomb of Cui Dun in Later Yan contained chicken bones.

魁

十六国北燕

铜 通高15.3厘米、通长33厘米、口径24.8厘
米、底径13.9厘米

1965年北票西官营子北燕冯素弗墓出土

辽宁省博物馆藏

大圆勺形加曲柄、矮圈足、足内平底。口下及腹部各有三周弦纹。勺柄接铸于勺体外壁，柄端铸一个长形龙头，龙顶处独角甚长，贴顶向后，角尖折而翘起。双长目分于两侧，长吻前伸，露上下两排巨齿。铜魁是一种较常见的盛食器，所盛之食有肉羹及酱。据古籍《易洞林》记载，"魁"为盛食器，自汉有之。朝阳袁台子壁画墓出土的铜魁及铜钵中则均盛有羊脊椎骨，后燕崔遹墓出土的铜魁内也盛有鸡骨。

19 (I–19)

Container

Sixteen Kingdoms, Northern Yan (407 –36)

Bronze; H. 17.5 cm, Diam. (mouth) 23 cm, Diam. (bottom) 22.1 cm

Excavated in 1965 from the tomb of Feng Sufu (d. 415), Xiguanyingzi, Beipiao

Liaoning Provincial Museum

尊

十六国北燕

铜　高17.5厘米、口径23厘米、底径22.1厘米

1965年北票西官营子北燕冯素弗墓出土

辽宁省博物馆藏

A round, straight-mouthed, short cylindrical *zun* vessel with straight walls and a flat bottom is supported by three hoof-shaped feet. The exterior of this vessel is decorated with three sets of "string pattern" decorations. All three feet were separately cast and then attached to the lower end of the vessel, and the attachment marks are clearly visible. This vessel has a balanced shape and was crafted with good workmanship. The term "尊" (*zun*) is often used to refer to practical wine vessels that appeared during the Warring States period (475–221 BCE). During the Han dynasty and later, the prevalence of drinking culture made the *zun* the primary type of vessel used for serving wine, with common forms being the three-legged cylindrical shape and the three-legged basin. The bronze vessel excavated from the tomb of Feng Sufu follows the design of the three-legged cylindrical *zun* that has been in use since the Han dynasty.

圆形直口矮筒状、直壁平底、三兽蹄足，该尊的外壁饰三组弦纹。三足均系另行铸就，然后接铸于尊壁下端，接铸痕迹清楚。此器形体规整，铸工较好。尊，即"樽"，常用来指代战国时期出现与使用的日常实用酒器。两汉时期，饮酒文化的盛行使尊成为主要的盛酒用器具类型，常见三足筒形与三足盆形两种。冯素弗墓出土的这件铜尊，即依照汉代以来的三足筒形尊的造型制作。

20 (I–20)

Basin

Sixteen Kingdoms, Northern Yan (407 –36)

Bronze; H. 6.6 cm, Diam. (mouth) 29.3 cm, Diam. (bottom) 19.6 cm

Excavated in 1965 from the tomb of Feng Sufu (d. 415), Xiguanyingzi, Beipiao

Liaoning Provincial Museum

弦纹洗

十六国北燕

铜 高6.6厘米、口径29.3厘米、底径19.6厘米

1965年北票西官营子北燕冯素弗墓出土

辽宁省博物馆藏

This open-mouthed *xi* vessel has a wide folded rim with a slightly concave rim surface, a round lip, shallow belly, and a rounded bottom. The bronze vessel excavated from the tomb of Feng Sufu is of excellent quality and craftsmanship, likely a customized creation as opposed to a mass-produced one. According to the ancient text *Xu Han Shu* [Continuation of the Book of Han], when feudal lords, nobles, princesses, dukes, and generals died, the imperial court bestowed twenty-four objects for their funerary rites. These unique bronze vessels from the Feng Sufu tomb may belong to the category of "bestowed objects" by the Northern Yan ruler, reflecting the deep sinicization of the Xianbei in their funeral culture.

敞口宽折沿，沿面略下凹，圆唇，浅腹，圜底。冯素弗墓出土的铜器铜质精良，铸工亦佳，不同于一般的明器，应是专门制作的。据古籍《续汉书·礼仪志下》，诸侯王、贵人、公主、公、将军，办理丧事时，宫廷将赐二十四物。由此推测，冯素弗墓这批特殊的铜器属于北燕王朝的"赐器"也不无可能，反映了慕容鲜卑连同北燕在丧葬文化上汉化的深度。

21 (I–21)

Tripod pot

Sixteen Kingdoms, Former Yan (337–70)
Bronze; H. 5.8 cm, Diam. (mouth) 5.2
cm, Diam. (bottom) 7.4 cm
Excavated in 1998 from tomb No. 196 at
Lamadong, Beipiao
Liaoning Provincial Institute of Cultural
Relics and Archaeology

The vessel has a straight mouth, a short neck, round shoulders, a flat
bottom, and at the bottom, three feet at the edge that are too small to
be functional. The vessel's shoulders have two rings, and one of them
holds an eight-shaped iron chain link. There are continuous patterns
of deer motifs on the shoulders and the belly of the vessel, with six
deer heads connecting in each of the two layers. These deer motifs are
filled with dense patterns and below the motifs, near the bottom, there
is an additional layer of continuous diamond-shaped patterns. The three-
footed design of this bronze vessel with deer motifs is likely the result
of a transition from three-footed vessels to flat-bottomed vessels during
the Wei-Jin period. It can also be seen as a simplified form of the bronze
wine vessel known as a *houlou* (cat. no. 22), perhaps reflecting the shift
from a nomadic lifestyle to settled agricultural living.

鹿纹三足罐

十六国前燕
铜　高5.8厘米、口径5.2厘米、底径7.4厘米
1998年北票南八家乡四家板村喇嘛洞墓地
ⅡM196出土
辽宁省文物考古研究院藏

直口、短颈、圆肩、平底，底部侧缘有仅具象征性的三个实心足。该罐肩
部有双系，其一内衔"8"形铁链节。肩、腹部刻有上下两层连续鹿纹的
图案，每层六只鹿首尾衔接，鹿纹内外分别以致密的篦纹和双重波浪纹填
充，鹿纹以下近底部加饰一道多重连续菱形纹。这件鹿纹三足铜罐的三足
造型，应是魏晋时期由三足器向平底器转化的结果，或可视为铜鍪镂（见
图录第22号）的一种简化形式，或许反映了从游牧生活到安居的农耕生活
的转变。

22 (I–22)

Wine vessel

Western Jin Dynasty (265–317)
Bronze; H. 9.7 cm, Diam. (mouth) 9.5
cm, Diam. (rim) 11 cm
Excavated in 1998 from tomb No. 315
at Lamadong, Beipiao
Liaoning Provincial Institute of
Cultural Relics and Archaeology

With a large mouth and rounded lip, a narrowed neck, bulging belly, and a round
bottom, this vessel has symmetric double rings on its neck. There is an inscription
carved on the lower part of the vessel's rim: "Made in Luoyang on the 20th of the
third month of the third year of Yuankang, three *sheng* of bronze *houlou*, weighing
two *jin*, first." The bronze *houlou* is a type of cooking vessel from the Han dynasty, so
named because the shape of the lid resembles connected mountain peaks with rugged
summits. There are not many excavated bronze *houlou* vessels, and they mainly date to
the middle and late Western Han period. This bronze container, dating to the third year
of Yuankang (293), is labeled as a "bronze *houlou*." It is similar in style to the bronze
vessels called "鍪" (*mou*) during the Qin and Han periods. In the Han dynasty, terms
like 鍪 (*mou*), 锜 (*qi*), 镂 (*lou*), and 鍢镂 (*houlou*) all referred to types of cauldrons.
The three-footed bronze jar with deer (cat. no. 21) and a bronze vessel with handle
excavated from the same tomb are also continuations of cauldron-like vessels from
the Han dynasty, showing changes in their forms during the Wei-Jin period to adapt to
regional and cultural preferences.

"元康三年"铜鍢镂

西晋

铜　高9.7厘米、口径9.5厘米、腹径11厘米
1998年北票南八家乡四家板村喇嘛洞墓地
ⅡM315出土
辽宁省文物考古研究院藏

侈口圆唇，束颈鼓腹圜底，颈部具对称双系，该鍢镂口沿下部刻一行字："元康
三年三月廿日，洛阳冶造，三升铜鍢镂，重二斤，第一。" 铜鍢镂是汉代的一
种炊食器，因其器盖造型犹如山峰相连、山巅岖嵘而得名。铜鍢镂出土的数量不
多，年代主要为西汉中晚期。这件元康三年（293）的青铜容器，自铭为"铜鍢
镂"，与秦汉时期铜鍪造型相似。汉代的鍪、锜、镂、鍢镂等，都是釜一类器物
的名称。同墓地出土的鹿纹三足铜罐及提梁铜器，均应是汉代青铜器中"釜"属
的鍪、镂等的延续，在魏晋时期为适应地域民族习俗而产生形制上的变化。

23 (I–23)

Vessel in the shape of a tiger

Sixteen Kingdoms, Northern Yan
(407–36)
Bronze; H. 23.1 cm, L. 38.5 cm,
Weight 6.3 kg
Excavated in 1965 from the tomb of
Feng Sufu (d. 415), Xiguanyingzi,
Beipiao
Liaoning Provincial Museum

虎子

十六国北燕
铜　高23.1厘米、通长38.5、重6.3千克
1965年北票西官营子北燕冯素弗墓出土
辽宁省博物馆藏

This exquisitely cast bronze tiger (*huzi*) features an elevated head and raised tail. It exudes a fierce demeanor. With its jaws wide open and its body hollow throughout, the tufted mane extends from the back of the neck, forming a handle that connects to the tail ridge. Curled hair resembling wings emerges from under the armpits. Apart from the intricate cast patterns covering its body, fine lines are etched on the neck, back, chest, and tail to depict fur.

According to archaeological findings, this type of so-called "虎子" (*huzi*) tiger statuette first appeared in the Spring and Autumn period. It was commonly found in tombs dating from the Han and the Six Dynasties. Such vessels were crafted from a range of materials, such as pottery, celadon, bronze, and lacquer, with ceramic being the most prevalent. Several hypotheses regarding usage have been proposed, including as a wash basin, a drinking vessel, drink container, chamber pot, and more. The bronze tiger unearthed from the tomb of Feng Sufu of Northern Yan exhibits a vivid form and exquisite ornamentation, making it a rare find that showcases the cultural amalgamation between North and South.

这件铸造精美的铜卧虎子昂首翘尾，状态凶猛。虎口大张，通体中空。颈后鬣毛伸长成为提梁，连于脊尾。腋下出卷毛如双翼，周身除铸出花纹外，在颈、背、胸、尾各处又刻划细线表示毛鬣。从考古发现所见，虎子这一类造型的器物最早出现在春秋时期，常见于两汉魏晋南北朝时期的墓葬中，质地有陶、青瓷、铜、漆木等，尤以陶瓷质地者居多，有用作清器、饮器、盛酒器、裒器等说法。北燕冯素弗墓出土的这件青铜虎子，造型生动、纹饰精美，尚属罕见，体现着南北交融的社会风尚。

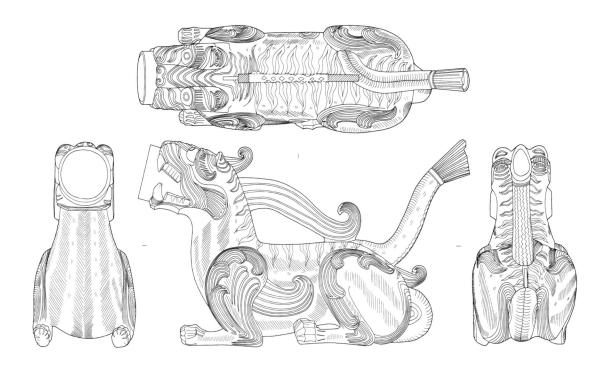

24 (I–24)

Iron stand

Wei-Jin period (220–420)
Bronze; H. 54.9 cm, Diam. (bottom)
27 cm
Found in 1976 at Tieling Smelting
Factory, Likely from the Chaoyang
area
Liaoning Provincial Museum

This trumpet-shaped object has a spherical base crowned by a tall, slender column. It has a bear-like beast sitting atop the column, and the column itself has a hole for inserting objects. Among the unearthed artifacts from the Wei-Jin period, there is a type of object called a "熨人" (yunren). According to the ancient text *Donggong jiu shi* [Anecdotes of the Eastern Palace] the *yunren* was used to hold irons or lamps, essentially functioning as a stand. The hole in the column would be used to insert the long handle of an iron or a lamp. From Tang dynasty poetry depicting scenes of daily life, there are records referring to "extinguish[ing] the lamp to iron clothes," which seems to describe a scenario where both a lamp or an iron was used, indicating the dual purpose of such objects.

熨人

魏晋
铜　高54.9厘米、底径27厘米
传朝阳地区出土，1976年铁岭地区有色金属
熔炼厂拣选
辽宁省博物馆藏

通体呈喇叭状，底座球冠形，上有高柱，瘦长体，铸有兽状柱头，柱身有一孔可插放器物。在考古出土的魏晋时期的器物中，有一种用于承托熨斗或灯盏器物座的器具名为"熨人"，见于古籍《东宫旧事》的记载。"熨人"是放熨斗的架子，柱孔既可插置熨斗的长柄，也可插置行灯的长柄。从反映唐人生活场景的唐诗中可见，有记载"停灯熨衣"之事，似描述了灯具与熨斗一举两用的场景。

25 a and b (I–25)

Two ceremonial pole finials in the form of a dragon's head

Sixteen Kingdoms, Northern Yan (407–36)

Gilded bronze; 25a: H. 16.5–16.9 cm, W. 12.–15.3 cm; 25b: H. 15.7 cm, W. 8.4 cm

Excavated in 1965 from the tomb of Feng Sufu (d. 415), Xiguanyingzi, Beipiao

Liaoning Provincial Museum

Gilded bronze dragons form the decorative finials of two ceremonial poles. Each has a hooked shape, with a round socket cast at the lower end for inserting the long pole. The upper end tapers gradually, bending downward with a dragon's head cast at the front. The dragon heads are finely crafted, with relief-like features such as eyebrows, ears, mouth, and horns, all deeply carved, and there are additional finely incised horizontal lines in many places. The long horns extend backward, with the horn tips standing upright. The dragon's mouth is open with a protruding tongue, and the front of the tongue forms a small flat disc with a hole pierced through it. Among the six gilt pole finials unearthed from the Feng Sufu tomb, many have lost their gilding, and the casting of the sockets is not uniform, with variations in the thickness of the poles' surfaces. Four bronze pole finials from the tomb of Feng Sufu's wife are not gilded and have a similar dragon head design. From excavated artifacts, it is evident that remnants of wood chips or wooden handles are found inside the sockets, and in one of the pole finials from the tomb of Feng Sufu, a sixty-centimeter-long wooden pole was discovered inside the socket. This indicates that the finial was likely used as a decorative element for a ceremonial pole, possibly in the possession of the tomb's occupant during their lifetime.

25a

25b

螭首杆头

十六国北燕

鎏金铜 25a高16.5～16.9厘米、宽 12～15.3
厘米 25b高 15.7厘米、宽 8.4厘米
1965年北票西官营子北燕冯素弗墓出土
辽宁省博物馆藏

此两件器物为仪仗长杆的杆头饰件，器形如钩，下端铸出圆銎以插长杆，上端渐细，弯转垂下，垂下的前端铸出龙首。龙首铸作较精，造型如浮雕，眉、耳、口、角刻作深峻，又多外加刻横线细纹。长角贴器身后伸，角尖直立，张口伸舌，舌前端出为小平盘，穿孔。冯素弗墓所出的6件鎏金铜杆头，鎏金多有脱落，杆头的銎口铸造并不规范，器壁厚薄不一；二号墓冯素弗妻属墓所出的4件铜杆头均未鎏金，且大小形制，特别是杆头龙首的造型基本一致。从出土实物看，这类器物均在銎内残留木屑或木柄，其中在冯素弗二号墓的1件杆头銎内还发现存长为60厘米的木杆，应是仪仗长杆的杆头饰件。杆头并应系有下垂的旌幢流苏之类。此或为墓主生前所用之物而作为随葬品。

26 (I–26)

Deer sculpture

Sixteen Kingdoms, Former Yan (337–70)
Bronze; H: 10.4 cm, L. 31 cm
Excavated in 1998 at Lamadong, Beipiao
Liaoning Provincial Institute of Cultural
Relics and Archaeology

鹿形饰件

十六国前燕
铜　高10.4厘米、通长31厘米
1998年北票南八家乡四家板村喇嘛洞墓地IM7
出土
辽宁省文物考古研究院藏

This bronze deer is formed by assembling several pieces, creating a three-dimensional sculpture. The deer's neck stretches forward while its head arcs backward, looking over its shoulder, and each of its two antlers branches into five flat tines. The deer's back resembles that of a tortoise: it has a short tail and there is a rectangular perforation on each side of its abdomen. In the archaeological remains of the Three Yan culture in western Liaoning, two types of deer-shaped ornaments have been unearthed, one made of bronze and the other made of lead. Both were found around the waist of the tomb occupants. The exact function of these deer-shaped ornaments remains a mystery.

由铜片裁制组合，呈立体雕塑状。鹿首引颈回眸，两支鹿角各分五叉平伸，龟背状鹿身置短尾，腹两侧各有一长方形穿带孔。在辽西地区的三燕文化遗存中，曾出土两种鹿形饰件，一为铜制，一为铅制，出土时均位于墓主人的腰部。此种鹿形饰具体为何作用，尚是未解之谜。

27 (I–27)

Mirror inscribed with "long-lasting prosperity with many generations"

Han-Jin Period (206 BCE–420 CE)
Bronze; Diam. 15.5 cm, T. 0.5 cm
Excavated in 1953 from a tomb in
Sandaohaozidong, Liaoyang
Liaoning Provincial Museum

The mirror has a round knob with interior patterns in the shape of a persimmon stem interlocking with that of eight continuous arcs, with the inscription "*chang yi zi sheng*," meaning "long-lasting prosperity with many generations." Bronze mirrors were essential everyday items for ancient Chinese people and were often included as burial objects. According to Chinese customs, bronze mirrors were believed not only to serve the practical function of reflection, assisting people in adjusting their appearance and attire, they also possessed cultural significance, symbolizing the ability to draw lessons from the past and assess one's conduct. There is a famous saying "using a bronze mirror to adjust one's clothing and headgear" that emphasizes the importance of self-reflection and self-cultivation. Inscriptions on mirrors often convey auspicious words and phrases. In this bronze mirror, the phrase "*chang yi zi sheng*" is synonymous with "*chang yi zi sun*," a common auspicious inscription found on objects from the Han dynasty (206 BCE–220 CE). It expresses hope for the enduring prosperity and success of one's descendants.

"长宜子生" 镜

汉晋
铜　直径15.5厘米、厚0.5厘米
1953年辽阳三道壕子东墓地出土
辽宁省博物馆藏

圆钮座，柿蒂纹内向八连弧纹，间有"长宜子生"四字。铜镜是中国古人必不可少的生活用具，也多用于随葬。在中国文化习俗中，铜镜不仅有映照的实际功能，即"以铜为镜，可以正衣冠"之说，并由此上升到借鉴古今、衡量品行的文化层面，有"以古为镜，可以知兴替；以人为镜，可以明得失"的名言；还可寄托情感、辟邪祈福，如有"破镜重圆"的说法，而使铜镜具有许多特殊含义。镜上铭文因此也流行吉言隽语。此铜镜的"长宜子生"与"长宜子孙"同义。"长宜子孙"是汉代器物上常见的吉语铭文，意思是希望自己的大家族式生活和家业能够世代久长，子子孙孙发达兴旺。

28 (I–28)

TLV mirror

Han-Jin Period (202 BCE–420 CE)
Bronze; Diam. 17 cm, T. 1 cm; Knob:
Diam. 2.5 cm, W. (hole) 1 cm
Excavated in 1955 from tomb no.1 at
Sandaohao yaoye gongchang dayao xi
caitu qu, Liaoyang
Liaoning Provincial Museum

This mirror has a flat round knob with a pointed top. The back is decorated with a pattern of a *bo* game board and birds, with the pointed top as the bird's eye. The inscription reads: "The mirror I made is really good. The bronze from Xuzhou is clear and bright." Xuzhou was not historically known for bronze production, so "bronze from Xuzhou" should be understood similarly to the expression "learning from Luoyang," where Xuzhou and Luoyang serve as symbolic references to China as a whole. The *bo* board pattern emerged during the Qin and Han dynasties (221 BCE–220 CE), developed during the Western Han period (206 BCE–25 CE), thrived during Wang Mang's Xin dynasty (9–23), and then declined during the Six Dynasties (220–589). The *bo* board pattern embeds ancient Chinese cosmological belief in the *yin–yang* and Five Elements, making it a popular decorative motif during that period.

鸟纹博局镜

汉晋
铜　直径17厘米、厚1厘米、钮径2.5厘米、
钮孔宽1厘米、高0.5厘米
1955年辽阳三道壕窑业工厂大窑西采土区一
号壁画墓出土
辽宁省博物馆藏

扁平圆钮，钮顶有一小乳钉；钮座外饰博局鸟纹，以乳钉做鸟目，外有一周铭文带："吾作大竟（镜）真是好，同（铜）出徐州清且明兮。"徐州历史上并非产铜之地，以"同（铜）出徐州"为铭辞同"师出洛阳"一样，只是用徐州、洛阳两地代指中国。博局纹饰产生于秦汉之际，发展于西汉，盛行于王莽时期，消失于魏晋南北朝。博局纹饰蕴藏着当时人们的宇宙观念、阴阳五行思想，因此成为当时较流行的纹饰。

29 (I–29)

Seal of the Duke of Fanyang

Sixteen Kingdoms, Northern Yan
(407–36)
Gold; H.1.9 cm, W. 2.35 cm, L. 2.27
cm, Weight 100 g
Excavated in 1965 from the tomb of
Feng Sufu (d. 415), Xiguanyingzi,
Beipiao
Liaoning Provincial Museum

This seal glows with a golden brilliance. It has a square base and a tortoise-shaped knob. The tortoise has eyes and a hollow belly. In the center of the tortoise's back there is a small circular patterned belt, with six and seven interconnected circles on each side, symbolizing the constellations of the Southern Dipper and Northern Dipper. The edge of the tortoise's back is irregularly engraved with connecting arcs. The four feet of the tortoise are also carved with claw patterns. The seal surface is carved in seal script in negative relief with the inscription "*Fanyanggong zhang*" [Seal of Duke of Fanyang] in two rows, with a square border around the characters.

"范阳公章"印

十六国北燕
金 通高1.9厘米、印面长2.27厘米、宽2.35
厘米、重100克
1965年北票西官营子北燕冯素弗墓出土
辽宁省博物馆藏

"范阳公章"金质色澄光亮。方座龟钮。龟口目均具，腹下中空。龟背中间刻小圆圈纹带，两边分刻双线连接的圆圈六个和七个，象征南斗、北斗星座，龟背周边刻不规则的连弧纹，龟的四足还刻划出足爪纹样。印面錾刻篆书阴文"范阳公章"两行四字，字外有方形边栏。

30 (I–30)

Seal of the Duke of Liaoxi

Sixteen Kingdoms, Northern Yan
(407–36)
Gilded bronze; H. 2.75 cm, W. 2.22
cm, L. 2.46 cm
Excavated in 1965 from the tomb of
Feng Sufu (d. 415), Xiguanyingzi,
Beipiao
Liaoning Provincial Museum

"辽西公章" 印

十六国北燕
鎏金铜　通高2.75厘米、印面长2.46厘米、宽
2.22厘米
1965年北票西官营子北燕冯素弗墓出土
辽宁省博物馆藏

The "*Liaoxigong zhang*" [Seal of Duke of Liaoxi] is made of gilded bronze. It has a rectangular body and a tortoise-shaped knob. The tortoise's body has only the basic shape but no fine details or decorations. The seal surface is carved in seal script in negative relief with the inscription "*Liaoxigong zhang*" in two rows, and there is a border line carved around the inscription. The characters are shallow and irregularly shaped, indicating that this seal was likely made as a burial object for the tomb occupant.

Seals, which came into use as early as the Warring States period (475–221 BCE), are important objects in Chinese culture to indicate one's identity. Both of the two seals in the exhibition, along with others, were found in the same tomb, confirming that the tomb occupant was Feng Sufu (d. 415), the imperial minister of Northern Yan. Feng Sufu, the younger brother of Northern Yan ruler Feng Ba, played a significant role in establishing the Northern Yan regime and was granted the title of Duke of Fanyang. He held important positions such as Palace Attendant, General of Chariots and Cavalry, and Grand Chancellor. Later, his title was changed to Duke of Liaoxi, and he served as the Grand Marshal, effectively governing Northern Yan. He made significant contributions during his time. Feng Sufu died in the seventh year of Taiping (415). His brother Feng Ba returned to his funeral seven times to mourn him with deep sorrow.

"辽西公章" 印为铜铸鎏金。印体呈长方形，龟钮。龟体仅具外形，无细部纹线装饰。印面系单刀划刻篆书阴文"辽西公章"两行四字，周边划刻边线，印文刻划极为细浅，字体亦不规整，故此印应系专为墓主人殉葬所制之明器印。

玺印是中国文化中重要的信物，以证身份，自战国始流行。以上两印和其他"车骑大将军""大司马章"等印章，同出于一墓，故得以确认本墓主人为北燕宰相冯素弗（？—414或415）。冯素弗，北燕皇帝冯跋之弟，助兄建立北燕政权，封范阳公，拜侍中、车骑大将军、录尚书事，后改封辽西公，任大司马职，治理北燕，居功厥伟。一说卒于北燕太平七年（415），及葬，燕王冯跋七临之，哭之哀恸。

31 (I–31)

Inkstone

Sixteen Kingdoms, Northern Yan
(407–36)
Stone; L. 26.8 cm , W. 23.7 cm, H. 7.8 cm
Excavated in 1965 from the tomb of
Feng Sufu (d. 415), Xiguanyingzi,
Beipiao
Liaoning Provincial Museum

This rectangular inkstone has four legs and features various carved elements on its surface. These carvings include a rectangular ink reservoir, a square ink bed, a ewer-shaped water container, and a pen rest. The pen rest has a carved groove for holding brushes, with the brush tips facing upward and a bifurcation at the end. The sides of the inkstone are carved with a wave pattern. In the year 294 CE, Murong Wei (Former Yan) relocated to Daji City, which marks the beginning of a more settled lifestyle for the Xianbei people. It was during this time that the Dongxiang, an institution which promoted the teachings of Confucian classics, was established. In 342 CE, Murong Wei's son Murong Huang moved the capital to Longcheng ("Dragon City") and repurposed the old palace into a school. He personally compiled the *Tai shang zhang* [Superior classic] to replace the Han dynasty-era textbook *Ji jiu pian* [Spontaneous classic] and conducted examinations for students at the Dongxiang. This move attracted a large number of talents to Dragon City. Later, Emperor Feng Ba of Northern Yan also encouraged education and issued decrees to establish an Imperial Academy for Confucian learning in the Dragon City. This Han-style stone inkstone may serve as evidence of Northern Yan's efforts of sinicization.

砚

十六国北燕
砂岩青石　长26.8厘米、宽23.7厘米、高7.8
厘米
1965年北票西官营子北燕冯素弗墓出土
辽宁省博物馆藏

长方形四足，砚面的不同位置雕出长方形砚池、方形墨床、耳杯形水池和笔榻，榻上刻出笔槽，笔锋向上，笔尾出一分叉。砚侧线雕水涛纹。公元294年慕容廆移居棘城，开始定居下来，始有 "东庠" 之设，教学内容以儒家经典为主。342年慕容廆之子慕容皝迁都龙城，将旧宫辟为学校，并亲编《太上章》，用以代替汉代的识字课本《急就篇》，还亲临东庠考学生，大批人才都随之聚集到龙城。北燕皇帝冯跋励精图治，下诏在龙城 "营建太学" 和 "国子学"，教学儒家经典。这件汉制石砚台或可为北燕汉化措施的物证之一。

32 (I–32)

Fragment inscribed with " 令 使 " (*ling shi*)

Sixteen Kingdoms, Former Yan (337–70)
Grey pottery; H. 4.3–10.7 cm, W. 13.4 cm, T. 1.6 cm
Excavated in 2000 at Beipiao
Liaoning Provincial Institute of Cultural Relics and Archaeology

"令使" 铭陶片

十六国前燕
黄褐陶　高4.3～10.7厘米、宽13.4厘米、厚1.6厘米
2000年北票金岭寺建筑遗址出土
辽宁省文物考古研究院藏

The clerical script inscription *"ling shi"* is found on this fragment of pottery. The characters were carved casually with a metal, bamboo, or hard wooden instrument before the object was fired in the kiln. Because a knife was used instead of a brush, the strokes are mostly sharp and slender, made without hesitation or pressure, and the dots and lines are emphasized with pressing. The characters have a square structure, and the horizontal strokes are long, while the left-falling and right-falling strokes are stretched out. This pottery fragment is from a site dating back to the Former Yan period.

隶书"令使"，见于一件残筒瓦背上，以金属或坚硬的竹木器在未入窑烧制前的陶坯上随意所刻。因以刀代笔，故撇、捺头尾多尖细，没有顿按，点画重按，结体近方。横长，撇、捺舒展。该建筑址为前燕时的遗存。

33 (I–33)

Pottery fragments with rubbings

Sixteen Kingdoms, Northern Yan (407–36)
Pottery, L. 32 cm, W. 23 cm
Excavated in 2002 at North Avenue of Chaoyang
Liaoning Provincial Institute of Cultural Relics and Archaeology

陶瓮残片与拓片

十六国北燕
陶　长32厘米、宽23厘米
2002年朝阳北大街出土
辽宁省文物考古研究院藏

The running script inscription "the thirteenth year of the Taiping reign, artisan Pan Yuan from Sun Long" is found on the shoulder of a ceramic jar (a) and was carved after firing. The calligraphy appears hurried and stiff, with thin and consistent strokes, often cursive. Another running script inscription, "the eleventh year of the Taiping reign, artisan [illegible] from Sun Long" is found on the shoulder of another ceramic jar (b). This inscription was carved using a blunt bamboo or wooden instrument before firing, resulting in thicker, cursive strokes. "Taiping" refers to a period of Northern Yan under Emperor Feng Ba's rule (409–30 CE).

行书"太平十三年孙龙造匠潘愿"，见于一件陶瓮肩上，系烧制后所刻，字迹潦草生硬，笔画纤细无变化，多连属。行书"太平十一年四□孙龙造□匠□□"，见于另一件陶瓮肩上，系烧制前用较钝的竹木器所刻，因此笔画较粗，多连属。"太平"为十六国北燕冯跋在位时的年号（409 — 430）。

a

b

34 (I–34)

Facsimiles of rubbings of Cui Yu's tomb inscriptions

Sixteen Kingdoms, Later Yan (384–407)
Paper: L. 58 cm, W. 55 cm, T. 10 cm
Excavated in 1979 from the tomb of Cui Yu at Yaojingou, Shi'ertaixiang, Chaoyang
Original in collection of Chaoyang Museum

崔遹墓表拓片仿品

原件为十六国后燕

纸质　长58厘米、宽55厘米、厚10厘米
原件于1979年朝阳十二台乡姚金沟崔遹墓出土
原件现藏于朝阳博物馆

This vertical inscription in clerical script is found on a tomb tablet, which reads "the tenth year of Latter Yan, Cui Yu, governor of Changli from Qinghe Wucheng." According to his biographies in the *Wei Shu* [Book of Wei] and *Bei Shu* [History of the Northern Dynasties], Cui Yu was the elder brother of Cui Cheng, and his courtesy name is Ningzu. He served as the secretary of the Later Yan ruler Murong Chui, and was the governor of Fanyang and Changli counties.

During the Wei-Jin and Sixteen Kingdoms period, many ethnic groups in the west of Liaoning, including Murong Xianbei, did not have their own scripts. The sinicization of education in the Yan state led to the use of Chinese characters in the region during this period. Unearthed artifacts include inscriptions on seals, ceramic tiles, bronzes, stone and brick tomb tablets, and mural painting inscriptions. These inscriptions feature scripts such as clerical script, regular script, and running script, indicating the coexistence of various calligraphic styles in western Liaoning during this period. Likely no later than the early Eastern Jin period (317–420), the updated regular script style arrived and became prevalent in the region.

墓表竖刻隶书"燕建兴十年昌黎太守清河武城崔遹"三行十五字，后燕建兴十年为 395 年。据《魏书》及《北史》里的《崔逞传》，崔遹是崔逞的兄长，字宁祖，曾做过后燕慕容垂的尚书左丞，任范阳、昌黎二郡太守。

魏晋十六国时期活动于辽西地区的慕容鲜卑等都没有本民族的文字，燕国立国后采取的汉化教育，使辽西地区这一时期通行的文字是汉字。目前所见实物均为考古所得，有印章、陶瓦文、铜器铭刻、砖石墓表、壁画题记五类，有隶书、楷书、行书等，可见三燕时期辽西地区也是篆、隶、楷、行诸体并行，而且不晚于东晋初年，新体的楷书就已经在辽西地区流行了。

燕建興十年

昌黎大守清

河武城崔遹

35 (I–35)

Buddha statuette

Northern Wei (386–534)
Red pottery; H. 22 cm
Excavated in 2003 from Chaoyang
Liaoning Provincial Institute of
Cultural Relics and Archaeology

This molded clay sculpture of a Buddha had a surface covered in a coat of white pigment. The Buddha has a prominent *ushnisha* (a cranial protuberance indicating Buddha's wisdom), full cheeks, long and slender eyebrows, narrow eyes, a straight nose, and a smile on its small mouth. There is an *urna*, another symbol of wisdom, between the eyebrows. The earlobes extend to the shoulders. The Buddha is depicted in the lotus position, with hands folded in front. A section of robe is draped over the otherwise bare right shoulder. The collar of the robe on the left shoulder features carved folds. One side of the Buddha's face and the back of the shoulders appear slightly grayish-black, as if exposed to fire. The style of this sculpture is consistent with the artistic style of Northern Wei-period Buddhist statues, particularly those found in the Northern Pagoda of Chaoyang. Because of the fragility of clay, most surviving Buddhist statues are made of stone, making sculptures like this one, though small and roughly made, relatively rare.

佛坐像

北魏

红陶　高22厘米

2003年朝阳老城三号地点03CL②出土

辽宁省文物考古研究院藏

模制，表面施白色化妆土。佛像头顶有肉髻凸起，面颊丰满，长眉细眼，直鼻小口，面似微笑，眉间有白毫，双耳落垂于肩。结跏趺坐，双手合于腹前系禅定印。披袒右袈裟，袈裟一角搭于右肩，在左肩所披袈裟的领子处刻有折叠的褶皱纹。此身像是如来佛身躯。面部一侧及肩背部略灰黑，似经火烧。此像风格与朝阳北塔北魏造像风格一致。历史遗存的佛像多为石质，因陶易碎而很难保存。此件陶佛坐像虽然粗糙且尺寸小，但不常见。

36 (I–36)

Tile with lotus pattern

Sixteen Kingdoms, Former Yan (337–70)

Grey pottery: L. 56 cm, Diam. 17 cm

Excavated in 2000 at Beipiao

Liaoning Provincial Institute of Cultural
Relics and Archaeology

莲花纹筒瓦

十六国前燕

灰陶　通长56厘米、当面直径17厘米

2000年北票金岭寺建筑遗址出土

辽宁省文物考古研究院藏

This barrel tile is a building component used to cove the eaves of a roof. The molded tile-end design consists of six lotus-petal forms and linear ornamentation bounded between concentric circles.

筒瓦是建筑构件，遮挡屋檐所用。此件其面为圆形，采用模印图案。单栏六界格，当心圆凸，外有弦纹两周。饰六瓣莲花纹，每界格内饰一朵莲瓣，衬几何形叶纹。

37 (I–37)

Cup

Sixteen Kingdoms, Northern Yan (407–36)
Glass; H. 7.7 cm, Diam. (mouth) 9.4 cm
Excavated in 1965 from the tomb of Feng
Sufu (d. 415), Xiguanyingzi, Beipiao
Liaoning Provincial Museum

This cup is deep green in color, with a pure translucence.The surface of the vessel shows signs of erosion and exhibits a brilliant purple and yellow iridescence. The vessel has a slightly widened large mouth with a small round lip, and the mouth curves slightly inward. It has a straight body with a slightly raised center on the bottom, likely caused by the pressure applied by the blowing of glass during the manufacturing process. There are also adhesive scars or remnants, which are marks left from the connection of the blowing tube during the blowing process and were later removed after the vessel was formed. The overall shape of the vessel has gentle curves that make it easy to handle.

杯

十六国北燕
钠钙玻璃　高7.7厘米、口径9.4厘米
1965年北票西官营子北燕冯素弗墓出土
辽宁省博物馆藏

深绿色，质地纯净透明。器表有侵蚀，闪紫黄色绚光。大口微侈，小圆唇，口下略收，直身，底心上凸，为制器时吹棒顶压所致，亦有粘疤残痕，系吹制时连接吹管之处在成器后被敲掉吹管留下的残疤。整个器形曲线柔和，便于把握。

38 (I–38)

Bowl

Sixteen Kingdoms, Northern Yan
(407–36)
Glass; H. 4.1 cm, Diam. (mouth) 13
cm, Diam. (bottom) 4.4 cm
Excavated in 1965 from the tomb of
Feng Sufu (d. 415), Xiguanyingzi,
Beipiao
Liaoning Provincial Museum

This glass bowl is made of light green translucent glass with a smooth and clear texture, featuring small air bubbles. The vessel has a large mouth and a short body with a small ring foot. The curved surface gradually straightens upward, and after cutting along the mouth, it is pinched inward using pliers and adhered to the inner wall, forming an inward-folded rim. This process leaves a concave-line indentation along the outer edge of the mouth. The round bottom is nearly flat, with a slight upward convexity at the center of the base. The outer base is made by winding and attaching circular glass strips to form a small foot ring, with a scar or remnant at the center of the foot. This vessel is made by blowing a large glass bubble and then cutting it. The overall design features clean lines and a pure color, making it a rare masterpiece.

Five glass vessels were unearthed from the tomb of Feng Sufu of Northern Yan, including a duck-shaped object, two bowls, a cup, and a fragment. These precious glass vessels, which appear in a rather large grouping, represent the earliest and largest corpus of glassware unearthed in China. They were all produced through free-form blowing and are made of sodium carbonate glass, classifiable as glass of Roman origin. It is highly likely that these glass vessels were products of the northeastern provinces of the Roman Empire and were brought into Northern Yan along the Silk Road through the Rouran Khaganate. They provide valuable material evidence for the study of the Silk Road on the steppes and hold significant historical and artistic value.

碗

十六国北燕

钠钙玻璃　高4.1厘米、口径13厘米、底径4.4
厘米

1965年北票西官营子北燕冯素弗墓出土

辽宁省博物馆藏

淡绿色透明玻璃，质地光洁明彻而有小气泡。大口矮身，小圈足。近口处渐成直壁，口沿经切割后以钳具夹使内卷贴于内壁，成为一个内卷沿，因此在口外沿留下一周凹线状夹痕。圆底近平而底心向上微凸。外底以圆体玻璃条盘卷粘贴成为一个小圈足，足心有一粘疤残痕。此器以吹制的大玻璃泡切割做成。整体造型线条简洁，色泽纯洁，是不可多得的精品。

北燕冯素弗墓出土有鸭形器、碗、杯、钵等 5 件玻璃器，这些珍贵的玻璃器，数量较多且成一组出现，是中国出土的年代较早而数量又最多的一批玻璃器。这批玻璃器皿都是无模吹制成型，均为普通的钠钙玻璃，可以归类到罗马玻璃中，很可能是罗马帝国东北行省的产品。这批玻璃器是经丝绸之路，由草原汗国柔然带入北燕的，是研究草原丝绸之路重要的实物资料，具有重要的历史和艺术价值。

Mural Art of Three Yan

II

第二部分
三燕的壁画艺术

II

The tradition of mural painting of the Three Yan period (337–436) was the continuation of a practice that traces back to the early Han and Wei dynasties (since 3rd century BCE). Themes and techniques found in murals illustrating pavilions and government officials from the Han and Wei periods in the Beiyuan No.1 tomb in Liaoyang, show similarities with those in the Yuantaizi tomb in Chaoyang from the Three Yan period. Continuity is evident in the style and techniques employed by artists—from figuration to the methods used to apply colors. The murals in this exhibition illustrate the tradition using replicas of the original tomb paintings. The selection of ancient mural reproductions exhibited here begins with the depiction of pavilions from the Beiyuan No.1 tomb of the Han and Wei dynasties and is followed by mural fragments of a building from the tomb of Feng Sufu of the Northern Yan at Yuantaizi. The exhibition continues with the mural of gate guardians from the Yuantaizi tomb, and offers glimpses of daily life, such as portraits of the tomb owner and court ladies, offerings of food, meal preparation, plowing, archery, and more. The murals also feature depictions of the celestial creatures that symbolized the four cardinal directions in ancient times: Qinglong (Azure Dragon), Baihu (White Tiger), Zhuque (Vermilion Bird), and Xuanwu (Black Tortoise). Additionally, there are images of the Gold Bird, symbolizing the sun, as well as depictions of animals like the black bear.

Taking the structure of the Yuantaizi mural tomb as an example, the main chamber of the tomb is rectangular, constructed entirely of green sandstone slabs and stones, and comprises a tomb passage, an entrance, side chambers, and niches. A rectangular sloping tomb passage is located in front, with the tomb entrance in the middle of the south wall, sealed by a square stone slab. The murals within the tomb are strategically placed, with the sun depicted on the top of the tomb chamber, and the four mythical creatures arranged according to the orientation of tomb walls. For instance, the Qinglong (Azure Dragon) representing the east is painted in the front part of the east wall below a hunting scene, and the Xuanwu (Black Tortoise) representing the north is painted in the upper part of the north niche. Various murals depict scenes of nomadic life, plowing, meals, etc. The mural on the front part of the west wall portrays an offering of food to the tomb's owner. The mural creation process generally involved applying a layer of mud wattle to the stone walls of the tomb chamber, allowing it to dry, and then applying a layer of lime approximately 1.5–2 centimeters thick. Finally, murals were painted using red, yellow, green, ochre, and black water-based pigments.

三燕的壁画技法传承有序，最早可见于汉魏时期，如辽阳北园一号壁画墓中的楼阁、府吏的题材壁画，其描绘人物形象的角度、色彩的运用和画工的技法等，与前燕时期的朝阳袁台子壁画墓中的相关文物都有相似之处，可见壁画题材和技法都得以延续。这部分展品为壁画摹本，首先展现选自汉魏时期辽阳北园一号墓葬的楼阁图，然后展现冯素弗墓葬壁画的建筑残图，接着以袁台子墓葬壁画的门吏图开启对该墓葬壁画所描绘的各种生活场景的观赏，如墓主人像、仕女像、奉食图、膳食图、牛耕图、骑射图等，以及袁台子墓葬中古代用来界定东西南北四个方向的象征——青龙、白虎、朱雀、玄武四神图，还有代表太阳的金乌和动物的形象，如黑熊。

墓葬的结构以袁台子壁画墓为例，该墓室主体呈长方形，全部以绿砂岩石板、石条构筑，由墓道、墓门、耳室、壁龛组成。前有长方形坡状墓道，墓门置于南壁中部，门口以一方形石板封堵。壁画在墓葬内的位置，如太阳图在墓室顶部，四神图也基本按照墓室四壁的方向排列，如代表东方的青龙图绘于东壁前部狩猎图的下方，代表北方的玄武图绘于北壁龛上部，各壁面间则表现游牧、牛耕、膳食的各种生活场景，以及位于西壁前部、描绘墓主人饮食的奉食图等。壁画制作的步骤一般是先以石条搭建好墓室后在墓壁上涂抹黄草泥，待其阴干后涂上厚约1.5～2厘米的白灰面，然后用红、黄、绿、赭、黑等色进行绘制。

39 (II–1)

Gate Tower

Original: between Han and Wei (3rd c. CE)
H. 125 cm, W. 184.5 cm (three sections)
Facsimile painted from tomb mural
excavated at Beiyuan of Liaoyang in 1994
Liaoning Provincial Museum

楼阁图

汉魏时期
纸本　分摹于三幅画纸。画心纵125厘米，横
184.5厘米
1944年据辽阳北园一号墓壁画临摹
辽宁省博物馆藏

A multi-tiered pavilion with double-eaved roofs is adorned with black tiles and vermilion railings and features red doors with cyan-colored locks. Phoenix statues stand facing each other at the roof ridge, with long crimson flags planted on both sides, adorned with scarlet ribbons. A woman sits in the middle story. On the upper story, a bird with a long tail and large eyes stands to the right of the ridge, turning its head in surprise as if about to take flight. In the distance, a man stands naked with his knees covered, pulling a bow as if ready to shoot the bird. Below the pavilion, various performances such as handstands, juggling, sword dancing, wheel dancing, archery, and animal dances are taking place. Two officials are seen beneath the pavilion, originally inscribed with the three characters "minor prefectural official." The two officials are facing left and standing with clasped hands. This mural depicts a scene of revelers enjoying entertainment from an elevated pavilion.

重檐三层的阙楼，黛瓦朱栏，赤户青锁，立凤相对于屋脊，左右并植赤色长旗，上结朱绶。中层坐一妇人。上层右垂脊上立一鸟，长尾巨目，作回首惊顾欲飞状，远方立一人，裸而着蔽膝，弯弓向鸟作势欲射。楼阁下为倒立、弄丸、跳剑、舞轮、反弓、兽舞等百戏乐舞。位于楼阁之下，有属吏二人，原题有"小府吏"三字。二人左向，拱手而立。表现登高娱乐之状。

40 (II–2)

Architectural Structures

Original: Sixteen Kingdoms, Northern
Yan (407–36)
H. 114 cm, W. 175 cm
Facsimile painted from tomb mural
of Feng Sufu excavated at Beipiao in
1965
Liaoning Provincial Museum

This mural is located on the west wall of Feng Sufu's burial chamber. It depicts
a tall gate-tower-like structure with two tiers and double-eaved roofs, with
brackets beneath each eave. The framework under the lower tier's eaves is
particularly clear. Above the sloping ridge of the lower tier's corner eave, there
is an animal, with what appears to be claw-like feet and folded wings on the
left side, crouching on the ridge, facing outward. At both ends under the eaves,
there are two female attendants on each side. All four attendants are dressed in
red jackets with cyan collars and colorful striped skirts. On the left side, the first
of the two attendants holds something in her arms and appears to be carrying
trays or plates. The attendant at the back on the right side is in a similar posture.
Between the two groups of attendants, four black dogs leap in front of the pillars;
under the eaves, there are four long-tailed black birds.

建筑物图

十六国北燕

纸本　纵114厘米、横175厘米
1965年据北票西官营子北燕冯素弗墓壁画临摹
辽宁省博物馆藏

图像位于墓内石椁的西壁。一座高大的门楼式建筑，重檐两层，檐下均有
拱架，下层檐下的构架比较清晰。下层角檐的斜脊之上，还有一个动物，
可见其类似兽爪的足，左面似有敛垂的翼，蹲在脊上，面向外。檐下左右
两端各立两个侍女，四人都穿缥青领的红襦，下着彩条裙。左端两个侍
女，前者臂部有物，似乎是捧持杯盘。右端后面的侍女与此相同。两对侍
女之间，可见四只黑狗腾跃于门柱之前，檐下亦见四只长尾的黑鸟。

41 (II–3)

Door Guardian

Original: Sixteen Kingdoms,
Former Yan (337–70)
H. 85.4 cm, W. 42.9 cm
Facsimile painted from tomb
mural excavated at Yuantaizi,
Chaoyang in 1982
Liaoning Provincial Museum

门吏图

十六国前燕
纸本　画心纵85.4厘米、横42.9厘米
1982年据朝阳袁台子壁画墓临摹
辽宁省博物馆藏

42 (II–4)

Door Guardian

Original: Sixteen Kingdoms,
Former Yan (337–70)
H. 87 cm, W. 48 cm
Facsimile painted from tomb mural
excavated at Yuantaizi, Chaoyang
in 1982
Liaoning Provincial Museum

门吏图

十六国前燕
纸本 画心纵87厘米、横48厘米
1982年据朝阳袁台子壁画墓临摹
辽宁省博物馆藏

To the left of the pillars inside the doorway
of the tomb chamber stands a guardian
figure wearing black headgear. He has a
square face, a high nose, and a red mouth
with prominent teeth, and he is dressed in
a wide-sleeved long black robe and black
boots. To the right of the pillars, another
guardian also wears black headgear. The
figure has a square face, an open mouth
with exposed teeth, fierce-looking eyes,
and a beard. He wears a long square-
collared, wide-sleeved robe and boots, and
holds a long spear in both hands. Featuring
exaggerated and intriguing characteristics,
the guardians are depicted with skillful
and smooth technique and share many
similarities with the guardian figures seen
in later periods.

位于墓室门内立柱左侧的门吏戴黑
帻，方脸高鼻，红嘴獠牙，着广袖长
衣黑靴。位于立柱右侧的门吏也戴黑
帻，亦为方脸，张嘴露齿，瞋目张
须，着方领广袖长衣，着靴，双手执
长矛。门吏的画法娴熟流畅，形象夸
张而有趣，与后世的门神相似。

43 (II–5)

Hunting Scene

Original: Sixteen Kingdoms, Former
Yan (337–70)
H. 58.5 cm, W. 85.5 cm
Facsimile painted from tomb mural
excavated at Yuantaizi, Chaoyang in
1982
Liaoning Provincial Museum

The mural is located on the front part of the east wall. In the mural, the tomb
occupant is seen riding on a black horse galloping with its head held high. The
horse's saddle and bridle are fully detailed, and even the decorations on its neck
are clear. The tomb occupant is draped in a black headdress and is dressed in a
short square-collared, red-cuffed, light green jacket, with a waist sash, yellow
pants, and black shoes. On his back, he wears a black arrow quiver containing
four arrows, with black feathers and red tassels at the arrowheads. The rider
holds a bow in his left hand and aims, pulling the bowstring to prepare for a shot.
A herd of deer and sheep flee before the horse. Behind the horse, there is another
person wearing black headgear and yellow, square-collared attire with black
pants and black shoes. This person is holding a whip in his left hand, urging
the horse onward. Below, the painting depicts undulating mountains and trees,
following the artistic style of landscape paintings from the Wei and Jin dynasties.

狩猎图

十六国前燕
纸本　画心纵60厘米、横87.4厘米
1982年据朝阳袁台子壁画墓临摹
辽宁省博物馆藏

图像位于东壁前部。图中墓主人骑在昂首奔驰的黑马上，马鞍勒俱全，鞴
及颈銮饰都很清晰。主人裹黑帻，身着方领、红袖口浅绿色短衣，束腰
系带，黄裤黑鞋。身背黑色箭囊，囊中装四支箭，箭尾端有黑羽红缨，左
手执弓，右手拉弦瞄准待射。马前方有群鹿、黄羊，正飞驰奔逃。马后一
人，黑帻方领，黄衣黑裤，黑鞋，左手扬鞭催马。下方画起伏的山峦及树
木，画法与魏晋时代的山水画风格一致。

44 (II–6)

Procession Scene

Original: Sixteen Kingdoms, Former
Yan (337–70)
H. 42.7 cm, W. 65.4 cm
Facsimile painted from tomb mural
excavated at Yuantaizi, Chaoyang in
1982
Liaoning Provincial Museum

The mural is located in the upper part of the niche on the east wall. In the upper left corner of the picture, an ox cart is depicted, with oxen harnessed to the yoke. The cart has a high canopy, a front curtain, and is adorned with rows of decorative tassels. Next to it, a herder wearing black headgear and a short blue jacket appears to be leading the oxen. In front of the ox cart, to the left and right, two individuals wearing black headgear, short jackets, long pants, and black shoes ride side by side on horseback. The combination of the ox cart scene and the hunting scene likely represents a comprehensive depiction of a hunting expedition, portraying the tomb occupant's role as a leader during the hunt, with followers trailing behind.

车骑图

十六国前燕
纸本 画心纵42.7厘米、横65.4厘米
1982年据朝阳袁台子壁画墓临摹
辽宁省博物馆藏

图像位于东壁壁龛上部。画面左上方绘一牛车，黄牛驾辕，车上高篷，前有门帘，上缀成排的泡饰。旁有车夫一人，黑帻，蓝色短衣，作牵牛姿态。牛车前方左右各有一人，均黑帻短衣，长裤黑鞋，骑于马上并列而行。车骑图与狩猎图，应是整幅连壁大作的出猎场面，象征主人出猎时前导后从的图景。

45 (II–7)

Plowing Scene

Original: Sixteen Kingdoms, Former
Yan (337–70)
H. 43 cm, W. 69.3 cm
Facsimile painted from tomb mural
excavated at Yuantaizi, Chaoyang in
1982
Liaoning Provincial Museum

The mural is located at the top of the niche on the west wall, depicting two oxen
in red and yellow harness, plowing. The man driving the oxen and plow has
a round face, wears black headgear, a square-collared short jacket with black-
trimmed edges at the collar and cuffs, a waist sash, and long pants. He holds
the plow with his left hand and wields a whip with his right hand. In front of
the oxen, two individuals stand side by side, both wearing black headgear,
short jackets in green with black-trimmed edges at the collar and cuffs, and
waist sashes. They appear to be assisting with the plowing. The painting style is
relatively simple, with the bodies of the two oxen directly colored without ink
outlines, giving the image a fresh and distinctive character.

牛耕图

十六国前燕
纸本　画心纵43厘米、横69.3厘米
1982年据朝阳袁台子壁画墓临摹
辽宁省博物馆藏

图像位于西壁龛顶部，绘红、黄二牛挽犁耕作。一扶犁者圆脸，黑帻，着
方领短衣，领边、袖口均镶黑边，束腰长裤，左手扶犁，右手扬鞭赶牛。牛
前并列二人，黑帻，着青色短衣，领边、袖口亦镶黑边，束腰，似在协助耕
作。画法较为简洁，两牛牛身直接用颜色涂绘，不用墨线勾勒，很有特色。

46 (II–8)

Man with an Ox Cart

Original: Sixteen Kingdoms, Former
Yan (337–70)
H. 31.6 cm, W. 49.7 cm
Facsimile painted from tomb mural
excavated at Yuantaizi, Chaoyang in
1982
Liaoning Provincial Museum

The mural is located in the southern part of the east wall of the eastern chamber.
It depicts a single ox cart with black wheels and shafts, a high canopy, a low
barrier in front of the canopy, high canopy frames on both sides, and ribbons
on top. The ox cart driver is dressed in a black headdress, a short jacket, black
pants, and black shoes.

牛车图

十六国前燕
纸本   画心纵31.6厘米、横49.7厘米
1982年据朝阳袁台子壁画墓临摹
辽宁省博物馆藏

图像位于东耳室东壁的南部。绘牛车一乘，黑轮辕，高篷，篷前有矮挡
隔，篷两侧有高篷架，顶有飘带。车夫一人，黑帻短衣，黑裤黑鞋。

47 (II–9)

Food Preparation Scene

Original: Sixteen Kingdoms, Former Yan (337–70)

H. 52.5 cm, W. 82.7 cm

Facsimile painted from tomb mural excavated at Yuantaizi, Chaoyang in 1982

Liaoning Provincial Museum

膳食图

十六国前燕

纸本　画心纵52.5厘米、横82.7厘米

1982年据朝阳袁台子壁画墓临摹

辽宁省博物馆藏

The mural is located at the rear of the east wall and features three individuals. The person on the right wears black headgear, a square-collared garment with black outlines at the collar and cuffs, and long pants. He wields a knife in his right hand and an unidentified object in his left hand as he leans over a chopping board. Next to the chopping board, a square plate contains vegetables, and beneath it, there are containers such as barrels and jars. The person in the middle wears similar attire and is engaged in actions similar to the man mentioned earlier. In front of him, there are three rows of cups and plates. On the left side, a woman with her hair in a high bun and wearing a square-collared garment is busy before the stove. There is a pot on the stove, and behind the woman sits a five-tiered bamboo steamer.

图像位于东壁后部，画中三人。右一人黑帻，着方领短衣，领边和袖口镶黑边，长裤，右手持刀，左手持物，俯首于俎案上作切菜姿态。俎旁置盛菜的方盘，下置樽、魁等器。中间一人装束、动作均与前同，前置三排杯盘。左边一女子，高髻，着方领衣，忙于灶前。灶上置釜，女子身后有一五层笼屉。

48 (II–10)

Offering Food and Libation

Original: Sixteen Kingdoms, Former Yan (337–70)

H. 53.3 cm, W. 98.9 cm

Facsimile painted from tomb mural excavated at Yuantaizi, Chaoyang in 1982

Liaoning Provincial Museum

The mural is located at the front of the west wall, featuring a row of seven individuals. Starting from the left, the first person wears headgear, has a round face, thick eyebrows, large eyes, a high nose, red lips, and is turning his head to look around. He wears a black square-collared, wide-sleeved garment, with a waist sash, and black shoes. In his right hand, he holds a long knife with a red tassel hanging from the hilt. His left hand is pressed against his chest. The second person wears black headgear, a short garment with a waist sash, black pants, and black shoes. Both hands are joined in front, as if holding something. The third person wears black headgear, a yellow garment, and a belt tied and hanging at the back. Both hands are held together in front, as if holding something. The fourth person wears black headgear, an orange garment, a belt hanging at the back, orange pants, and black shoes. He is carrying a tray with three cups placed on it. The fifth person wears black headgear, an orange garment with black-trimmed edges at the collar, and a sash hanging at the back. He wears black pants and black shoes, and he holds a bottle with both hands in front of his chest. The sixth person has a round face, wears black headgear, an orange garment with black-trimmed edges at the collar and cuffs, a sash hanging at the back, black pants, and black shoes. He holds a ladle in his left hand and a spoon in his right hand. The seventh person's appearance is unclear, and only the hands are visible in a gesture that suggests offering a plate. Above the heads of the fifth and sixth individuals there are ink inscriptions. Currently, only parts of the inscription can be deciphered, such as "February… tomb… tomb offering," which are in regular script. There is also a partial mural of a dragon head above the head of the first person. Based on the remaining murals and inscriptions, it is inferred that this scene depicts the funeral custom of offering food and drinks as part of a burial ceremony to honor the deceased.

奉食图

十六国前燕

纸本　画心纵53.3厘米、横98.9厘米

1982年据朝阳袁台子壁画墓临摹

辽宁省博物馆藏

图像位于西壁前部，一列七人。左起第一人头戴冠，脸方圆，浓眉大眼，高鼻，朱唇，呈回首张望姿态。着黑方领广袖短衣，束腰系带，穿黑鞋。右手执环首长刀，环首有朱缨下垂，左手按于胸前。第二人黑帻，短衣束腰，黑裤黑鞋，双手合于胸前，似捧物。第三人黑帻，黄色短衣，腰带挽结飘垂于身后，双手合于胸前作捧物状。第四人黑帻，橙色短衣，腰带飘于身后，橙色裤，黑鞋，双手捧案，案上置耳杯三件。第五人黑帻，橙色短衣镶黑领边，飘带飘于身后，黑裤黑鞋，双手捧樽于胸前。第六人方圆脸，黑帻，着方领橙色短衣，领边、袖口镶黑边，腰系带飘垂于身后，黑裤黑鞋，左手提魁，右手提勺。第七人形貌不清，仅见双手作捧盘状。在第五、六人头上部有墨书题铭，现只可识出"二月己……子……殡背万……墓……墓奠"等楷书字样。在第一人头上部还残存一龙首。从残存图像和题铭推测，此图描绘了以酒水饭食供奉祭奠亡者的丧葬习俗。

49 (II–11)

Portrait of Tomb Occupant

Original: Sixteen Kingdoms, Former
Yan (337–70)
H. 80.3 cm, W. 65.2 cm
Facsimile painted from tomb mural
excavated at Yuantaizi, Chaoyang in
1982
Liaoning Provincial Museum

The mural is located in the west niche of the front chamber. Curtains tied with
tassels and flowing crimson ribbons hang high at the top of a portrait. There are
screens on the left and right. The tomb occupant is wearing a black cap and is
seated on a couch below the curtains. He has an oval face, thick eyebrows, big
eyes, a high nose, red lips, and a long beard. He is dressed in a right-folded red
robe with a black collar and wide sleeves. His left hand is placed flat in front
of his chest and abdomen, while his right hand holds a fly-whisk in front of his
right shoulder. To the left, behind the screen, there are two maids with high buns
and indistinct faces wearing long robes with square collars. To the right, behind
the screen, there is another maid with a high bun. The lower part of the picture
has become indecipherable.

主人像

十六国前燕
纸本　画心纵80.3厘米、横65.2厘米
1982年据朝阳袁台子壁画墓临摹
辽宁省博物馆藏

图像位于前室西龛内。画面上方帷幕高悬，帷帐挽结，下垂朱带，左右有
屏障。主人坐于帐下方榻之上，戴黑冠，面长圆，浓眉大眼，高鼻红唇，
大耳留须，身着右衽红袍，黑领广袖。左手平放于胸腹之前，右手执塵尾
于右肩前。左方屏后立二侍女，高髻，着方领长衣，面目不清。右方屏后
亦立侍女，仅见高髻。下部画面已模糊不清。

50 (II–12)

Female Attendants

Original: Sixteen Kingdoms, Former
Yan (337–70)
H. 53.2 cm, W. 64.9 cm
Facsimile painted from tomb mural
excavated at Yuantaizi, Chaoyang in
1982
Liaoning Provincial Museum

The mural is located on the south wall in front of the tomb occupant's portrait. In the upper part of the picture, four individuals in procession face the tomb occupant's portrait. The two individuals on the right hold objects in their hands, while due to erosion, only the heads of the left two figures are visible. All four individuals have double-looped high buns adorned with horizontal red hairpins. Their faces are round, with curved eyebrows, large eyes, high noses, and red lips, and their foreheads and cheekbones are painted with red pigment. They are dressed in square-collared long robes, and their attire is colorful. The lower part of the mural has become blurred and unclear.

仕女图

十六国前燕
纸本　画心纵53.2厘米、横64.9厘米
1982年据朝阳袁台子壁画墓临摹
辽宁省博物馆藏

图像位于主人像前面的南壁上。上部画面东西并列四人，均面向墓主人。西面二人站立，手捧器物。东面二人由于白灰面脱落，仅见头部。四人均双环高髻，横贯朱笄，面部方圆，弯眉大眼，高鼻，朱唇，额、颧骨部均涂朱，着方领长袍，装束艳丽。下部已漫漶不清。

51 (II–13)

Female Attendant Drawing Water

Original: Sixteen Kingdoms, Northern
Yan (407–36)
H. 18 cm, W. 24.5 cm
Copy of facsimile painted from
tomb mural excavated at Goumenzi,
Chaoyang in 1975
Original in collection of Chaoyang
Museum

The well structure appears to be made of wood, with a pulley mounted on the frame. A woman is drawing water by pulling a long rope. Her hair is drawn into a double-looped bun adorned with colored ribbons. Locks of hair frame both sides of her face. She is dressed in a two-toned skirt, with her eyebrows, eyelashes, lips, and cheeks all tinted with red pigment.

汲水图

仿本 十六国北燕
纸本　纵18厘米、横24.5厘米
原件于1975年朝阳县沟门子乡北庙生产队
（今东山村）北庙M1壁画墓出土
原件现藏于朝阳博物馆

井架似为木制，架上安滑轮，汲水女子手拽长绳打水。女子头顶结双环髻，系彩带，两鬓垂发，身着间色裙，眉间、眉梢、口唇及脸颊均点染红彩。

52 (II–14)

Azure Dragon—Symbol of the East

Azure Dragon—Symbol of the East
Original: Sixteen Kingdoms, Former Yan (337–70)
H. 65.5 cm, W. 110.5 cm
Facsimile painted from tomb mural excavated at Yuantaizi, Chaoyang in 1982
Liaoning Provincial Museum

青龙图

十六国前燕
纸本　画心纵65.5厘米、横110.5厘米
1982年据朝阳袁台子壁画墓临摹
辽宁省博物馆藏

53 (II–15)

White Tiger—Symbol of the West

Original: Sixteen Kingdoms, Former Yan (337–70)
H. 62 cm, W. 104.5 cm
Facsimile painted from tomb mural excavated at Yuantaizi, Chaoyang in 1982
Liaoning Provincial Museum

白虎图

十六国前燕
纸本　画心纵62厘米、横104.5厘米
1982年据朝阳袁台子壁画墓临摹
辽宁省博物馆藏

54 (II–16)

Vermilion Bird—Symbol of the South

Original: Sixteen Kingdoms, Former Yan (337–70)

H. 28.9 cm, W. 41 cm

Facsimile painted from tomb mural excavated at Yuantaizi, Chaoyang in 1982

Liaoning Provincial Museum

朱雀图

十六国前燕

纸本 画心纵28.9厘米、横41厘米

1982年据朝阳袁台子壁画墓临摹

辽宁省博物馆藏

55 (II–17)

Black Tortoise with Snake—Symbol of the North

Original: Sixteen Kingdoms, Former Yan (337–70)

H. 39.5 cm, W. 60.5 cm

Facsimile painted after original tomb mural excavated at Yuantaizi, Chaoyang in 1982

Liaoning Provincial Museum

玄武图

十六国前燕

纸本 画心纵39.5厘米、横60.5厘米

1982年据朝阳袁台子壁画墓临摹

辽宁省博物馆藏

The Azure Dragon, White Tiger, Vermilion Bird, and Black Tortoise, collectively known as the "Four Symbols" in Chinese culture, are common themes in tomb mural paintings from the mid-Western Han period onward. They often appear alongside celestial images in tombs to symbolize heaven. Tracing their historical origins, these Four Symbols first emerged and were employed in military formations, becoming protective deities for marching and warfare. In Han dynasty tombs, representations of the Four Symbols were frequently painted on the four walls of burial chambers, symbolizing the four cardinal directions (east, south, west, and north, as they are rendered in Chinese, in contrast to the customary Western listing of north, south, east, and west). In ancient times, people divided heaven into four palaces, each associated with one of the Four Symbols: the Azure Dragon, the White Tiger, the Vermilion Bird, and the Black Tortoise (depicted as a tortoise entwined with a snake). Essentially, this division represented the sky's four quadrants, with each quadrant formed by connecting seven prominent constellations, and named based on the shapes formed by these constellations. The eastern palace, resembling the shape of a dragon, was named the Azure Dragon; the western palace, resembling the shape of a tiger, was named the White Tiger; the southern palace, with constellations forming a bird shape, was named the Vermilion Bird; and the northern palace, with constellations resembling a tortoise, was named the Black Tortoise. As a result, the Green Dragon, White Tiger, Vermilion Bird, and Black Tortoise became the guardians of heaven, warding off evil and harmonizing the forces of *yin* and *yang*.

In the murals of the Yuantaizi tomb, the mural of the Azure Dragon is located in the lower part of the eastern wall, just below the hunting scene painted on the front part of the wall. It depicts an Azure Dragon with an upturned head, an open mouth revealing a red tongue, and a sinuous body with stretched legs, a coiled tail, and outspread wings, exuding a vigorous and majestic aura. The intricate details of the dragon's horns, mane, elbow fur, claws, and scales are depicted vividly. Above the dragon, there is a Vermilion Bird depicted with outstretched wings in a flying posture. The mural of the White Tiger is located in the lower part of the western wall, below the scene of an offering table painted on the front part of the wall. Both the White Tiger and the Vermilion Bird in the painting are constructed using ink lines. The White Tiger has an open mouth, bared teeth, round eyes, an upturned head, a sinuous body, and a raised tail, and appears to be galloping. Above the tiger, there is a Vermilion Bird depicted flying with an upturned head and outspread wings. The mural of the Vermilion Bird is located in the lower part of the eastern wall, below the hunting scene, and is rendered primarily using black and red lines. The exact content of this artwork is no longer discernible, and it is speculated to be a fragment of a Vermilion Bird mural. The mural of the Black Tortoise is located in the upper part of the north wall. In the painting, the tortoise is depicted in light green, with its head raised and its body resting on the ground, entwined by a long serpent.

青龙、白虎、朱雀、玄武被称为"四神"，是西汉中期以来墓葬壁画中常见的题材，常与天象图一起出现在墓葬中作为天的象征。追溯历史，最早四神形象出现并被运用于军容军列中，成为行军打仗的保护神。在汉墓当中，四神像多绘于墓室四壁，以表示东、西、南、北四个方向。在上古时代，古人把天分为东西南北四宫，分别以青龙（苍龙）、白虎、朱雀、玄武（一种龟形之神）为名。实际上是把天空分为四部，将每部分中的七个主要星宿连线成形，以其形状命名。东方的角、亢、氐、房、心、尾、箕形状如龙，所以称东宫为青龙或苍龙；西方七星奎、娄、胃、昴、毕、觜、参形状如虎，称西宫为白虎；南方的井、鬼、柳、星、张、翼、轸联为鸟形，称朱雀；北方七星斗、牛、女、虚、危、室、壁，其形如龟，称玄武。于是，青龙、白虎、朱雀、玄武又成为镇守天宫的四神，辟邪恶、调阴阳。

朝阳袁台子壁画墓中，其青龙图像位于东壁前部狩猎图下部。绘一昂首、张嘴露红舌的青龙，龙曲身张足，卷尾，双翼后摆，雄健而有气势。龙角、鬣、肘毛、爪和麟甲等都描绘得细致而生动。白虎图像位于绘于西壁前部奉食图的下部。画白虎、朱雀，皆墨线构图。白虎张嘴露齿，双目圆睁，昂首曲身扬尾，作奔腾姿态。朱雀图像位于绘于东壁前部狩猎图下部，以黑色和红色线条为主，图画内容已不识，推测应是朱雀图的残片。玄武图像位于北壁龛上部，画面中龟为浅绿色，昂首俯卧，被长蛇缠绕。

52 (II–14)

53 (II-15)

54 (II–16)

55 (II-17)

56 (II–18)

Gold Bird—Symbol of the Sun

Original: Sixteen Kingdoms, Former
Yan (337–70)
H. 8.7 cm, Diam. 19.5 cm
Facsimile painted after original
tomb mural excavated at Yuantaizi,
Chaoyang in 1982
Liaoning Provincial Museum

This mural is located above the hunting scene. The sun is painted vermilion, and within it, there is a golden three-legged crow with a long tail and wings spread in preparation for flight.

The concept of the golden crow has a long history in ancient Chinese mythology, with its basic composition being that of the "sun and bird." The image frequently appears in texts such as the *Chu Ci* 楚辞 (Verses of Chu), *Chanhai Jing* 山海经 (Classic of Mountains and Seas), *Huainanzi* 淮南子 (Masters of Huainan), and *Hanwu Gushi* 汉武故事 (Emperor Wudi of Han Dynasty's Story). In ancient Chinese mythology, the sun is the son of Emperor Jun and Xihe, and possesses both human and divine characteristics. It is the incarnation of the golden crow, a crow with three legs, and a flying sun bird. Therefore, it represents the sun. The golden crow holds an important place in China's ancient mythological system, playing significant roles in myths involving cultural progenitors the Queen Mother of the West, Fuxi and Nüwa, and Houyi shooting down the sun. It is a common theme in Han dynasty tomb paintings and exists in abundance in the murals, carved stone images, and image bricks of that period, reflecting its role as a symbol of longevity, rebirth, and protection.

太阳图

十六国前燕

纸本　画心横29.4厘米、纵28.3厘米、太阳直
径19.5厘米　金乌长12厘米、高8.7厘米
1982年据朝阳袁台子壁画墓临摹
辽宁省博物馆藏

图像位于狩猎图的顶盖上。太阳涂朱，内有一只金乌，三足，长尾，作昂首展翅状。

金乌在我国古代神话体系中由来已久，其基本组合就是"太阳与鸟"，它的形象多出现在《楚辞》《山海经》《淮南子》《汉武故事》等文献中。在中国古代神话中，太阳是帝俊与羲和的儿子，它们有人与神的特征，是金乌的化身，是长有三足的鸟，是会飞翔的太阳神鸟，所以，以此来代表太阳。金乌在我国古代神话体系中占有重要的地位，作为西王母、伏羲女娲、后羿射日等神话体系中的重要角色，在两汉墓葬绘画中成为常见题材，在两汉的壁画墓、画像石、画像砖等中大量存在，体现其具有长生、重生和辟佑作用。

57 (II–19)

Black Bear

Original: Sixteen Kingdoms, Former
Yan (337–70)
H. 21.3 cm, W. 32 cm
Facsimile painted after original
tomb mural excavated at Yuantaizi,
Chaoyang in 1982
Liaoning Provincial Museum

This mural is located on the upper stone pedestal of the west wall of the food
offering scene (cat. no. 47), but parts of the painting have been lost. Only a black
bear remains at the northern end, with upright ears, an open mouth with tongue
exposed, and front limbs and paws raised, apparently standing upright on its hind
limbs. The black bear is directly depicted using ink coloring without additional
outlining.

黑熊图

十六国前燕
纸本　画心纵21.3厘米、横32厘米
1982年据朝阳袁台子壁画墓临摹
辽宁省博物馆藏

图像位于西壁奉食图上部垫石上，画面脱落。北端仅存一黑熊，竖耳，张
嘴露舌，前肢、掌上举，下肢站立。黑熊直接用墨涂染而不加勾勒。

Gold Art of
Three Yan

III

第三部分
三燕的金饰艺术

III

According to historical records, after the Murong Xianbei, led by Mohuba, entered the Liaoxi region, a distinctive headdress called the *buyao* crown, meaning "swaying with steps" became popular. This ornament, originating from West Asia and adorned with shaking leaves, spread southward along the Steppe Route with the Murong Xianbei and became admired in the whole Liaoxi region. Moreover, it became a headpiece symbolizing the aristocratic status of the Three Yan states, serving as a significant feature of Three Yan culture. The exhibition displays various gold *buyao* ornaments, which mainly fall into two types: one resembling a flowering tree, and the other taking the form of a stand furnished with shaking leaves, both creating an elegant swaying effect. The name "Murong" may have originated phonetically from *buyao* and the exhibits here seem to support this point. They vividly evoke the image of the Three Yan people wearing gold *buyao* headdresses resembling a tree of golden flowers in full bloom, swaying gently in the wind, and radiating a myriad of lights. The Three Yan people had a fondness for gold ornaments such as earrings, bracelets, and belts. Through analysis of specimens, the gold content in their jewelry was determined to have reached a percentage of 85%–92%. The goldsmithing craftsmanship involved techniques like embossing, engraving, inlay, filigree, and soldering with gold beads. The ornaments featured various motifs, including dragons, phoenixes, honeysuckle, deer, Buddha statues, and others, revealing the influence of Central Plains culture as well as connections to Buddhism and the Silk Road. All these elements resulted in the creation of a unique form of gold ornament art in the Three Yan period.

古文献记载，慕容鲜卑由莫护跋率领进入辽西后，喜戴一种"步摇冠"。这种源于西亚的摇叶装饰，通过草原丝绸之路随慕容鲜卑南下传入，流行于辽西地区，成为表示三燕贵族身份和地位的特定冠饰，更是成为三燕文化的显著特征。展览中展出的多件金步摇基本属于两种类型，一种状如花树，一种为支架状冠式，加上摇叶，均可摇曳生姿，不仅印证了慕容鲜卑的"慕容"二字即"步摇"音讹而来，也生动地再现了三燕人头戴金步摇，如一树金花盛开，随风轻摆、万束光来的形象。三燕人钟爱金饰物，这能从耳饰、手饰、带饰等多方面体现出来。经标本测定，其金饰的含金量高达85%～92%；其制作工艺亦臻成熟，已知有锤鍱、镂刻、镶嵌、花丝、金珠焊缀等多种技法；其装饰有龙、凤、忍冬、鹿、佛像等多种纹饰，既表现了对中原文化的传承，又透露了与丝路和宗教的联系，形成了这种可用可赏的独特的金饰艺术。

58 (III–1)

Hat ornament

Western Jin (265–317)
Gold; H. 14.5 cm
Excavated in 1956–7 from tomb No. 2
at Fangshencun, Xusihuayingzixiang,
Beipiao
Liaoning Provincial Museum

The base of this golden *buyao* headdress is rectangular, with a central ridge and hollow cloud patterns on both sides. The perimeter is covered with numerous needle holes, indicating it was attached to a hat. Two pieces were unearthed at the same time, with the larger one measuring 5.2 cm in length and 4.5 cm in width at the base, and the smaller one measuring 4 cm in length and 3.5 cm in width at the base. A short and wide trunk extends from the base, with the larger piece branching into three main stalks, totaling sixteen smaller branches; the smaller piece has eleven branches, which wind around in loops and pass through peach-shaped gold leaves that sway and tremble in the wind. These two gold ornaments share a general resemblance to the gold crown ornaments found in the tomb of Feng Sufu, indicating that they are exclusive noble crown accessories of Xianbei and other Northern ethnic groups during the Six Dynasties period.

花树状步摇

西晋
金质 通高14.5厘米
1956—1957年北票徐四花营子乡房身村M2出土
辽宁省博物馆藏

这件金步摇的基部呈长方形，中间突起一脊，两侧为镂空云纹，周边满布针孔，可知为缝缀于冠帽之上。所出两件，大者基部长5.2厘米、宽 4.5厘米，小者基部长4厘米、宽3.5厘米。在基部上伸出短而宽的树干，大者分出三主枝，共出十六分枝；小者十一分枝，枝身缠绕为环，上穿桃形金叶，随风摇颤。这两件金饰与冯素弗墓出土的金冠饰大致相似，是两晋十六国时期鲜卑等北方民族的专属贵族冠用饰品。

59 (III–2)

Hat ornament

Sixteen Kingdoms, Former Yan (337–70)
Gold; H. 27.2 cm
Excavated in 1989 from tomb No.1 at
Tiancaogou, Xiyingzixiang, Chaoyang
Liaoning Provincial Institute of Cultural
Relics and Archaeology

This *buyao* headdress consists of a rectangular base and branches resembling flowering trees. In the middle of the base, there is a protruding central ridge, with symmetrically carved and deformed persimmon motifs on both sides. A row of grain-like patterns decorates the middle part of the raised edges, the surroundings of the protrusions, and the edges of the base. The branches are divided into two layers: in the front layer, from the bottom edge of the main branch at the hollowed-out part, another branch extends outward, further dividing into three branches, each with two rings and adorned with leaves; in the rear layer, the central part of the main branch is hollowed out, with six branches at the top, each coiled around a ring and holding leaves inside the ring.

花树状步摇

十六国前燕
金质　高27.2厘米
1989年朝阳西营子乡田草沟M1出土
辽宁省文物考古研究院藏

由矩形牌座和花树状缀叶枝干组成。牌座中部中间突起一脊，两侧对称镂刻变形柿蒂纹，凸棱中部和镂孔周围及牌座边缘均饰一行粟粒纹。枝干分前后两层：前层自主干镂空处底缘向外再出一枝干，上分三枝，每枝存二环，缀叶；后层片状主干中部镂空，干顶六枝，每枝绕环、环内衔叶。

60 (III–3)

Hat ornament

Sixteen Kingdoms, Former Yan (337–70)
Gold; Base: H. 5 cm, W. 4.6–4.8 cm;
Branches, W. 13.7 cm, L. 17.8 cm with
remaining 35 leafs
Excavated in 1989 from tomb No. 2 of
Tiancaogou, Xiyingzixiang, Chaoyang
Liaoning Provincial Institute of Cultural
Relics and Archaeology

This *buyao* headdress is composed of a nearly rectangular base and serpentine branches with dangling leaves. In the middle of the front side, there is a vertical tower-like structure, with four deformed leaf motifs carved out. A row of grain-like patterns adorns the surroundings of the openings and the edges of the base. In the center, slightly thicker round gold wires form a serpentine pattern. From the upper and lower parts, flat ribbon-like branches extend outward on both sides, with several smaller branches branching out at the ends of each; each branch holds one to two leaves within a ring. At the top, there are five additional branches, each also coiled around a ring and holding leaves.

花树状步摇

十六国前燕
金质　牌座长5厘米、宽4.6～4.8厘米　展宽约
13.7厘米　树状存长17.8厘米
1989年朝阳西营子乡田草沟M2出土
辽宁省文物考古研究院藏

由近矩形的牌座和花树状缀叶枝干组成。正面中部轧出竖楼并镂出四个变形蒂叶纹，镂孔周围和牌座边缘均饰一行粟粒纹。中间为略粗的圆体金丝，呈蛇行状，其中、下部各向两侧分出扁带状分枝，枝端又分出若干细枝，每枝绕环衔叶一至二片。顶部另分出五枝，每枝也绕环衔叶，存叶三十五片。

61 (III–4)

Hat ornament

Sixteen Kingdoms, Former Yan (337–70)
Gold; H. 20 cm, W. 4.5 cm
Excavated in 1989 from tomb No. 1 at
Tiancaogou, Xiyingzixiang, Chaoyang
Chaoyang County Museum

花树状步摇

十六国前燕
金质   底宽4.5厘米、残高20厘米
1989年朝阳西营子乡田草沟M1出土
朝阳县博物馆藏

The *buyao* was made entirely of gold and is divided into two parts: the base and the branches and leaves. The base of the *buyao* is rectangular in shape, with a vertical strip-shaped protrusion in the middle. The ridge is decorated with cone-point patterns, and on each side, there is a carved honeysuckle vine. The borders of the honeysuckle vine and the periphery of the base are adorned with cone-point patterns. As for the branches and leaves section, the central area is hollow, with one branch still connected at the bottom, now damaged. On both sides, there are five branches each, and at the top of each branch, there is a twist of gold wire forming a ring that holds dangling leaves.

以一金片制成，分基部和枝叶两部分，基部呈长方形，中部有竖条状凸起，脊部饰锥点纹，两侧各透雕一忍冬，忍冬边界及基部周边均饰锥点纹。枝叶部分，中部镂空，底连一枝，已残。两侧各有五分枝，顶部一分枝，每枝金丝拧环缀摇叶。

62 (III–5)

Hat ornament

Sixteen Kingdoms, Former Yan (337–70)
Gold: H. (total) 14 cm, W. 13 cm
Excavated in 1998 from tomb No. 7 of
Lamadong, Beipiao
Liaoning Provincial Institute of Cultural
Relics and Archaeology

花树状步摇

十六国前燕
金质　展宽约13厘米、通高14厘米
1998年北票南八家乡四家板村喇嘛洞墓地ⅠM7
出土
辽宁省文物考古研究院藏

This *buyao* headdress consists of a nearly rectangular base and branches resembling a budding tree. The center of the base has a vertical ridge, and there is a small hole at each of the four corners. The branches are divided into two layers: in the rear layer, the central part of the main branch is hollowed out, with a branch extending from the top and three branches on each side. Additionally, a supporting branch is riveted to the bottom edge of the central hollow part of the main branch, dividing into three branches. These are the branches of the front layer. Each layer of branches coils around a ring at its top and is adorned with a peach-shaped leaf.

The gold *buyao* ("step sway") is a unique headdress of the Murong Xianbei people and is formed by winding peach-shaped gold leaves on branches see earlier tree. It is distinct from the *buyao* used by ancient Chinese women as a hair ornament. This metal leaf decoration originated in Western Asia and was introduced to the northern regions through the Silk Road, spreading in the western Liaoning area and becoming a prominent feature of Three Yan culture. These gold *buyao* are often found in high-ranking noble tombs in the western Liaoning region and symbolize the status of the Murong nobility.

由近矩形的牌座和花树状缀叶枝干组成。牌座中部轧出竖棱，四角各具一针孔。干枝分前后两层：后层主干中部镂空，其顶端出一枝，两侧各分三枝。另于主干镂空处底缘中部铆接支干，上分三枝，此为前层枝干。每层分枝只在其顶端各绕一环并缀一片桃形叶，共缀叶十片。

金步摇是慕容鲜卑特有的一种冠饰，是在花树状枝干上缠绕桃形金叶形成的，不同于中国古代妇女使用的一种名为"步摇"的发饰。这种金属摇叶装饰源于西亚，是通过草原丝绸之路随北方游牧民族南下传入，流行于辽西地区，成为三燕文化的显著特征。这种金步摇多出土于辽西地区高等级的贵族墓葬，是慕容贵族身份的象征。

63 (III–6)

Buyao crown frame

Sixteen Kingdoms, Former Yan (337–70)
Gold; H. 20.5 cm, Wt. 55.5 g
Excavated in 1976 from tomb No.
4 at Wangzifenshan, Shi'ertaixiang,
Chaoyang,
Chaoyang County Museum

步摇冠

十六国前燕
金质　高20.5厘米、重55.5克
1976年朝阳十二台乡王子坟山M4出土
朝阳县博物馆藏

The upper part of the *buyao* resembles a tree-like structure with dangling leaves. In the middle, there is a semi-spherical top with a hollow sphere formed by two halves locked together, connected to the crown cage below. The crown cage is made of three long, flat strips of gold, each 1.4 cm wide, hammered into a semi-circular shape arranged in a "T" formation. Three holes are evenly drilled on both sides of the three gold strips, with gold wire wound inside the holes, and circular leaves attached above.

A similar golden headdress was found in the tomb of Feng Sufu from Northern Yan. Both are composed of several branches gathered into a bundle, adorned with leaves on the branches, and have a cap-like shape at the base. This similarity suggests a cultural inheritance.

上部似一花树，缀摇叶。中部的半圆球形顶部有一由两半圆泡合扣在一起的空心球体与下面的冠笼衔接。冠笼是以宽1.4厘米的三条长条形金片锤制的呈"T"形排列的半圆球状，三条金片两侧均匀钻孔，孔内绕金丝，上级圆形叶片。在北燕冯素弗墓发现的金步摇冠与之相似，均为由数枝集为一束，枝上缀叶，基部为帽笼之形，可见其传承。

64 (III–7)

Buyao crown frame

Sixteen Kingdoms, Former Yan (337–70)
Gold; H. 29 cm, W. 1 cm, Wt. 89 g
Excavated in 1965 from the tomb of Feng
Sufu (d. 415), Xiguanyingzi, Beipiao
Liaoning Provincial Museum

The frame consists of a top ornament and a cage crown structure. The top ornament has six branches, each winding around to form three loops, with a gold leaf passing through each loop. The branches are riveted onto a bowl-shaped base, which passes through a hollow, flattened sphere and connects to the beams of the cage crown. The cage crown's structure comprises two narrow gold strips crossing each other in a cross shape, with all four ends bending downward and draping over the crown. Along the sides of the gold strips, there is a row of small holes, presumably intended for attaching dangling gold leaves, which are now missing. One side of the intersecting gold strip is shorter, likely positioned at the front of the crown to accommodate the placement of the "*ti*" (the central part of the headdress). This type of floral ornament sways and trembles as one moves, hence its name "step-sway." A crown adorned with this kind of floral ornament is referred to as a "step-sway headdress." This noble headdress was used by various Northern ethnic groups, including the Xianbei, during the Jin dynasty (266–420) and the Sixteen Kingdoms period (303–439).

步摇冠

十六国北燕
金质　梁架宽1厘米、高29厘米、重89克
1965年北票西官营子北燕冯素弗墓出土
辽宁省博物馆藏

由顶花和笼冠的梁架构成。顶花六枝，每枝绕出三环，每环穿一金叶（步摇叶）。枝干铆在一钵形座上，下面穿过一空体扁球，连于笼冠的梁架上。梁架为两条窄金片作十字交叉，四端都弯而下垂，以笼覆于冠上。沿金片的两边各有一排小孔，原也应穿缀步摇金叶，金叶已缺失。作十字交叉的金片一面较短，当是位于冠的前面，以备安放冠"题"（即帽正）。这种花饰随行步而摇颤，故名"步摇"，戴有这种花饰的冠即"步摇冠"，是两晋十六国时期鲜卑等北方民族的一种贵族用冠。

65 (III–8)

Plaque with disk pendants

Western Jin (266–317)
Gold; H. 9 cm, W. 9 cm
Excavated in 1956–7 from tomb No. 2
at Fangshencun, Xusihuayingzixiang,
Beipiao
Liaoning Provincial Museum

透雕龙凤纹金珰

西晋
金质　长9厘米、宽9厘米
1956—1957年北票徐四花营子乡房身村M2出土
辽宁省博物馆藏

This thin square plaque has two diagonal lines perpendicular to each other that divide the square evenly into four sections. It is carved and pierced through to create four phoenixes. There are holes drilled around the perimeter and along the inner cross lines, where small circular gold pieces in the shape of floral leaves, known as "step-sway" leaves, are attached. The number of these leaves varies.

方形薄片，方形内两对角线垂直交叉，将方形均匀地分成四部分，镂空透雕四凤，四周边框及内十字边上均有钻孔，上系花叶状小圆金片即步摇叶片，枚数不等。

66 (III–9)

Plaque

Sixteen Kingdoms, Former Yan (337–70)
Gold; H. 8.9 cm, W. 8.9 cm
Excavated in 1989 from tomb No.1 at
Tiancaogou, Xiyingzixiang, Chaoyang
Chaoyang County Museum

方形金珰

十六国前燕
金质　长8.9厘米、宽8.9厘米
1989年朝阳西营子乡田草沟M1出土
朝阳县博物馆藏

Within the four triangular areas formed by the borders and diagonals on this thin square plaque, abstract dragon and phoenix patterns are symmetrically carved in pairs. There are two rows of grain-like patterns on both the borders and diagonals, and each of the four corners has two small holes.

This type of gold plaque is decorative. As evidenced by the presence of small holes in their four corners, such plaques were originally intended to be sewn or attached to other objects.

正方形薄片。在由边框和对角线所构成的四个三角区内两两对称镂出变形龙凤图案，边框和对角线上皆饰有两行粟粒纹，四角各具两个针孔。

此类薄片形金饰均为装饰之用，从其四角常有针孔可见，原应为缝缀于其他物品之上。

67 (III–10)

Cicada finial ornament

Sixteen Kingdoms, Northern Yan
(407–36)
Gold and stone; H. 7 cm, W. 6.6 cm,
Wt. 20 g
Excavated in 1965 from the tomb of
Feng Sufu (d. 415), Xiguanyingzi,
Beipiao
Liaoning Provincial Museum

Resembling the character "山" (mountain) in shape, this type of ornament sat at the front of a headdress, known as a "*ti*." The front is adorned with intricate gold wire patterns that coil around, and on either side of the gold wires, gold granules are applied as decoration. The central motif appears to be cicada-like, with double wings and grey stone beads as eyes, though only one bead remains. The empty spaces within the pattern are carved with openings, often backed with a plain piece of gold foil of the same size to serve as a cushion, sewn together. This type of ornament might have been worn by high-ranking officials, specifically those with the title of "侍中" (*shizhong*). Known as "*jindang*" (golden plaque) and with the "*chan*" (cicada) motif, this ornament is referred to as the "*jindang fu chan*."

蝉纹金珰

十六国北燕
金质、石珠　高7厘米、宽6.6厘米、重20克
1965年北票西官营子北燕冯素弗墓出土
辽宁省博物馆藏

状如"山"字形，为一种冠前的帽正，即"题"。正面以细金丝盘曲为纹，沿金丝的两侧又附金粟为饰。主体图案似为蝉形，旁有双翅，眼窝上缀灰石珠作目。图案的空隙处镂切出孔，背后常常复加一片同样大小的素面金箔作为衬垫，缝连一起。这种饰片可能为高级官员中有"侍中"名衔者所戴用，即"金珰"，加上蝉纹即所谓"金珰附蝉"。

68 (III–11)

Plaque

Sixteen Kingdoms, Former Yan (337–70)
Gold; H. 5.6 cm , W. (top) 4.2 cm; W. (bottom) 3.7 cm
Excavated in 1980 from tomb No. 2 at Yaoeryingzi brick factory, Shi'ertaixiang, Chaoyang,
Chaoyang County Museum

The gold plaque is in the shape of the character "山" (mountain). wider at the top and narrower at the bottom. Along the outer edge of the gold plaque, there are decorative cone-point patterns extending for two rounds. The gold plaque is evenly hammered and has a golden brilliance. It is probably the backing piece for the cicada-patterned golden plaque.

山形金珰

十六国前燕
金质　上宽4.2厘米、下宽3.7厘米、高5.6厘米
1980年朝阳十二台乡腰而营子砖厂M2出土
朝阳县博物馆藏

金珰呈"山"形，上宽下窄，沿金珰外边饰两周锥点纹，金珰锤鍱均匀，颜色金黄，应是蝉纹金珰的衬片。

69 (III–12)

Hat ornament with Buddha image and disk pendants

Sixteen Kingdoms, Northern Yan
(407–36)
Gold; H. 6.6 cm, W. 6.8–8.2 cm
Excavated in 1965 from the tomb of
Feng Sufu (d. 415), Xiguanyingzi,
Beipiao
Liaoning Provincial Museum

One side of this plaque bears an embossed image of a Buddha and two Bodhisattvas. The Buddha has elongated horizontal eyes and is seated in a meditative posture. On the other side, the plaque is adorned with dangling gold leaves, showcasing the distinctive characteristics of Murong Xianbei culture. This cultural artifact serves as important evidence of the early transmission of Buddhism and its development in Northern Yan, reflecting the growing influence of Buddhism in the Northern Yan region. This decorative piece represents the convergence of Central Plains tradition, Buddhism, and Murong Xianbei culture, leaving a profound impact on the culture of decorative arts in Northeast Asia.

压印佛像纹山形金珰

十六国北燕
金质　宽6.8～8.2厘米、高6.6厘米
1965年北票西官营子北燕冯素弗墓出土
辽宁省博物馆藏

一面压印一佛二菩萨像，佛像双目横长，跌坐作禅定印，一面缀步摇金叶，显示出鲜明的慕容鲜卑文化特色。这件文物是早期佛教东传和在北燕发展的重要物证，是佛教在北燕地区日益兴盛的一种反映。这种装饰品表现了中原文化、佛教文化与鲜卑文化的交汇融合，对东北亚金饰品文化的影响至为深远。

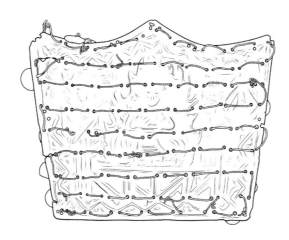

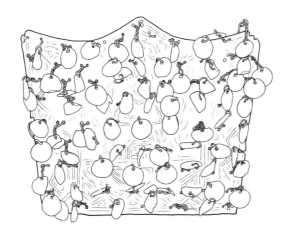

70 (III–13)

Earring

Sixteen Kingdoms, Former Yan (337–70)
Gold; Diam. 2.5 cm, L. 7.1 cm; Leaf: W.
0.3 cm, L. 0.6 cm
Excavated in 1998 from a tomb at
Lamadong, Beipiao
Liaoning Provincial Institute of Cultural
Relics and Archaeology

This earring consists of a ring and two gold pendants adorned with dangling leaves. The earring is made of curved gold tubes, forming a circular shape with both ends closed. Below the earring, there is a short chain, and below the chain, there are two layers of gold pendants. The upper layer of gold pendants is round with a flat top, and there are nine circular perforations near the bottom edge of the pendant. Inside these perforations, there are small chains and a dangling leaf on each. The lower layer of gold pendants has a similar shape to the upper layer but is slightly larger, and it holds eleven dangling leaves. Four dangling leaves are missing.

耳坠

十六国前燕
金质　通长7.1厘米、环径2.5厘米、宽0.3厘米、
摇叶长0.6厘米
1998年北票南八家乡四家板村喇嘛洞墓地出土
辽宁省文物考古研究院藏

由耳环和两个衔有摇叶的金泡组成。耳环用金管弯制而成，环形，两端闭合。耳环下连接短链，链下再连接上下两层金泡。上层金泡为圆形平顶，近金泡的底边有九个圆形穿孔，孔内衔小链和一枚摇叶。下层金泡形状与上层的相似，规格略大，衔有十一枚摇叶。残缺四枚摇叶。

71 (III–14)

Earrings

Sixteen Kingdoms, Former Yan (337–70)
Gold with agate bead; W. 2.2–3 cm, L: 8.2–8.7
cm; Leaf: W. 0.5–0.9 cm, L. 1–1.9 cm
Excavated in 1998 from tomb No. 17 at
Lamadong, Beipiao
Liaoning Provincial Institute of Cultural
Relics and Archaeology

The frames of these earrings are made from twisted gold wires and are divided into three layers: upper, middle, and lower. At the end of each branch on each layer there is a loop, and each loop holds a dangling leaf. In the lowest layer, there is an additional branch that extends downward and passes through a single agate bead.

Many gold earrings have been excavated in Murong Xianbei tombs, and they primarily fall into two main forms. One type has a circular ring at the top for passing through the earlobe, and the lower part consists of gold leaves for ornamentation. An example is the earrings (cat. no. 70) unearthed from Lamadong in Sijiaban Village, Nanbajia Township, Beipiao, in 1998. Another type features a pendant frame and hook made from twisted gold wires at the top, with multiple layers adorned with dangling leaves below. An example is the earrings discovered from burial site Ⅰ M17 at Lamadong in 1998. The dangling leaves on these gold earrings echo those on the "step-sway."

耳坠

十六国前燕
金质　通长8.2～8.7厘米、宽2.2～3厘米；叶长1～1.9
厘米、宽0.5～0.9厘米
1998年北票南八家乡四家板村喇嘛洞墓地Ⅰ M17出土
辽宁省文物考古研究院藏

以金丝拧成坠架，分上、中、下三层，每层枝权末端拧环各衔一圭形摇叶，最下层中间下延一枝，穿玛瑙珠一颗。

在慕容鲜卑墓中出土了许多金耳饰，基本上有两种形式。一种是上部有环形穿鼻，下部套接金叶垂饰的，如1998年北票南八家乡四家板村喇嘛洞墓地出土的耳坠饰（见图录第70号）；另一种是上部以金丝拧成坠架和挂钩，下部分层次地缀有摇叶装饰，如1998年北票南八家乡四家板村喇嘛洞墓地Ⅰ M17出土的耳坠饰。金耳饰上的摇叶运用与头饰的步摇装饰相互呼应，融为一体。

72 (III–15)

Ornaments

Sixteen Kingdoms, Former Yan (337–70)
Gold; H. (total) 4.85 cm, Diam. 4.3–5.1
cm, T. 1.1 cm
Excavated in 1989 from tomb No. 1 at
Tiancaogou, Xiyingzoxiang, Chaoyang
Chaoyang County Museum

锁形金坠

十六国前燕
金质　高4.85厘米；锁径4.3～5.1厘米、最厚处
1.1厘米
1989年朝阳西营子乡田草沟M1出土
朝阳县博物馆藏

The leaves on these ornaments are damaged. The ornament is made by interlocking two round gold pieces and then riveting them together along the edges. The lock body is round and convex on both sides, with a flat area in the center, and each side has a circular recess. The entire surface is decorated with a circular arrangement of granular patterns. Along the outer edge of the lock-shaped ornament, there are protrusions, and drilled holes arranged along the upper side. Through these holes, twisted gold wires are passed, forming loops and connecting dangling leaves. Additionally, there are double loops riveted at the notches along the upper edge. It is speculated that these ornaments were meant to be hung on either side of a headdress as decorations.

叶残缺。以两块圆形金片对扣，再铆合边缝而成。锁体两面圆凸，其内扁心处各有一圆窝，通体饰呈环状排列的粟粒纹。锁形饰的外缘出沿，沿上布列钻孔，孔内穿绞股金丝拧环并联缀摇叶。另在上缘外沿缺口处对铆双系，推测应是挂在冠的两侧为饰。

73 (III–16)

Thimble

Western Jin (266–317)
Gold; W. 1.2 cm, Diam. 1.8 cm, Wt. 3.6 g
Excavated in 1957 from tomb No. 2
at Fangshencun, Xusihuayingzixiang,
Beipiao
Liaoning Provincial Museum

This gold thimble was hammered into shape. Its surface features fine lines creating a diamond-shaped border, with circles chiseled within the borders. The inner surface is plain, without patterns, and has been polished smooth. In 1957, three tombs were discovered in Fangshen Village, Xusihuayingzi Township, Beipiao. They are in proximity and share consistent burial depth, all featuring tomb chambers constructed from stone slabs. In particular, the first and second tombs are adjacent to each other, have the same orientation, and share similar architectural features, suggesting a close connection between them. Based on the characteristics of the bronze mirror found in the first tomb and the gold shield decorations in the second tomb, as well as the bronze and pottery items from the third tomb, their dating appears consistent, indicating that all three tombs likely belong to the same period. Archaeologists, in conjunction with their analysis of the historical development of the burial site, suggest that these tombs might belong to the Xianbei tribe during the Jin dynasty. This gold thimble from a Murong Xianbei tomb serves as evidence of their cultural fusion with Han Chinese culture.

顶针

西晋
金质　宽1.2厘米、环径1.8厘米、重3.6克
1957年北票徐四花营子乡房身村M2出土
辽宁省博物馆藏

打制成型。表面以细线划菱形界格，在界格内满饰錾凿的圆窝点。内壁素面无纹，磨光。1957年北票徐四花营子乡房身村发现了3座墓葬，且距离较近，埋葬深度也一致，墓室均为石板砌筑，尤其是第一、二号两墓，墓室相邻，方向一致，结构相同，当有密切关系。从一号墓中的铜镜和二号墓中金质装饰品的特点，以及三号墓中的铜器和陶器来看，其时代很为一致，三墓应属同一时期。考古人员结合墓地的历史沿革，认为可能是晋代鲜卑族的墓葬。此件金顶针出土于慕容鲜卑墓中，当是其与汉文化融合的物证。

74 (III–17)

Ring inlaid with green and blue stones

Western Jin (266–317)
Gold; Diam. 2.5 cm, Wt. 1.44 g
Excavated in 1957 from tomb No. 2
at Fangshencun, Xusihuayingzixiang,
Beipiao
Liaoning Provincial Museum

嵌石戒指

西晋
金质　环径2.5厘米、重1.44克
1957年北票徐四花营子乡房身村M2出土
辽宁省博物馆藏

Made by soldering, this ring features embossed patterns on the top. In the central part, there is a green stone set in a bezel, with blue stones inset on the sides. Only five of the original stones remain, and around the insets, there are patterns of linked gold beads created using a welding technique. The ring is interrupted by a small gap.

打制而成，上有压印纹饰。中部镶嵌绿色玉石，旁侧镶嵌蓝色玉石，仅存五处，在镶嵌周围以金珠焊接工艺作联珠纹样。戒环中断，有一小缺口。

75 (III–18)

Ornament with turquoise inlay

Western Jin (266–317)
Gold; H. 1.2 cm, Diam. 0.7 cm
Excavated in 1957 from tomb No. 2
at Fangshencun, Xusihuayingzixiang,
Beipiao
Liaoning Provincial Museum

嵌石金珠

西晋
金质　高1.2厘米、直径0.7厘米
1957年北票徐四花营子乡房身村M2出土
辽宁省博物馆藏

This is an ornament made by joining gold sheets into a base, then inlaying gemstones such as turquoise, using a technique of soldering gold beads to decorate the surroundings of the inlays. Only two inlaid pieces remain. The spindle-shaped inlay design of this item bears a striking resemblance to the gold bead necklaces from the ancient site of Ur in Mesopotamia, dating from 2500 to 2400 BCE.

此为金片打制成胎，再镶嵌绿松石等宝石，以金珠焊接工艺，装饰镶嵌周围。镶嵌物仅存两处。此物的梭形镶嵌造型与西亚美索不达米亚乌尔遗址公元前2500年至前2400年的黄金串珠具有高度相似性。

76 (III–19)

Inlaid ornament

Sixteen Kingdoms, Former Yan (337–70)
Gold and turquoise; Diam. 0.9 cm, L. 3 cm
Excavated in 1989 from tomb No. 1 at
Tiancaogou, Xiyingzixiang, Chaoyang
Chaoyang County Museum

嵌松石管状饰件

十六国前燕
金质、松石　长3厘米、直径0.9厘米
1989年朝阳西营子乡田草沟M1出土
朝阳县博物馆藏

This ornament is made from gold sheets formed into a tubular shape, with circular gold sheets used to seal both ends. The surface of the tube is decorated with four rows of double-line, rice-grain-like stripes, with diamond-shaped granular stripes between each row. These stripes are inlaid with turquoise stones, with blue stones at both ends and green stones in the middle. The craftsmanship is exquisite and meticulous. This item was likely used as an accessory.

以金片制成管状，两端以圆形钻孔金片封堵。管表面饰以双行米粒状条纹四道，每道条纹间饰菱形米粒状条纹，纹中嵌有松石，两端松石为蓝色，中部两松石为绿色。制作精细，工艺讲究，应作为佩饰品。

77 (III–20)

Hairpin

Sixteen Kingdoms, Former Yan (337–70)
Gold; W. 3.3 cm, L. 8 cm
Excavated in 1998 from tomb No. 266 at
Lamadong, Beipiao
Liaoning Provincial Institute of Cultural
Relics and Archaeology

This gold hairpin is made by folding gold sheets ranging from 0.35 to 1.6 centimeters in width into a "U" shape, with the folded part being wider and the narrower part resembling the shape of a Chinese "*gui*" ornament. The hairpin, "*chai*" in Chinese, primarily serves the functions of securing the hair, fastening headwear, and adorning the hair. To some extent, it symbolizes one's social status and position and has been used in various dynasties. During the Wei-Jin and Sixteen Kingdoms period, these hairpins were typically made from a single piece of gold, featuring a slender pin with a pointed end and a wider section at the bending point.

钗

十六国前燕
金质　长8厘米、钗针间距3.3厘米
1998年北票南八家乡四家板村喇嘛洞墓地 II
M266出土
辽宁省文物考古研究院藏

以0.35～1.6厘米宽的金片条对折成"U"形，其弯折部较宽，尖部作圭首状。钗是戴在人头部的一种装饰物，主要功能是固发、固冠以及装饰头发，一定程度上是身份和地位的象征，在历代都有使用。魏晋十六国时期的钗，多为金片一体打造制成，钗针较细，端部较尖，中部弯折处宽。

78 (III–21)

Plaque

Sixteen Kingdoms, Former Yan (337–70)

Gold; W. 8.55 cm, L. 12.7 cm

Excavated in 1989 from tomb No. 1 at
Tiancaogou, Xiyingzixiang, Chaoyang

Chaoyang County Museum

This plaque is made by interlocking two semi-circular gold sheets and then riveting them together along the edges. Each of the straight edges has a hole at the intersection point. In the middle of the front side, there is an almost semi-circular frame, measuring 5.3 cm in length and 3.2 cm in width. There are no remaining inlays within the frame. The frame is surrounded by hammered and hollowed-out patterns depicting three-dimensional branch-like motifs that resemble distorted long-tailed phoenixes and striding dragons. On the raised patterns, the frame, and the edges of the ornament, there are one to two strands of gold wires attached, with small gold beads arranged densely on both sides of the wires. Additionally, there are sixteen small inlaid frames distributed along the edges of the ornament and the patterns, including crescent-shaped, droplet-shaped, and diamond-shaped ones, some of which still contain jade stones. Fourteen rivets are distributed on the back of the ornament.

半圆形牌饰

十六国前燕

金质　长12.7厘米、宽8.55厘米

1989年朝阳西营子乡田草沟M1出土

朝阳县博物馆藏

以两块半圆形金片对扣、再铆合边缝而成，其直边两端交角处各留一孔。正面中部为近半圆形框额，长5.3厘米、宽3.2厘米，框内嵌物不存。框额周围以锤鍱和镂空手法表现具有立体效果的枝蔓状纹缕，似为变形长尾凤和仃龙纹。在凸起的纹缕、框额和牌饰边缘上皆贴焊有一至两道金丝，金丝两侧再排列细密的金珠颗粒；另在牌饰边缘和纹络上分布有月牙形、液滴形和菱形小嵌框十六个，其中有的尚嵌有玉石。牌饰背面分布铆钉十四个。

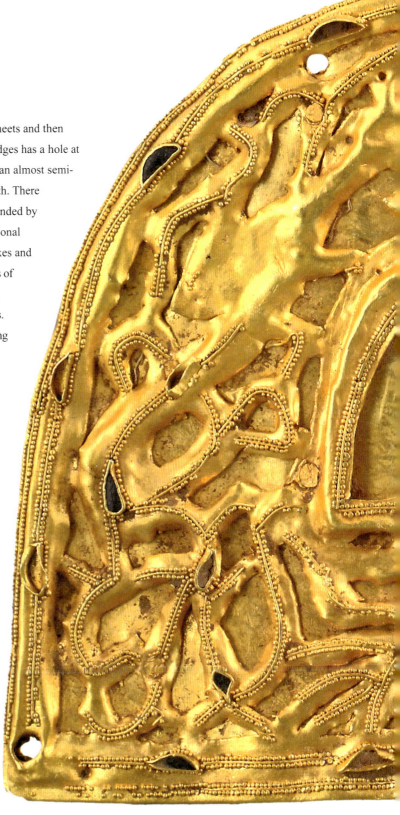

79 (III–22)

Crescent-shaped plaque with phoenix pattern

Western Jin (266–317)
Gold and jade; W. 5 cm., L. 14 cm,
Wt. 32.5 g
Excavated in 1956 from tomb No. 2
at Fangshencun, Xusihuayingzixiang,
Beipiao
Liaoning Provincial Museum

凤纹嵌玉新月形牌饰

西晋
金质 长14厘米、宽5厘米、重32.5克
1956年北票徐四花营子乡房身村M2出土
辽宁省博物馆藏

This plaque is in a crescent shape. In the center, a rectangular piece of green jade is inlaid, with each corner riveted. On either side of the jade piece, there are intricately carved opposing phoenix motifs, characterized by smooth lines. Around the edges, there are raised bead patterns, totaling eighteen, with small perforations on each bead pattern. At both ends of the crescent shape, there are four holes each, as if for threading ornaments, or for attaching to some kind of fabric as an accessory. This is a highly distinctive ornament with Xianbei characteristics.

片状，呈月牙形。中心镶嵌一长方形青玉石片，以金片作底衬，包住四边，以钉铆住四角。玉片的两侧镂刻相对的飞凤纹，线条流畅。周边起高突的联珠纹，共十八个，每个联珠纹上均密布细小孔眼。月牙形两端各有四孔，似穿线后悬项作饰，或钉在某种织物上作为衣饰。为极具鲜卑特色的饰物。

80 (III–23)

Crescent-shaped plaque

Sixteen Kingdoms, Former Yan (337–70)

Gold; W. 3.2 cm, L. 14.1 cm

Excavated in 1980 from tomb No. 6 at Wangzifenshan, Shi'ertaixiang brick factory, Chaoyang

Chaoyang County Museum

The edges of the crescent-shaped gold plaque are adorned with pointed cone-shaped patterns for two rounds, with three rows of pointed cone-shaped patterns in the middle. Between the patterns, the pointed cone-shaped patterns are zigzagging, with two holes drilled at each end. Traces of pointed cone-shaped patterns can also be seen on the back. Based on the holes at both ends, it is speculated that this plaque might have been used as an ornament sewn or attached to another object.

新月形牌饰

十六国前燕

金质 长14.1厘米、宽3.2厘米

1980年朝阳十二台乡砖厂王子坟山M6出土

朝阳县博物馆藏

月牙形金片边缘饰锥刺纹两周，中间饰锥刺纹三道，纹饰之间饰"之"字形锥刺纹，两端各钻两个穿孔。背面亦可见锥刺纹工艺痕迹。从其两端穿孔推测，或为缝缀于其他物件上之装饰物。

81 (III–24)

Bells

Sixteen Kingdoms, Former Yan (337–70)
Gold; Diam. 1.2 cm, Wt. 7.9 g
Excavated in 1980 from tomb No. 6 at
Wangzifenshan, Shi'ertaixiang brick
factory Chaoyang
Chaoyang County Museum

The round bells are made by riveting together two gold hemispheres, forming a hollow structure. At the top, there is a circular opening for threading, and at the bottom, there is an opening for the bell mouth. Inside, a grain of white sand serves as the bell's clapper, with a nose attached to the bell. These bells produce a pleasant sound when they jingle. Originally, they would have been strung together to form a loop and worn as ankle bells.

铃

十六国前燕
金质　每个直径1.2厘米、总重7.9克
1980年朝阳十二台乡砖厂王子坟山M6出土
朝阳县博物馆藏

圆形诸铃以两个轧制的金质半球体对扣铆接而成，空心，上具环形穿鼻，下留铃口，内含一白色砂粒作为铃胆，铃上连一鼻。锒铛作响，声音悦耳。原应是串联成环，系在踝部的脚铃。

82 (III–25)

Mold with two-deer motif

Western Jin (266–317)

Clay; W. 10.2 cm, L. 9 cm

Excavated in 1995 at Yuantaizicun,

Liuchengzhen, Chaoyang

Chaoyang County Museum

This mold is used for creating deer-patterned gold ornaments. Although it is a mold, its fine craftsmanship is still evident. During the Three Yan culture period, decorative pieces featuring deer patterns were common. These deer patterns depict either single deer in a standing position or groups of three deer, portraying a vibrant and lively scene.

双鹿纹范

西晋

灰陶　长9厘米、宽10.2厘米

1995年朝阳柳城镇袁台子村遗址出土

朝阳县博物馆藏

此为制作鹿纹金饰片时使用的模范。它虽是模范，但是仍可见其工艺之精细。以鹿为装饰纹样的饰片为三燕文化时期所常见，鹿纹或是相对站立，或是三鹿成群，充满生机。

83 (III–26)

Plaque with three-deer motif

Western Jin (266–317)
Gold; H. 7.1 cm, W. 8.7 cm
Excavated in 1960 from a tomb at
Bao'ansi, Yixian, Jinzhou
Liaoning Provincial Museum

This gold plaque is crafted into a rectangular shape using cutting techniques, with hammered patterns of three deer. The deer heads are all curved in one direction, and the antlers have a three-pronged shape, extending upwards. The heads are round and protrude from the surface, while the chests of the deer are also prominent, and the legs have distinct contours. There is a row of pointed cone-shaped patterns along the edge of the ornament with stitching holes arranged around it. Inside the ornament, there are two sets of one large and one small perforation, with some damage in the lower four corners. The ornament is relatively thick and heavy, and traces of hammering techniques can also be seen on the back. Stitching holes around the perimeter of the plaque suggest the means by which a decorative element was attached.

三鹿纹牌饰

西晋
金质　宽8.7厘米、高7.1厘米
1960年锦州义县保安寺古墓出土
辽宁省博物馆藏

金片以切割工艺制成长方形，锤鍱出三鹿纹饰。鹿头均曲向一侧，鹿角呈三枝丫形态，向上延伸；头呈圆形凸出表面，胸部亦凸出，腿凹凸分明。牌饰边缘有一排锥刺纹，四周有缝缀的排孔。在牌饰内圈有一大一小穿孔两组，下四角有残缺。牌饰较厚重，背面亦可见锤鍱工艺留下的痕迹。其四周的缝缀排孔，透露了其缝缀装饰物的用途。

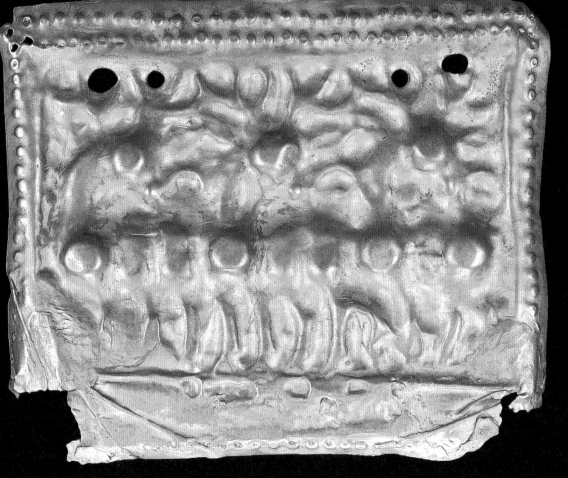

84 (III–27)

85 (III–28)

Belt buckle

Sixteen Kingdoms, Former Yan (337–70)
Gilt bronze; Cat. No. 84: W. 3.5 cm, L.
6.6 cm, T. 0.4 cm; Cat. No. 85: W.. 3.4, L.
7 cm, T. 0.5 cm
Excavated in 1998 from tomb No. 101 at
Lamadong, Beipiao
Liaoning Provincial Institute of Cultural
Relics and Archaeology

These two decorated pieces are likely the front and back ends of a leather belt. They could have been attached to a ribbon or leather strap between them. Both pieces are rectangular in shape and the same size. On the front side, there is a finely engraved and hollowed-out dragon pattern, surrounded by an additional border layer. Four or five rivets are used to secure it, along with a bronze backing plate. The front end of the piece with the buckle has a hole for threading a belt, and on the hole's side, there is a notch for the buckle tongue, although the buckle tongue is missing.

镂空带饰

十六国前燕
鎏金铜 第84号长6.6厘米、宽3.5厘米、缘厚
0.4厘米 第85号长7厘米、宽3.4厘米、缘厚0.5
厘米
1998年北票南八家乡四家板村喇嘛洞墓地
Ⅱ M101出土
辽宁省文物考古研究院藏

此两件带饰应为革带的首、尾两端，背衬铜片与此带饰之间或缀以丝带，或缀以革带。均为前圆后方的矩形，大小相同。正面錾刻镂空一龙纹，周边加贴一层边框，上铆四或五个钉，背衬铜片，其中带扣前端具穿带孔，孔侧具一扣槽，扣舌已失。

84 (III-27)

85 (III-28)

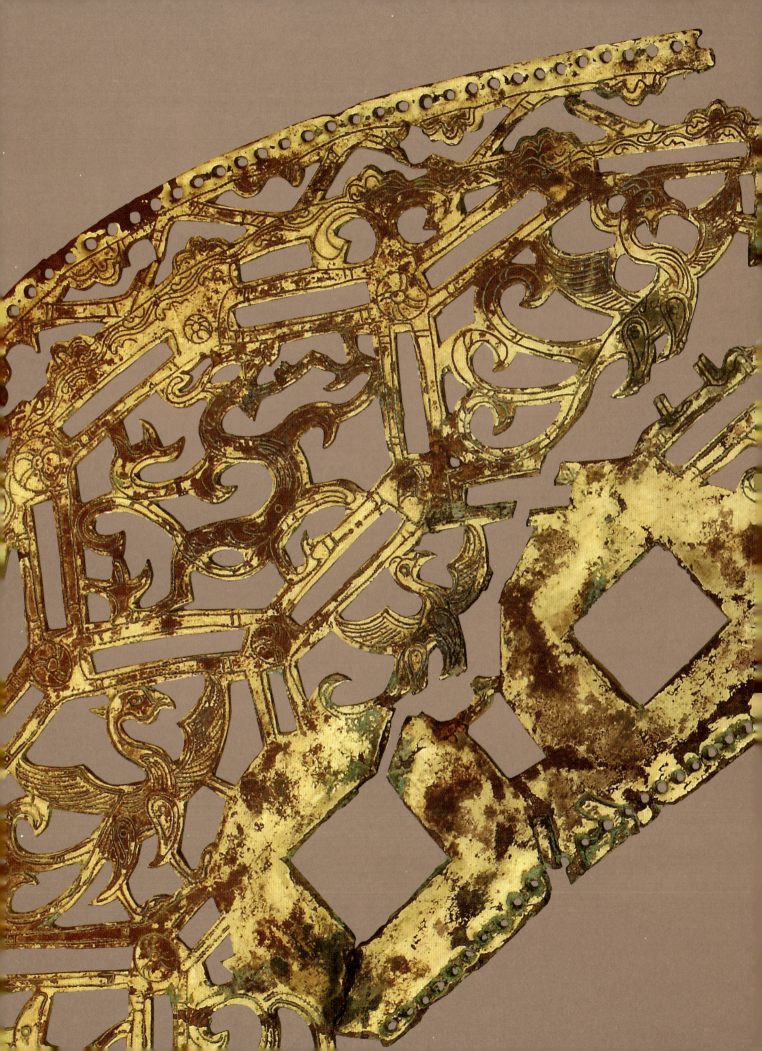

Equestrian Art
of Three Yan

IV

第四部分
三燕的马具艺术

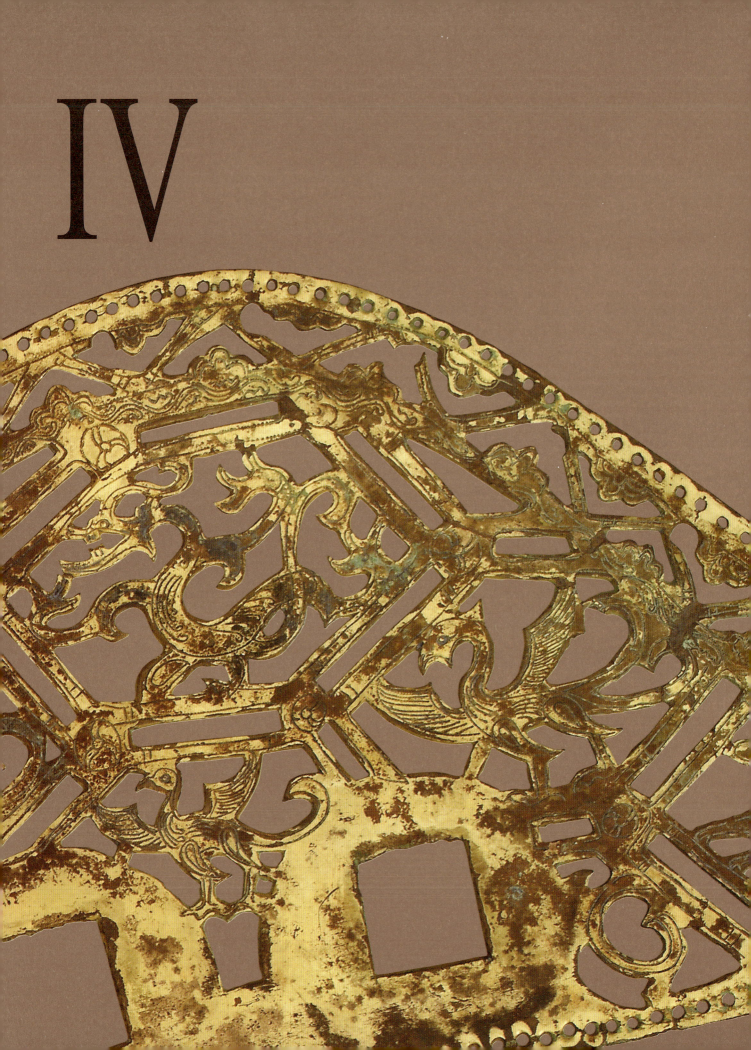

IV

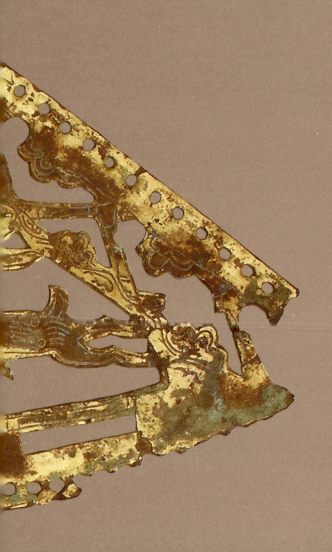

During the Wei, Jin, and Sixteen Kingdoms periods, the region was divided and local regimes frequently engaged in conflicts. It was during this time that armored cavalry emerged. The Three Yan states demonstrated the effectiveness of their armor in numerous wars, using a combination of defenses for both rider and horse. The rider's armor includes body armor, neck armor, and an iron helmet, while the horse's equipment comprises head armor and body armor. To the courageous Three Yan warriors, horses were more than just companions; they were comrades. Their love for horses was expressed through various horse accessories, from forehead pieces, chest armor, body armor, and tail shields for protecting the horses, to reins, saddle pommels, and stirrups for controlling the horses. Further embellishments included leaf decorations on the harness. The combination of well-armed warriors and fully equipped warhorses gave rise to the formidable armored cavalry. Armor unearthed from the Shi'ertai tomb in Chaoyang and the Lamadong cemetery in Beipiao provides evidence of the emergence of armored cavalry during the Three Yan period. The cavalry represented a significant advance in the equestrian level of the Xianbei, and was of crucial importance in the cultural and military history of northern ethnic groups. These mounted, armored warriors had a profound impact not only on Chinese history but also on world military history.

魏晋十六国时期地方政权割据、战乱频仍，重装骑兵开始出现。三燕的甲胄和马具，组成一套完整的"甲骑具装"，在诸多战争中发挥了作用。"甲骑具装"即人甲与马甲的合称。人甲包括身甲、颈甲、铁兜鍪等，马甲包括马胄、铠等。骁勇善战的三燕勇士与战马之间是伙伴，是战友，他们将对马的热爱演绎为各种马饰：从保护马首的当卢，到驾驭马匹的衔镳、鞍桥与马镫，到装饰攀胸的杏叶，再到保护马身的当胸、身甲，再到保护马尾的寄生。战马与骑兵，以马具为媒介，做到了合二为一——尖兵利器的武士加上全副武装的战马，构成了所向披靡的"重装骑兵"。朝阳十二台和北票喇嘛洞出土的甲骑具装实物，标志着三燕时期重装骑兵的出现，代表了鲜卑骑射文化的水平，在北方民族文化史和战争史上具有重要意义，甚而在中国历史乃至世界兵器史上都具有着十分重要的影响。

86 (IV–1)

Helmet

Sixteen Kingdoms, Former Yan (337–70)
Iron; H. (total) 34 cm
Excavated in 1998 from tomb No. 5 at
Lamadong, Beipiao
Liaoning Provincial Institute of Cultural
Relics and Archaeology

兜鍪

十六国前燕
铁　高34厘米；盔高23.5厘米；颈甲高10.5厘米
1998年北票南八家乡四家板村喇嘛洞墓地ⅠM5
出土
辽宁省文物考古研究院藏

The iron helmet was an important component of the armor suite at the time. This iron helmet, designed to protect the head, is made by riveting together strips of iron plates. In the central front portion, the plate forms a pointed shape, with the iron plates folding to the left and right sides from this central piece. Each of the five plates at the forehead has a symmetrical curved notch at the bottom edge. At the top gathering point, six rivets are used to connect to a round plate, and in the center, a tubular socket is also riveted.

铁兜鍪，是该时期铠甲装备"甲骑具装"的重要部分。作为保护头部的铁盔，以条状铁甲叶铆接而成，正面中部甲片呈圭首状，由此甲叶向左右两侧叠压，额部五片甲叶的底缘均裁出对称的弧形缺口，顶部收拢处铆六钉，扣接一圆形甲片，正中再铆接一管状插座。

87 (IV–2)

Knife

Sixteen Kingdoms, Former Yan (337–70)

Iron; W. 3.2 cm, L. 118 cm, T. 0.5 cm

Excavated in 1994 from Dapingfang,

Chaoyang

Chaoyang County Museum

The blade is long and straight, with a rounded ring-shaped pommel, suitable for use by cavalry. This weapon, considered a "knife" in Chinese, would be classified as a "sword" in English. Armed with sharp-edged weapons, the soldiers, together with fully equipped warhorses, formed the formidable "heavy cavalry," playing a crucial role in both Chinese and global military history.

环首刀

十六国前燕

铁　长118厘米、宽3.2厘米、厚0.5厘米

1994年朝阳大平房镇公皋村北山出土

朝阳县博物馆藏

刀身长且直，柄首圆环形，便于骑兵使用。尖兵利器的武士加上全副武装的战马构成了所向披靡的"重装骑兵"，这在中国历史乃至世界兵器史上具有着十分重要的地位。

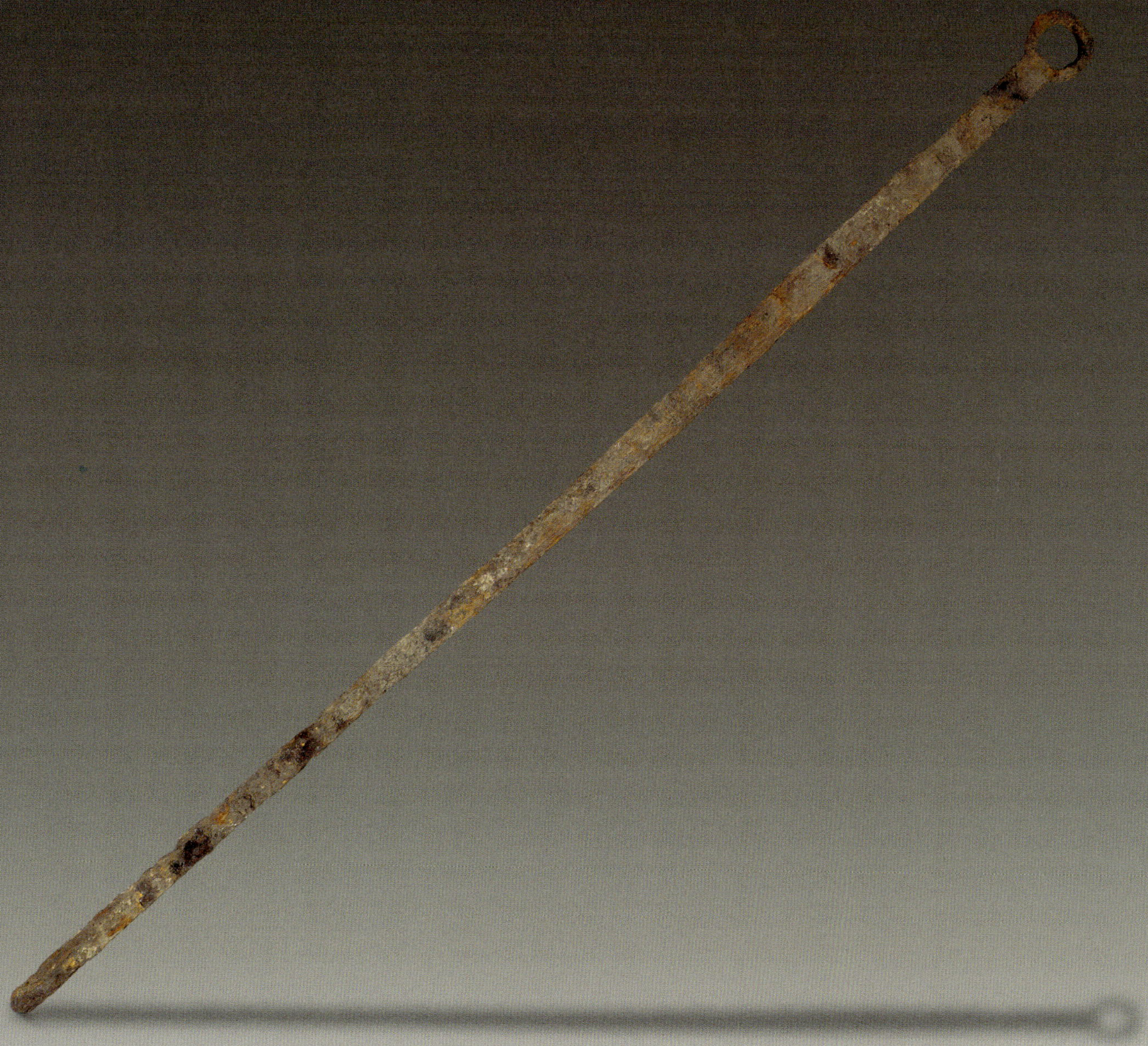

88 (IV–3)

Ornament from a quiver

Sixteen Kingdoms, Former Yan (337–70)
Gilt; H. 12.5 cm, W. 22 cm, T. 0.1 cm
Excavated in 2005 at Yaoeryingzi
hongzhuan yichang, Chaoyang
Chaoyang County Museum

This gilded plaque is in the shape of a mountain. Surrounding the central design of swirling cloud patterns symmetrically placed phoenixes soar with wings outstretched in flight, their patterns comprised of a series of finely chiseled continuous wedge-shaped points. The edges of the mountain shape are evenly punctured. This ornament is a part of the arrow quiver, which holds bows and arrows.

凤纹山形铜箭箙饰

十六国前燕
鎏金铜　宽22厘米、高12.5厘米、厚0.1厘米
2005年朝阳柳城镇腰而营子红砖一厂出土
朝阳县博物馆藏

山形。围绕正中间的卷云纹图案，左右为对称展翅飞舞的对凤，纹饰线条由连续錾刻的细密楔形点构成。山形边缘有均匀分布的穿孔，是为盛放弓箭之具的箭箙之一部分。

89 (IV–4)

Horse ornament

Sixteen Kingdoms, Former Yan (337–70)
Gilt bronze; H. 9.8 cm, W. 7.8 cm
Excavated in 1998 from a tomb at
Lamadong, Beipiao
Liaoning Provincial Institute of Cultural
Relics and Archaeology

This ornament is composed of a cross-shaped base, a
through strap, a tube, and a dangling leaf. Its bulbous convex
surface is cast with a semi-relief-style coiled dragon pattern,
with four nose rings and double-stranded straps passing
through the tube from the hole in the convex surface, then
bending the through straps to both sides to secure them to
the bellows belt. A dangling leaf hangs from the top of the
tube.

节约

十六国前燕
鎏金铜　高9.8厘米、宽7.8厘米；叶长4.8厘米、
宽3.9厘米
1998年北票南八家乡四家板村喇嘛洞墓地出土
辽宁省文物考古研究院藏

节约由"十"字形基座、穿条、套管和摇叶构成。节约
的泡状凸面上铸有半浮雕式盘龙纹，周边出沿并具四个
穿鼻，双股穿条经过套管自节约凸面中孔穿入，再将穿
条分向两侧弯折以固定在鞴带上，套管顶端挂摇叶。

90 (IV–5)

Ornaments in the shape of an apricot leaf

Sixteen Kingdoms, Former Yan (337–70)
Gilt bronze; W. 5.8 cm
Excavated in 1976 from tomb No. 4 at
Yuantaizicun, Shi'ertaixiang, Chaoyang
Chaoyang County Museum

The apricot leaves are decorations worn on the horse's chest, which can make the horse that wears them look spirited. These leaf-shaped pieces have a narrow top and a wide bottom, slightly tapered at the waist, with a straight upper end, and a transverse hole. They are connected to leather straps through bronze folding leaves, reinforced with three rivets.

杏叶

十六国前燕
鎏金铜　宽5.8厘米
1976年朝阳十二台袁台子M4出土
朝阳县博物馆藏

杏叶是马的攀胸上的装饰，可使佩戴上杏叶的马匹神采奕奕。该叶片呈上窄下宽的圭形，略有束腰，上端平直，有横穿，内穿铜折叶与革带连接，并有三个加固的铆钉。

91 (IV–6)

Pair of stirrups

Sixteen Kingdoms, Northern Yan (407–36)
Wood and gilt bronze; H. 23.2 cm, H. 25
cm; (both) W. 16.9 cm; H. 25 cm
Excavated in 1965 from the tomb of Feng
Sufu (d. 415), Xiguanyingzi, Beipiao
Liaoning Provincial Museum

This pair of horse stirrups (one slightly longer than the other) was unearthed from the tomb of Feng Sufu (d. 415). Each stirrup is formed from twisted mulberry wood strips, reinforced by a layer of gilded bronze plates nailed along the outer wall of the stirrup's circular base. A long projection at the top has a slot or "eye" for attaching stirrup leathers. These exquisitely crafted stirrups represent one of the masterpieces of gilded craftsmanship from the Northern Yan during the Sixteen Kingdoms period. They are the earliest pair of stirrups with a confirmed dating to have been discovered in an archaeological setting to date. Their appearance changed the history of cavalry: "When we think of medieval Europe, we think of knights in armor carrying heavy lances and riding on horseback, but that would have been impossible without stirrups, for such heavily weighted riders would have fallen off too easily. It was the Chinese invention of the stirrup which made Western medieval knights possible, and gave us the age of chivalry."[1] In Europe, where horse stirrups were called "Chinese boots," they were hailed as the "fifth great invention of China." The discovery of this pair of gilded bronze and wood-core stirrups provides important evidence of cultural exchange between East and West and China's contribution to the field of military technology.

铜鎏金木芯钉马镫

十六国北燕
鎏金铜、木　全高分别为23.2厘米和25厘米、宽
均为16.9厘米
1965年北票西官营子北燕冯素弗墓出土
辽宁省博物馆藏

这副马镫出土于辽宁北票北燕冯素弗墓。整体以桑木条揉拗做成镫圈，上为带孔的长柄，沿圈条的外壁包钉一层鎏金铜片。此马镫制工精美，为十六国时期北燕鎏金工艺品的代表作之一。它是目前考古发现最早的有绝对年代可考的双马镫。它们的出现改变了骑兵史。《中国：发明与发现的国度——中国科学技术史精华》（〔美〕罗伯特·K. G. 坦普尔著，陈养正、陈小慧、李耕耕等译，21世纪出版社，1995年12月版）一书中曾说："如果没有从中国引进马镫，使骑手能安然地坐在马上，中世纪的骑士就不可能身披闪闪盔甲，救出那些处于绝境的少女，欧洲就不会有骑士时代……中国人发明了马镫，使西方有可能出现中世纪的骑士，并赐予我们一个骑士制度的时代。"在欧洲，马镫被称为"中国靴子"，还誉其为"中国第五大发明"。如今，马镫被广泛应用在世界各地的各个骑马项目中，而出土于北燕冯素弗墓的这对铜鎏金木芯钉马镫，提供了东西方文化交流和中国在军事领域内做出贡献的重要物证。

[1] Temple, Robert. *The Genius of China: 3,000 Years of Science, Discovery, and Invention*, (New York) 1986.

92 (IV–7)

Ornaments with dragon motif

Sixteen Kingdoms, Former Yan (337–70)
Gilt bronze; H. 2 cm, Diam. 5.4 cm
Excavated in 1976 from tomb No. 4 at
Yuantaizicun, Shi'ertaixiang, Chaoyang
Chaoyang County Museum

镂雕龙纹鎏金铜泡饰

十六国前燕
鎏金铜　高2厘米、直径5.4厘米
1976年朝阳十二台袁台子M4出土
朝阳县博物馆藏

93 (IV–8)

Ornaments with dragon motif

Sixteen Kingdoms, Former Yan (337–70)
Gilt bronze; H. 2 cm, Diam. 5
cm, T. 0.23 cm
Excavated in 1978 from a Xianbei tomb,
Yaoeryingzi brick factory, Shi'ertai,
Chaoyang
Chaoyang County Museum

镂雕龙纹鎏金铜泡饰

十六国前燕
鎏金铜　高2厘米、直径5.3厘米、厚0.23厘米
1978年朝阳十二台公社腰而营子砖厂鲜卑墓出土
朝阳县博物馆藏

These ornaments are gilded on the surface and have a hemispherical shape. Carved with dragon patterns, they appear to be accessories for a horse bridle, possibly depicting a phoenix.

During the Three Yan period, horse equipment was made from materials such as bronze, gilded bronze, iron, and metal-wrapped wooden cores, created through casting or forging methods. The most common themes in decorative patterns of Three Yan culture horse equipment include phoenixes, dragons, deer, rabbits, honeysuckle, cloud patterns, and more. These patterns are expressed through individual motifs, matching motifs, multi-sided continuous motifs, combination motifs, and border motifs. They were often adorned using techniques such as engraving, relief carving, and gilding.

表面鎏金，呈半球状，镂雕龙纹，似为鸾镳附件。

三燕时期的马具由铜、鎏金铜、铁、木芯金属包片等材质经铸造或打制方式制作而成。三燕文化马具装饰纹样中最常见的题材有凤、龙、鹿、兔、忍冬、云纹等。表现形式有单独纹样、适合纹样、多方连续纹样、组合纹样、边饰纹样。多采用錾刻、减地镂空、鎏金等复合工艺装饰。

92 (Ⅳ-7)

93 (Ⅳ-8)

94 (IV–9)

Horse ornament

Sixteen Kingdoms, Former Yan (337–70)
Gilt bronze; H. 17.5 cm, W. 11–27.8 cm
Found at Lamadong, Beipiao, 1998
Liaoning Provincial Institute of Cultural
Relics and Archaeology

The outer frame of this ornament is nearly fan-shaped, with a relatively straight bottom edge, and both sides have outer arcs. There are pairs of small holes at the groove openings to secure the hollow fan surface inside the groove and attach the circular dangling leaves. The fan surface consists of two pieces, one in front and one in back, both vertically hollowed out with a modified honeysuckle pattern, totaling thirty-eight branches. Additionally, there are seven rows of circular dangling leaves fixed with silver wire attached to the honeysuckle pattern. At the upper edge of the fan surface, there is still a row of hollowed-out apricot leaves remaining.

"*Jisheng*," a part of the armor harness, is a unique type of horse harness in ancient China. It is placed at the end of the horse saddle, with the "fan surface" standing above the horse's hindquarters. Its purpose is to shield the rider's back and prevent attacks from behind. This type of harness was popular from the Sixteen Kingdoms period of Eastern Jin dynasty to the early Tang dynasty.

寄生

十六国前燕
鎏金铜　宽11～27.8厘米、高17.5厘米
1998年北票南八家乡四家板村喇嘛洞村征集
辽宁省文物考古研究院藏

外框近扇形，底边较平直，两侧外弧，槽口处皆有两个一组的小孔，用以固定槽内的镂空扇面和系缀圆形摇叶。扇面为前后两片，均为竖向镂空的变形忍冬纹，共三十八枝，另有七行以银丝固定的圆形摇叶附缀在忍冬纹上，扇面上缘尚存一排镂空的杏叶。

寄生是中国古代一种很特别的马具，是甲骑具装的一部分，它置于马鞍末端，"扇面"立于马尻上方，以障藏骑乘者的背部，起到防止敌人从背后袭击的作用，流行于东晋十六国到唐朝初年。

95 (IV–10)

Horse ornament

Sixteen Kingdoms, Former Yan (337–70)
Iron; W. 13.7–29.6 cm, L. (total) 66 cm
Excavated in 1988 from tomb No. 88M1
at Shi'ertaixiang brick factory, Chaoyang
Liaoning Provincial Institute of Cultural
Relics and Archaeology

This ornament consists of three parts: a face mask, protective cheek plates, and a lip guard. The face mask is constructed from five strips of iron, with the front piece folded up in a crown-like shape. The cheek plates are made up of three strip-shaped iron plates and one arc-shaped iron plate, each placed on either side of the face mask. Each of the lower edges has three corresponding clasps and perforations. There are also arc-shaped notches at the locations of the horse's eyes on both the cheek plates and the face mask. The tongue-shaped lip guard is attached to the front of the face mask. These three parts are connected by iron pins, allowing them to rotate and be folded when not in use. This is the first complete piece of horse armor found in China.

马胄

十六国前燕
铁　面罩通长66厘米、宽13.7～29.6厘米；护颊
板长36.5厘米、宽18.7厘米；护唇片高7.8厘米、
宽8厘米
1988年朝阳十二台乡砖厂88M1出土
辽宁省文物考古研究院藏

由面罩、护颊板、护唇片三部分组成。面罩由五块条形铁片铆制，额前护片折起，其形如冠。护颊板由三块条形和一块弧形铁片拼成，分别置于面罩两侧，其下缘各具三个对应的带卡和穿孔，在两颊板和面罩之间的马眼位置上均留有弧形缺口，舌形护唇片则接在面罩前端。此三部分均以铁销相连，可以转动，不用时还可以折叠，是国内发现的第一件完整的马胄实物。

96 (IV–11)

Horse ornaments (two pieces)

Sixteen Kingdoms, Former Yan (337–70)
Gilt bronze; 96a: H. 38 cm, W. 13.5 cm;
96b: H. 41.7 cm, W. 16.5 cm
Excavated in 1995 from tomb No. 5 at
Lamadong, Beipiao
Liaoning Provincial Institute of Cultural
Relics and Archaeology

A *danglu* is a bronze piece cast in an upside-down gourd shape to protect the horse's face. With rings and hanging leaves in the shape of peaches, this pair of *danglu* strongly features Xianbei's decorative equestrian art style.

当卢

十六国前燕
鎏金铜　96a宽13.5厘米、高38厘米　96b宽16.5
厘米、高41.7厘米
1995年北票南八家乡四家板村喇嘛洞墓地M5出土
辽宁省文物考古研究院藏

形似倒置的琵琶形，上部顶端铆一短柱，顶端向两侧分开，似可作置缨之用；下部条片中起脊，当卢周边穿孔用铜丝套管缀摇叶。

96a

96b

97 (IV–12)

Wing-shaped plaques

Sixteen Kingdoms, Former Yan (337–70)
Gilt bronze; W. 6.2 cm, L. 13 cm, T. 0.2 cm
Excavated in 1976 from tomb No. 4 at
Yuantaizicun, Shi'ertaixiang, Chaoyang
Chaoyang County Museum

This horse harness ornament was likely installed on the lower edge of the front saddle bridge. It is made from a 0.2-cm-thick cast bronze plate using techniques such as carving and drilling and its shape is similar to a bird's head. The surface is gilded, the bottom edge is straight, and the upper part features a single phoenix with outstretched wings. The phoenix has a curved neck, raised chest, and curved and raised feathers. It is standing on two legs, and its wings and tail feathers are intricately carved with lines, creating a clear and detailed image. There are four rectangular openings in the central part of the piece, and honeysuckle patterns on the left and right sides. In the lower section, there are two identical phoenixes. At the top of the bird's head, there is a circular through-hole. The back has no carvings. The plaques show traces of slight rusting and retain fine patterns.

透雕翼形鞍桥包片

十六国前燕
鎏金铜　长13厘米、宽6.2厘米、厚0.2厘米
1976年朝阳十二台袁台子M4出土
朝阳县博物馆藏

系马具饰件，大约是安装在前鞍桥内缘下的饰片。以0.2厘米厚的铸制铜板和镂、錾、钻等工艺方法制成，近似鸟首形。表面鎏金，底边平直，上部镂一展翅单凤，凤曲颈挺胸展双翼，双足站立，双翼及尾部以錾刻线条构成羽毛，形象清晰；中部的中心部位镂刻长方形四孔，左右各镂一忍冬纹；下部镂刻双凤，双凤姿态一致。鸟首顶端钻一圆形透孔，背面无錾刻，轻度锈蚀，保留有细绢纹。

98 (IV–13)

Horse ornaments

Sixteen Kingdoms, Former Yan (337–70)
Gilt bronze; H. 13.5 cm, L. 27 cm, T. 0.1 cm
Excavated in 1976 from tomb No. 4 at
Yuantaizicun, Shi'ertaixiang, Chaoyang
Chaoyang County Museum

透雕翼形鞍桥包片（前桥）

十六国前燕
鎏金铜　长27厘米、高13.5厘米、厚0.1厘米
1976年朝阳十二台袁台子M4出土
朝阳县博物馆藏

This pair of ornamental wing-shaped pieces is installed on the inner edge of the saddle bridge. The functional purpose is twofold: first, to reduce the space on the inner edge of the saddle bridge, making it conform to the horse's spine, and second, to connect and secure the breastplate of the saddle to the horse's rear girth. Based on their excavated positions and their shapes and sizes, they were originally installed on the inner edge of the front bridge of the saddle. Both wing-shaped pieces are carved with composite patterns consisting of tortoiseshell and phoenix motifs, and they each have square, rectangular, or strip-shaped holes. The edges are engraved with continuous phoenix patterns, and there are numerous nail holes around the periphery.

这两件饰件是一组翼形片，其作用一是缩小鞍桥内缘的空间，使之与马脊相吻合，另一作用是连接固定鞍的攀胸与马尻鞧带。根据出土位置和它的形状大小来看，它原本是安装于马鞍前桥内缘的。两块翼形片上均镂刻由龟背纹和凤纹组成的复合纹饰，分别带有条状矩形或正方形孔，边缘处则刻以连续凤鸟纹带，周边密布钉孔。

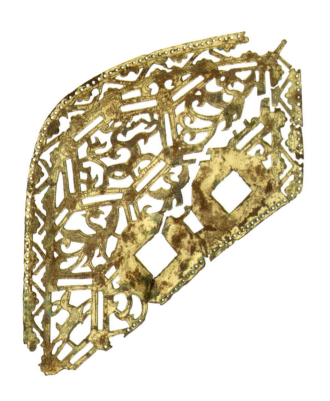

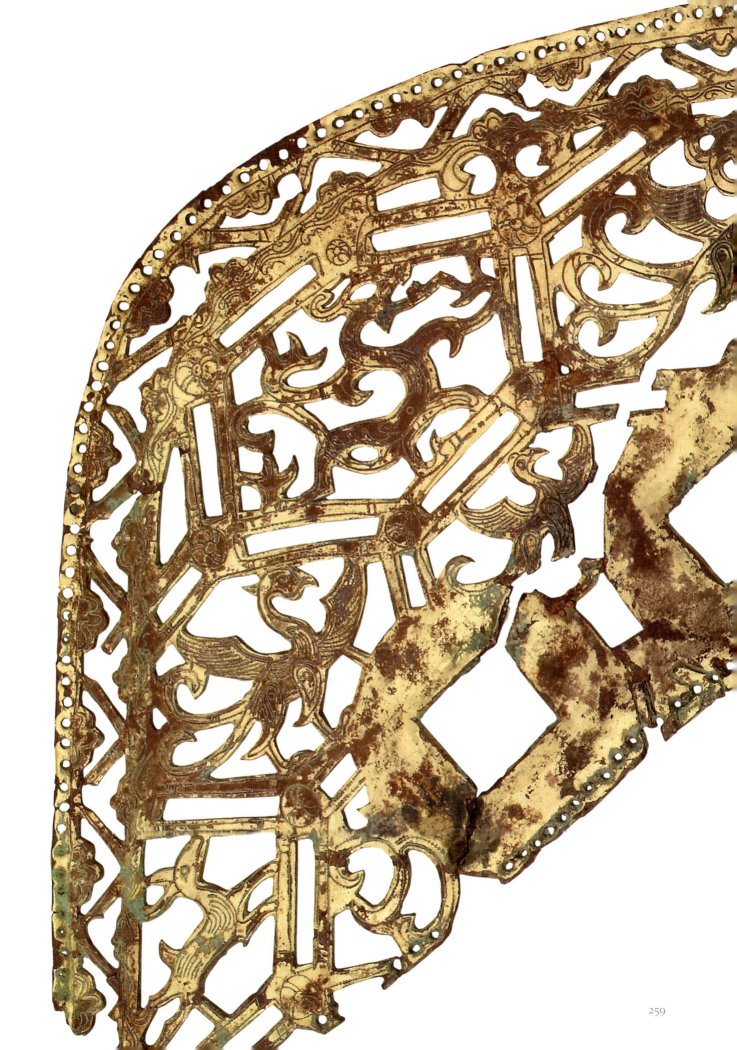

99 (IV–14)

Horse ornaments with phoenix motif

Sixteen Kingdoms, Former Yan (337–70)
Gilt bronze; H. 31 cm, W. 57 cm, T. 0.1 cm
Excavated in 1976 from tomb No. 4 at
Yuantaizicun, Shi'ertaixiang, Chaoyang
Chaoyang County Museum

龙凤纹鞍桥包片（后桥）

十六国前燕
鎏金铜　宽57厘米、高31厘米、厚0.1厘米
1976年朝阳十二台袁台子M4出土
朝阳县博物馆藏

The saddle bridge ornament is installed on the edge of the saddle bridge surface to protect the saddle and secure the saddle's shape. Based on its position when it was unearthed and its height, this saddle bridge ornament was originally installed on the rear bridge of the saddle. It is handcrafted with intricate carvings. The overall shape is like an inverted "U." The upper horizontal part is relatively wide, forming an upward curved arch, and the central lower part protrudes from the edge. Both ends gradually curve downward. The entire surface is adorned with continuous hexagonal tortoiseshell patterns, with a central motif of a dragon surrounded by other images such as phoenixes, all intricately engraved using point-carving techniques.

鞍桥饰件是安装于鞍桥表面边缘的饰件，起到了保护马鞍、固定鞍形等作用。这件鞍桥饰件根据出土位置和它的高度来看，它原本安装于鞍的后桥。錾刻手制。整体呈倒"U"形。上横额较宽，作上隆弧形，下缘中央部位凸出。两端向下弧转渐收。通体透錾六方连续的龟背纹，以中央团龙图案为中心，其间平面采用点刻法饰龙、凤等图像。

Gold from
Dragon City

龙城
之金

Masterpieces of
Three Yan from Liaoning
337–436

辽宁三燕文物选萃
337—436

Appendices 附录

Appendix 1   Lineage of Three Yan

Murong Xianbei and Former Yan (220–370)

Year	Name	Titles, posthumous titles, and era names
220	Mohuba	Prince Shuaiyi (meaning "Prince of Righteousness")
244	Muyan	Commander-in-Chief, Wise Prince of the Left
?–283	Shegui	Chanyu of Xianbei
284–333	Murong Wei	Duke of Liaodong, Chanyu of Xianbei
334–348	Murong Huang	Prince of Yan (337 CE, establishing Former Yan) Posthumous name: Emperor Wenming, temple name: Taizu, tomb name: Longping
349–360	Murong Jun	Posthumous name: Emperor Jingzhao, temple name: Liezu, tomb name: Longling Era names: Yuannian (349–351); Yuaxi (352–356); Guangshou (357–360)
360–370	Murong Wei	Posthumous name: Emperor You Era name: Jianxi (360–370)

Later Yan (384–407)

Year	Name	Titles, posthumous titles, and era names
384–396	Murong Chui	Posthumous name: Emperor Chengwu, temple name: Shizu, tomb name: Xuanpingling Era names: Yanyuan (384–385); Jianxing (386–396)
396–398	Murong Bao	Posthumous name: Emperor Huimin, temple name: Liezong Era name: Yongkang (396–398)
398–401	Murong Sheng	Posthumous name: Emperor Zhaowu, temple name: Zhongzong, tomb name: Xingpingling Era name: Jianping (398); Changle (399–401)
401–407	Murong Xi	Posthumous name: Emperor Zhaowen Era name: Guangshi (401–406); Jianshi (407)

Northern Yan (407–436)

Year	Name	Titles, posthumous titles, and era names
407–409	Gao Yun (Murong Yun)	Posthumous name: Emperor Huiyi Era Name: Zhengshi (407–409)
409–430	Feng Ba	Posthumous name: Emperor Wencheng, temple name: Taizu, tomb name: Changguling Era name: Taiping (409–430)
431–436	Feng Hong	Posthumous name: Emperor Zhaocheng Era name: Taixing (431–436)

附录一 三燕世系表

慕容鲜卑与前燕世系表（238—370）

年　代	本　名	称号（封号、谥号、庙号）、年号
220	莫护跋	率义王
244	木延	大都督、左贤王
？—283	涉归	鲜卑单于
284—333	慕容廆	辽东郡公、鲜卑单于
334—348	慕容皝	燕王（337 年称燕王，是为前燕） 谥文明皇帝，庙号太祖，墓号龙平
349—360	慕容儁	谥景昭皇帝，庙号烈祖，墓号龙陵 　　　元年（349—351） 　　　元玺（352—356） 　　　光寿（357—360）
360—370	慕容暐	谥幽皇帝 　　　建熙（360—370）

后燕世系表（384—407）

年 代	本 名	称号（封号、谥号、庙号）、年号
384—396	慕容垂	谥成武皇帝，庙号世祖，墓号宣平陵 燕元（384—385） 建兴（386—396）
396—398	慕容宝	谥惠愍皇帝，庙号烈宗 永康（396—398）
398—401	慕容盛	谥昭武皇帝，庙号中宗，墓号兴平陵 建平（398） 长乐（399—401）
401—407	慕容熙	谥昭文皇帝 光始（401—406） 建始（407）

北燕世系表（407—436）

年 代	本 名	称号（封号、谥号、庙号）、年号
407—409	高云（慕容云）	谥惠懿皇帝 正始（407—409）
409—430	冯跋	谥文成皇帝，庙号太祖，葬长谷陵 太平（409—430）
431—436	冯弘	谥昭成皇帝 太兴（431—436）

Appendix 2　Major Events of Three Yan

Years	Events（Important archaeological sites and relics）
238 CE Second year of the Jingchu era under Emperor Ming	Sima Yi, Grand Commandant of Wei, attacked the kingdom of Yan led by Gongsun Yuan. Mohuba of the Murong Xianbei, who was awarded the title Prince Shuaiyi for his participation in Sima Yi's campaign, settled his clan in Liaoxi, north of Jicheng.
244 CE Fifth year of the Zhengshi era under Emperor Cao Fang	Guan Qiujian, an inspector and general of Wei, led a military campaign against Goguryeo. Murong Muyan, son of Mohuba, was awarded the title Commander-in-Chief for his contribution to the campaign.
281 CE Second year of the Taikang era under Emperor Wu of Jin	Murong Xianbei began raids in Changli.
	Jin dynasty tombs were discovered in Liaoning, revealing inscribed tiles from the second year of Taikang.
289 CE Tenth year of the Taikang era under Emperor Wu of Jin	Murong Wei surrendered to the Jin dynasty and was appointed Chief of Xianbei. He relocated the clan to Qingshan in Tuhe. His brother, Tuyuhun, led some of the clan to move westward, and a branch of Murong Xianbei has been living in the northwest ever since.
294 CE Fourth year of the Yuankang era under Emperor Hui of Jin	Murong Wei moved the capital to Jicheng, promoted agriculture, and implemented laws of the Central Plains.
	Three stone tombs were discovered in Beipiao, Liaoning.
302 CE Second year of the Yongning era and first year of the Tai'an era under Emperor Hui of Jin	The Yuwen clan besieged Jicheng. Murong Wei counterattacked and defeated the enemy.
	A tomb from the second year of the Yongning era was discovered in Changsha in the 1950s, featuring an equestrian figure with a triangular-shaped stirrup on the left side, the earliest of its kind known.
307 CE First year of the Yongjia era under Emperor Huai of Jin	Murong Wei proclaimed himself the Da Chanyu (supreme leader) of the Xianbei.

Years	Events（Important archaeological sites and relics）
313 CE First year of the Jiaxing era under Emperor Min of Jin	Scholars from the Central Plains flocked to Murong Hu for his wise and prudent governance. By the second year of the Jianxing era (314), tens of thousands of exiles from the Central Plains had turned to Murong Wei.
321 CE Fourth year of the Daxing era under Emperor Yuan of Jin	Jin dynasty promoted Murong Wei as the military Commander-in-Chief of Pingzhou and Dongyi, General of Chariots and Cavalry, Governor of Pingzhou, and Duke of Liaodong. Murong Wei established the Royal Academy, where his son, Murong Huang, and others received education.
333 CE Eighth year of the Xianhe era under Emperor Cheng of Ji	Murong Wei died, and his son, Murong Huang, succeeded him. Murong Ren, Huang's brother, rebelled against him. Huang sent his brother Murong You and the marshal Dong Shou to suppress the rebellion.
334 CE Ninth year of the Xianhe era under Emperor Cheng of Ji	Jin dynasty appointed Murong Huang Grand General Who Guards the Army, Governor of Pingzhou, and Duke of Liaodong.
336 CE Second year of the Xiankang era under Emperor Cheng of Jin	Murong Huang led his army across the frozen Bohai Sea from Changli to defeat his brother Murong Ren. Dong Shou, who had surrendered to Ren, and Gao Chong fled to Goguryeo. Dong Shou died and was buried in Goguryeo. His tomb was identified as the Anak Tomb No. 3 in Pyongyang, North Korea. Inside the tomb, there is an inscription that reads, "In the thirteenth year of the Yonghe era," an era under Emperor Mu of Jin, revealing that he had been serving the Jin dynasty since he fled to Goguryeo.
337 CE Third year of the Xiankang era under Emperor Cheng of Eastern Jin	Murong Huang declared himself Prince of Yan, establishing the Former Yan.
341 CE Seventh year of the Xiankang era under Emperor Cheng of Jin	Murong Huang built the city of Longcheng to the north of Liucheng and renamed Liucheng Longcheng county.
342 CE Eighth year of the Xiankang era under Emperor Cheng of Jin	Murong Huang relocated the capital to Longcheng and built palaces. In November, he launched attacks from two directions, north and south, against Goguryeo and reached the fortress city of Hwando, burning its palaces and destroying the city before he returned.

Years	Events（Important archaeological sites and relics）

342 CE Eighth year of the Xiankang era under Emperor Cheng of Jin	In 1982 a tomb from Former Yan was discovered in Yuantaizi, Liaoning, resembling the Wei and Jin mural-decorated tombs in Liaoyang. The mural depicted the tomb's owner sitting and holding a fly-wisk, similar to one in the portrait in Dong Shou's tomb.
345 CE First year of the Yonghe era under Emperor Mu of Jin	Murong Huang stopped using Jin's era name and proclaimed his twelfth year. By this time, nearly 100,000 households from Goguryeo, Baekje, Yuwen, and Duan Xianbei had migrated to Murong's capital city.
348 CE Fourth year of the Yonghe era under Emperor Mu of Ji	Murong Huang died, and his son, Murong Jun, succeeded him.
350 CE Sixth year of the Yonghe era under Emperor Mu of Ji	Murong June moved the capital from Longcheng to Ji. He captured the city of Ye in 352, proclaimed himself emperor, established the state of Yan, and declared the era name Yuanxi.
357 CE First year of the Shengping era under Emperor Mu of Ji	Murong Jun relocated the capital to Ye.
	Tombs from Former Yan were discovered in Xiaomingtun, Henan, near Ye.
360 CE Fourth year of the Shengping era under Emperor Mu of Ji	Murong Jun died, and was succeeded by his son, Murong Wei.
370 CE Fifth year of the Taihe era under Emperor Fei of Jin	Former Qin's Fu Jian attacked the city of Ye and captured Murong Wei. Former Yan fell.
384 CE Ninth year of the Taiyuan era under Emperor Xiaowu of Jin	During Former Qin's chaos, Murong Chui, son of Murong Huang, proclaimed himself Prince of Yan and established the Later Yan, declaring the era name Yanyuan. In 386, he claimed the title of emperor in Zhongshan and changed the era name to Jianxing.
	Cui Yu's tomb from Later Yan was discovered in Chaoyang, Liaoning in 2003. Two stone tablets were found and the epitaph reads, "In the Jianxing tenth year of Yan (395), prefect of Changli from Qinghe Wucheng, Cui Yu." Cui Yu's name appeared in the *Book of Wei and History of the Northern Dynasties* (in the biography of Cui Cheng).
385 CE Tenth year of the Taiyuan era under Emperor Xiaowu of Jin	Murong Chong of Western Yan proclaimed himself emperor.

Years	Events（Important archaeological sites and relics）
394 CE Nineteenth year of the Taiyuan era under Emperor Xiaowu of Jin	Later Yan's troops entered Zhangzi County and killed Murong Yong. Western Yan fell.
397 CE First year of the Long'an era under Emperor An of Jin	Murong Bao, son of Murong Chui and the Later Yan monarch, moved the capital from Zhongshan back to Longcheng.
398 CE Second year of the Long'an era under Emperor An of Jin	Murong De, brother of Murong Chui, declared himself Prince of Yan, establishing Southern Yan.
407 CE Third year of the Yixi era under Emperor An of Jin	Gao Yun killed Murong Xi (who had become ruler in 401) and seized the throne. In 409, Gao Yun was killed by his attendants, Li Ban and Tao Ren, and Later Yan fell. Feng Ba, a Han Chinese, succeeded to the throne and retained the dynasty name Yan, establishing the Northern Yan and declaring the era name Taiping.
410 CE Sixth year of the Yixi era under Emperor An of Jin	Liu Yu of the Jin dynasty captured Murong Chao. Southern Yan fell.
411 CE Seventh year of the Yixi era under Emperor An of Jin	The ruler of the northern grasslands, Yujiulü Hulü of the Rouran, made peace with Feng Ba and offered a tribute of three thousand horses, with a request to marry Feng Ba's daughter, Princess Lelang.
415 CE Eleventh year of the Yixi era under Emperor An of Jin	Feng Ba's brother, the Grand Marshal, Duke of Liaoxi, and Attendant-in-chief Feng Sufu died. He accomplished remarkable achievements in the establishment of Northern Yan.
	The tomb of Feng Sufu, probably part of the Feng family cemetery, was discovered in Beipiao, Liaoning in 1965.
436 CE Second year of the Taiyan era under Emperor Taiwu of Northern Wei	Northern Wei attacked Northern Yan, whose ruler Feng Hong destroyed Longcheng and fled with his people to Goguryeo. Northern Yan fell.
	Tomb No. 126 of Niizawa Senzuka ancient tombs was discovered in Nara, Japan in 1988. Dated to the mid-fifth century, it contains a number of burial objects that can be compared with those from the tomb of Feng Sufu.

附录二 三燕史事年表

年 代	重要史事（重要考古遗迹及遗物）
公元 238 年 魏明帝景初二年	魏太尉司马懿率师讨公孙渊。慕容鲜卑之莫护跋，以从司马懿伐公孙渊有功，拜率义王，始建国于棘城之北
公元 244 年 魏齐王正始五年	魏幽州刺史毌丘俭击高句丽。慕容鲜卑莫护跋之子、左贤王木延从征有功，加号大都督
公元 281 年 晋武帝太康二年	慕容鲜卑始寇昌黎
	辽宁发现晋墓，出土有晋"太康二年"铭瓦当等
公元 289 年 晋武帝太康十年	慕容廆降晋，拜为鲜卑都督。 同年，慕容廆迁居徒河之青山，其庶兄吐谷浑率众西迁，慕容鲜卑一支自此流居西北
公元 294 年 晋惠帝元康四年	慕容廆移居大棘城。教民农桑，用中原法制
	辽宁北票房身发现晋代石椁墓三座
公元 302 年 晋惠帝永宁二年太安元年	宇文鲜卑大素延率众十万围棘城，慕容廆出击，大素延大败
	长沙晋永宁二年墓出土有马俑，一件马俑左腹出现三角形马镫形象，这是迄今所知最早的马镫形象资料
公元 307 年 晋怀帝永嘉元年	慕容廆自称鲜卑大单于
公元 313 年 晋愍帝建兴元年	中原士夫纷纷往依慕容廆，人才济济，随才授任。慕容廆政事修明，爱重人物，至建兴二年（314）中原流民归于慕容廆者已数万家
公元 321 年 东晋元帝大兴四年	晋迁授慕容廆都督平州东夷诸军事，车骑将军，平州牧，封辽东郡公。廆设东庠，世子慕容皝等束修受业

续表

年 代	重要史事（重要考古遗迹及遗物）
公元 333 年 东晋成帝咸和八年	慕容廆卒，子慕容皝嗣立。皝弟慕容仁据平郭叛皝，皝遣弟慕容幼、司马冬寿讨伐
公元 334 年 东晋成帝咸和九年	东晋遣使拜慕容皝为镇军大将军、平州刺史、辽东公
公元 336 年 东晋成帝咸康二年	慕容皝讨伐慕容仁，自昌黎践冰而进，杀仁而还。冬寿、高充奔高句丽
	冬寿死葬高句丽，墓即平壤安岳 3 号古墓。墓内题记有"永和十三年（357）"，知冬寿居高句丽之后，一直奉晋朔
公元 337 年 东晋成帝咸康三年	慕容皝称燕王，是为前燕
公元 341 年 东晋成帝咸康七年	慕容皝筑龙城，改柳城为龙城县
公元 342 年 东晋成帝咸康八年	慕容皝迁都龙城，营制宫庙，号新宫曰和龙宫 十一月，慕容皝发兵自南北二道击高句丽，入丸都，焚其宫室，毁丸都而归
	辽宁朝阳袁台子前燕石椁墓，以石板支筑，颇似辽阳魏晋壁画墓形制。壁画有墓主人执麈尾正面坐像，与冬寿墓绘墓主人方法相同
公元 345 年 东晋穆帝永和元年	慕容皝始不用晋年号，自称十二年。 此时高句丽、百济、宇文、段氏鲜卑徙慕容都城民众已近十万户
公元 348 年 东晋穆帝永和四年	慕容皝死，子慕容儁继之
公元 350 年 东晋穆帝永和六年	慕容儁自龙城迁都于蓟。352 年取邺，称帝，国号燕，建元元玺

年　代	重要史事（重要考古遗迹及遗物）
公元 357 年 东晋穆帝升平元年	慕容儁迁都于邺
	河南滑台县（距邺城甚近）孝民屯发现 154 号墓等前燕墓葬
公元 360 年 东晋穆帝升平四年	慕容儁死，子暐嗣位
公元 370 年 东晋海西公太和五年	前秦符坚克邺，俘慕容暐，前燕至是灭亡
公元 384 年 东晋孝武帝太元九年	前秦乱，慕容皝子慕容垂逃离苻秦，自称燕王，建元曰"燕元"，是为后燕。386 年，即皇帝位于中山，改元建兴
	朝阳姚金沟发现后燕崔遹墓。出土石墓表两块。铭曰："燕建兴十年（395）昌黎太守清河武城崔遹。"崔遹名字在《魏书》和《北史》之《崔逞传》中均有记载
公元 385 年 东晋孝武帝太元十年	西燕慕容冲称帝
公元 394 年 东晋孝武帝太元十九年	后燕兵入长子，杀慕容永，西燕亡
公元 397 年 东晋安帝隆安元年	后燕主、慕容垂之子慕容宝自中山还都龙城
公元 398 年 东晋安帝隆安二年	慕容垂之弟慕容德称王，是为南燕
公元 407 年 东晋安帝义熙三年	高云杀慕容熙，即帝位，后燕亡。409 年高云近侍离班、桃仁杀高云。汉人冯跋继立，仍号燕，是为北燕。建元太平
公元 410 年 东晋安帝义熙六年	晋刘裕擒慕容超，南燕亡

续表

年　代	重要史事（重要考古遗迹及遗物）
公元 411 年 东晋安帝义熙七年	北方草原的柔然可汗斛律与冯跋和亲，献马三千匹，又聘跋女乐浪公主为妻
公元 415 年 东晋安帝义熙十一年	北燕大司马、辽西公、侍中冯素弗卒。素弗为冯跋长弟，在建立冯氏北燕时功勋卓著
	辽宁北票西官营子于 1965 年发现冯素弗墓，所葬之处应为冯氏陵园"长谷陵"
公元 436 年 北魏太武帝太延二年	北魏攻北燕，北燕主冯弘毁龙城，率众走高句丽，北燕亡
	日本奈良县橿原市新泽千尺冢 126 号古坟，随葬品多有可与冯素弗墓相互对照研究者，其时代约为五世纪中期

Appendix 3　Process of Mural Painting

Using the Yuantaizi mural tomb in Chaoyang as an example:

Archaeological excavations of the mural-decorated Yuantaizi tomb in Chaoyang, Liaoning have revealed the method of creating murals, as shown in the following steps and illustration:

Step 1: Build the tomb chamber with large stone blocks and slabs.

Step 2: Apply a layer of mixed straw and mud on the surface of the stone walls of the chamber.

Step 3: When the mud dries, apply a layer of lime about 1.5 to 2 centimeters thick atop the mud.

Step 4: Paint murals on the lime surface with red, yellow, green, ochre, and black water-based pigments.

附录三　壁画制作步骤

以朝阳袁台子壁画墓为例。

在对辽宁朝阳袁台子壁画墓进行考古发掘时发现，该墓的壁画制作步骤如下图所示：

第一步，以大型条石块、石板搭建起石室墓；

第二步，在墓室墙壁的石块表面涂抹一层黄草泥；

第三步，在黄草泥阴干后，在其表面涂抹一层厚约1.5～2厘米的白灰面；

第四步，在白灰面上用红、黄、绿、赭、黑等色绘制壁画。

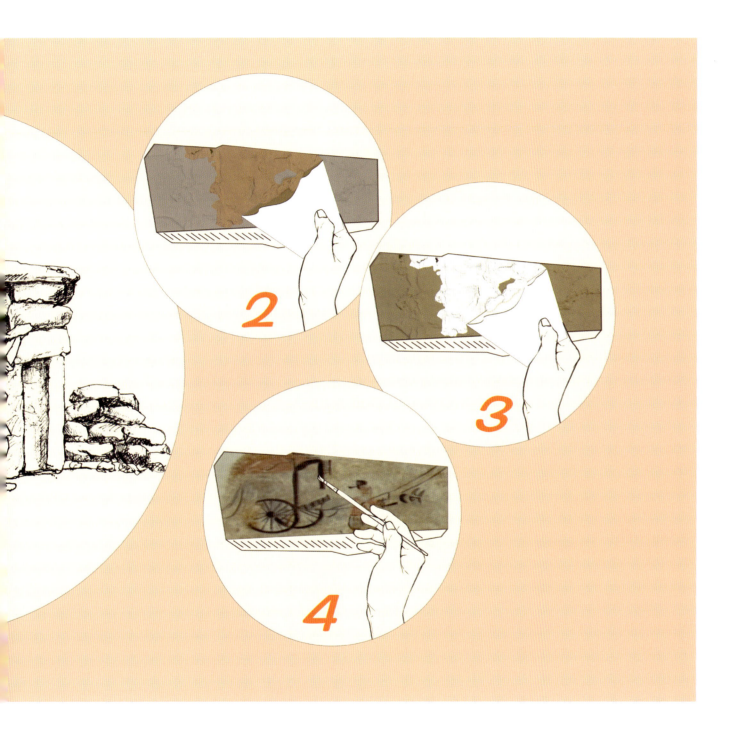

Appendix 4　Techniques of Goldsmithing

The goldsmithing techniques of the Three Yan culture include hammering, inlay, filigree, and bead soldering. These techniques reveal that the far-reaching influence of their featured *buyao* "swaying-leaf" or "step-sway" ornament extended from Central Asia to the East, after being absorbed by the Murong Xianbei clan, and then spreading further to Northeast Asia.

1. Swaying leaves

Originating in West Asia, swaying-leaf ornaments were particularly popular in the Liaoxi region from the third to the fifth centuries. In addition to the golden *buyao* headdresses, swaying metal leaves were also used as decoration on belts, earrings (fig. 1), and horse harnesses. Metal ornaments with swaying leaves of different sizes and textures have become a distinctive feature of the Three Yan culture.

2. Craftsmanship

Through the examination of surface patterns, edges, and finishing traces of the artifacts, it can be determined that production generally involves multiple processes such as hammering, engraving, openwork, wire making, bead making, soldering, and inlay. These techniques are used not only to give shape to the artifacts, but also to create decorative patterns on their surfaces.

Fig. 1　Gold earrings from Tomb IM17 of Lamadong cemetery in Beipiao, Liaoning (cat. no. 71).

　　The hat plaque with cicada pattern unearthed from the Feng Sufu tomb of Northern Yan is a good example (fig. 2), on which various holes can be seen. The plaque is made of a thin gold sheet, engraved using chisels of different sizes and cutting tips, and then pounded with a small hammer. Chisel marks can be found in certain areas. Due to the limited size of the pattern, the metalwork is not very refined.

　　Also visible on this artifact are filigree and bead-soldering techniques. The filigree process leaves a spiral pattern on the surface of the wire, giving the false impression that two strands of flat wire are wrapped around a round wire (fig. 3 and fig. 4). However, the end of the wire reveals that it is made up of a single flat wire. The wire was twisted and then rolled or drawn into a thin wire with a narrow spiral pattern. Rows of round gold beads are soldered to the wire on either side of the wire before all are soldered together to the base sheet. A pair of round "eyes" is inlaid in the center of the gold plaque, providing the finishing touch and bringing the cicada to life.

Fig. 3

Fig. 2   Gold ornamental plaque with cicada pattern used to decorate official hats, with openwork detail of the graphic pattern. One "eye" is missing and one is intact. From Feng Sufu Tomb of Northern Yan (cat. no. 67).

Fig. 4   Detail of filigree on gold ornamental plaque (cat. no. 62).

Process of metal wire making

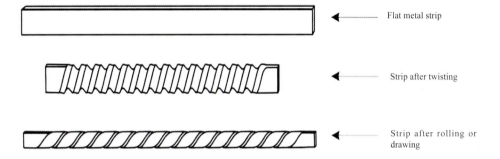

Flat metal strip

Strip after twisting

Strip after rolling or drawing

3. Patterns

In the Three Yan culture, decorative patterns such as dragons, phoenixes, deer- (or goat-) head phoenixes, divine beasts, and lotus and honeysuckle flowers were commonly used on horse harnesses (fig. 5). Most of these patterns can be found in the murals and illustrated stones of Han dynasty tombs in the Central Plains. Han tomb murals and illustrated stones are one of the main sources of Three Yan harness patterns. The continuous hexagon pattern and the symmetrical phoenix pattern may have originated in the Western Regions and been transmitted by Eurasian nomads.

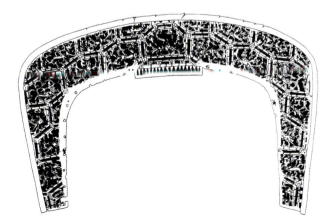

Fig. 5   Openwork hexagonal pattern on saddle pommel decorative sheath unearthed from Tomb 88M1, Shi'ertai brick factory, Chaoyang. Drawing from Liaoning Provincial Institute of Cultural Relics and Archaeology, Chaoyang County Museum, "Chaoyang shiertai brick factory 88M1 fajue jianbao" [Briefing on the Excavation of Tomb 88M1, Shi'ertai brick factory, Chaoyang], *Wenwu* [Cultural Relics] 1997.11: 28, fig. 25

Other sample patterns from Three Yan artifacts:

The dragon pattern is seen on the gilded openwork bronze saddle pommel decorative sheath unearthed from Tomb 88M1, Shi'ertai brick factory, Chaoyang. Drawing from Tian Likun, "Sanyan wenhua maju zhuangshi wenyang yanjiu" [A study of the decorative patterns of horse tack of Three Yan culture], in *Caitong Ji* [Caitong Collection], Cultural Relics Publishing House, 2016: 277, fig.3.

The symmetrical phoenix pattern is found on the middle part of the gilded openwork bronze saddle pommel decorative sheath unearthed from Xigou Village, Zhangjiyingzi, Beipiao, Liaoning. Drawing from Tian Likun, "Sanyan wenhua maju zhuangshi wenyang yanjiu" [A study of the decorative patterns of horse tack of Three Yan culture], in *Caitong Ji* [Caitong Collection], Cultural Relics Publishing House, 2016: 280, fig. 6-4.

The divine beast pattern is seen on the gilded openwork bronze saddle pommel decorative sheath unearthed from Lamadong cemetery, Beipiao, Chaoyang County Museum collection. Drawing from Tian Likun, "Sanyan wenhua maju zhuangshi wenyang yanjiu" [A study of the decorative patterns of horse tack of Three Yan culture], in *Caitong Ji* [Caitong Collection], Cultural Relics Publishing House, 2016: 280, fig. 6-7.

The hunter pattern is seen on the left side of
the gilded openwork bronze saddle pommel
decorative sheath unearthed from a tomb in
Sanhe Village, Qidaoling, Chaoyang, Chaoyang
County Museum collection. Drawing from
Tian Likun, "Sanyan wenhua maju zhuangshi
wenyang yanjiu" [A study of the decorative
patterns of horse tack of Three Yan culture], in
Caitong Ji [Caitong Collection], Cultural Relics
Publishing House, 2016: 281, fig.7-3.

The honeysuckle pattern is seen on the
circular gilded bronze ornament with a central
perforation and motifs unearthed from Xigou
Village, Zhangjiyingzi, Beipiao, Chaoyang
County Museum collection. Drawing from Tian
Likun, "Chaoyang faxian de sanyan wenhua
yiwu ji xiangguan wenti" [The Three Yan culture
remains found in Chaoyang and related issues],
Wenwu [Cultural Relics] 1994:11. 21, fig. 4-2, 3.

附录四 金饰工艺

三燕文化金饰工艺的基本技术，主要包括了锤鍱、镶嵌、花丝、金珠焊接等。为其特征的摇叶装饰自中亚地区向东延伸，为慕容鲜卑所吸收，之后又向东北亚地区传播，深远影响。

1. 摇叶

金属摇叶装饰起源于西亚，3—5世纪在辽西地区特别流行，除用于冠上的金步摇外，在带具、耳饰、马具上也都用摇叶作装饰。大小不一、质地不同的金属摇叶，成为三燕文化的显著特征。

2. 工艺

通过对文物表面纹饰、线条及加工痕迹的观察，可以确定其制作大体包括锤鍱、錾刻、镂空、掐丝、搓丝、吹珠、焊接、镶嵌多道工序。这些工艺除了用于器物造型的制作，还用于装饰纹样的塑造。

以北燕冯素弗墓出土的蝉纹金珰为例，在其器形工艺上可见有錾刻镂空而成的各种几何形镂孔，系用各种大小、刃形不同的錾子，用小锤敲击薄金片表面制成，局部保留下来了錾子加工的痕迹，由于镂空花纹较小，制作精度受限。同样在此器物上可见花丝及金珠焊接工艺。花丝工艺使金丝表面呈现螺旋纹，细部结构好像两股扁丝缠在一根圆丝上，通过金丝末端结构来看，可以确定金丝是由单股扁素丝搓制而成，再经过捻压或拔丝最终使旋纹间距变小。金丝两侧紧密排列着较为圆润的金珠，两者熔融焊接在一起，也同时焊接在下面的基体上。在金珰中央位置以镶嵌工艺制成的一对"玉眼"则为其造型画龙点睛。

图 1　图录第 71 号，辽宁北票喇嘛洞 Ⅰ M17 出土的耳坠

图 2　图录第 67 号，北燕冯素弗墓出土的蝉纹金珰，尚存一目。錾刻镂空而成的几何形镂孔细节

图 3　图录第 67 号，蝉纹金珰上的镂空工艺特写

图 4　图录第 67 号，蝉纹金珰上的花丝与金珠焊接工艺特写

花丝制作工艺流程图

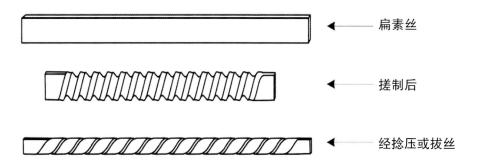

←　扁素丝

←　搓制后

←　经捻压或拔丝

3. 纹饰

三燕文化常见有龙、凤、鹿（羊）首凤、神兽、莲花纹、忍冬纹等纹饰，它们多见于马具之上，这些纹样大都可以在中原地区汉代壁画墓和画像石墓中见到，可以说汉墓壁画和画像石是三燕文化马具纹样的主要来源之一。而六方连续纹样、对凤纹等可能都与西域和欧亚草原文化有关。

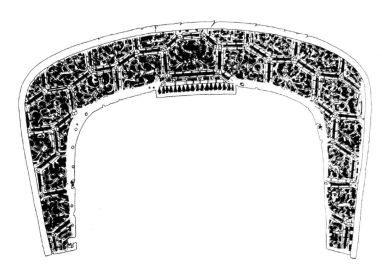

图 5　减地镂空六边形装饰纹样，见于朝阳十二台砖厂 88M1 出土的铜鎏金镂孔鞍桥包片，线图出自辽宁省文物考古研究所、朝阳市博物馆：《朝阳十二台乡砖厂 88M1 发掘简报》，《文物》1997 年第 11 期，第 28 页，图 25

三燕文物中所见其他图案举例

龙纹，见于朝阳十二台砖厂88M1出土的鎏金铜镂孔鞍桥包片。该线图出自田立坤《三燕文化马具装饰纹样研究》，《采铜集》，文物出版社，2016，第277页，图3-3。

对凤纹，见于朝阳博物馆藏朝阳北票章吉营子乡西沟村古墓出土的鎏金铜减地镂空鞍桥包片正中。该线图出自田立坤《三燕文化马具装饰纹样研究》，《采铜集》，文物出版社，2016，第280页，图6-4。

神兽纹，见于朝阳博物馆藏朝阳北票喇嘛洞墓地出土的鎏金铜减地镂空鞍桥包片左侧。该线图出自田立坤《三燕文化马具装饰纹样研究》，《采铜集》，文物出版社，2016，第280页，图6-7。

狩猎纹，见于朝阳博物馆藏朝阳七道岭乡三
合成墓出土鎏金铜錾刻鞍桥包片的左侧。该
线图出自田立坤《三燕文化马具装饰纹样研
究》，《采铜集》，文物出版社，2016，第
281页，图7-3。

忍冬纹，见于朝阳博物馆藏北票章吉营子乡
西沟村古墓出土的铜鎏金镂孔忍冬纹圆形饰
件。该线图出自田立坤《朝阳发现的三燕文
化遗物及相关问题》，《文物》1994年第11
期，第21页，图4-2、图4-3。

Gold from
Dragon City

龙城
之金

Masterpieces of
Three Yan from Liaoning
337–436

辽宁三燕文物选萃

337—436

Selected Bibliography　参考书目

[1] An Jiayao. "Fengsufu mu chutu de boliqi" [Glassware unearthed from the Feng Sufu tomb] in *Taolichengxi ji—Qingzhu anzhimin xiansheng bashi shouchen* [Anthology in celebration of An Zhimin's 80th Birthday], The Chinese University of Hong Kong Center of Chinese Archaeology and Art (2004): 377–87.

[2] ————. "Zhongguo de zaoqi boli qimin" [Early glassware in China]. *Kaogu xuebao* [Journal of Archaeology] 1984.4: 417.

[3] *Bei shi* [History of the Northern Dynasties] (vol. 98), "Ruru zhuan, xiongnu yuwen mohuai, tuhe duanjiuliuyu, gaoche" [Biography of Rouran, Yuwen Mohuai of Xiongnu, Duanjiuliuyu of Tuhe, and Gaoche], Zhonghua Book Company (1974): 3251.

[4] Cao, D., Zheng, Y., Bao, Q. *et al* "Ancient DNA sheds light on the origin and migration patterns of the Xianbei Confederation," *Archaeological and Anthropological Sciences*. November 24, 2023.15: 1–12.

[5] Holcombe, Charles. "Foreign Relations," Chapter 13:297. Edited by Albert E. Dien and Keith N. Knapp. *The Cambridge History of China: II: The Six Dynasties 220–589*. Cambridge University Press, London, 2019.

[6] ————. " The Xianbei in Chinese History," *Early Medieval China*, 2019: Fan Ye 范晔 (398–446), *Hou Han shu* 后汉书 (Beijing: Zhonghua shuju, (1965): 90.2985.

[7] Chen Dawei. "Liaoning beipiao fangshencun jinmu fajue jianbao" [Briefing on the excavation of Jin tomb in Fanshen Village, Beipiao, Liaoning]. *Kaogu* [Archeology] 1960.1: 24–26.

[8] *Jiu tang shu* [Old book of Tang] (vol. 83), *Xuerengui liezhuan* [Biography of Xue Rengui], Zhonghua Book Company. (1975): 2781. Also in *Xin tang shu* [New book of Tang] (vol. 3), *Xuerengui liezhuan* [Biography of Xue Rengui], Zhonghua Book Company. (1975): 4140–41.

[9] Juliano, Annette L. and Judith A. Lerner. *Monks and Merchants, Silk Road Treasures from Northwest China*. New York: Harry N. Abrams, Inc and Asia Society (2001).

[10] Laursen, Sarah. "Leaves that Sway: Gold Cup Ornaments from Northeast China," dissertation, University of Pennsylvania, 2011: 13–14 (UMI Number 3463014).

[11] Liaoning Provincial Institute of Cultural Relics and Archaeology, Nara National Research Institute for Cultural Properties of Japan, *Dongbeiya kaoguxue luncong* [Northeast Asia Archaeology Series], Science Publishing House, 2010. Liaoning Provincial Institute of Cultural Relics and Archaeology, Nara National Research Institute for Cultural Properties of Japan, *Liaoxi diqu dongjin shiliuguo shiqi ducheng wenhua yanjiu* [Research on the culture of Eastern Jin and Sixteen Kingdoms capitals in the Liaoxi region], Liaoning People's Publishing House, 2017.

[12] Lin Gan 林幹 . *Dong-Hu shi* 东胡史 (Huhehaote: Nei-Menggu renmin chubanshe (2007): 71–72.

[13] Liu Ning. "Beiyan rouran yu caoyuan sichou zhilu—cong fengsufu mu chutu de boliqi tanqi" [Northern Yan, the Rouran khaganate and the Steppe Road— from glassware unearthed in the Feng Sufu tomb], *Beiyan fengsufu mu* [Feng Sufu Tomb of Northern Yan], Cultural Relics Publishing House (2015): 238–45.

[14] Liu Yonghua, *Zhongguo gudai che yu maju* [Ancient Chinese chariots and horse equipment], Shanghai Lexicographical Publishing House, (2002): 205–206.

[15] Müller, Shing, Thomas O. Höllmann, and Sonja Filip, eds. *Early Medieval North China: Archaeological and Textual Evidence*. (In English and Chinese) (Asiatische Forschungen, 159), Wiesbaden: 2019.

[16] Pan Ling. "Duibufen yu xianbei xiangguan yicun niandai de zaitantao" [Reconsideration of the dating of some remains associated with the Xianbei], *Bianjiang kaogu yanjiu* [Archaeological research on the frontier] (vol. 13), Science Publishing House, 2013: 215.

[17] Serruys, Henry. "A Note on China's Northern Frontier," *Monumenta Serica* (vol. 28) 1969: 442–46.

[18] Su Bai. "Dongbei, Neimenggu diqu de xianbei yiji jilu zhiyi" [Remains of Xianbei in the Northeast and Inner Mongolia: A collection of Xianbei remains, vol. 1]. *Wenwu* [Cultural Relics] 1977.5: 46.

[19] *Sui shu* [Book of Sui] (vol. 84). "Beidi tiele zhuan" [Biography of Beidi and Tiele], Zhonghua Book Company (1974): 1879.

[20] Tao Liang and Lu Yeping, "Fengsufu mu taoqi zonghe kaocha" [A comprehensive examination of pottery from the Feng Sufu tomb]. *Beiyan fengsufu mu* [Feng Sufu Tomb of Northern Yan], Cultural Relics Publishing House, 2015: 278–83.

[21] Tian Likun, "Guanyu beipiao lamadong sanyan wenhua mudi de jige wenti" [Questions around the Lamadong cemetery of the Three Yan culture]. *Liaoning kaogu wenji* [Liaoning Archaeological Anthology], Liaoning Ethnic Publishing House, 2003: 263–67.

[22] Tian Likun, "Jicheng xinkao" [New examination of Jicheng]. *Liaohai wenwu xuekan* [Journal of Cultural Relics of Liaohai] 1996.2: 117–22.

[23] Tian Likun, "Liufang lianxu wenhyang kao" [An examination of the seamless pattern] in *Xinguoji—Qingzhu linyun xiansheng qishi huadan lunwenji* [Anthology in celebration of Lin Yun's 70th birthday], Science Publishing House, 2009.

[24] Tian Likun, "Qianyan de liangge lite jiazu" [Two Sogdian families of Former Yan], in *Literen zai zhongguo—kaogu faxian yu chutu wenxian de xin yinzheng* [Sogdians in China, new corroboration of archeological discoveries and excavated documents], Science Publishing House, 2014: 532–41.

[25] Waldron, Arthur. *The Great Wall from History to Myth*. Cambridge, England and New York: Cambridge University Press, 1990.

[26] *Wei shu* [Book of Wei] (vol. 103), *Ruru, xiongnu yuwen mohuai, tuhe duanjiuliuyu, gaoche zhuan* [Biography of Rouran, Yuwen Mohuai of Xiongnu, Duanjiuliuyu of Tuhe, and Gaoche], Zhonghua Book Company. (1974): 2291.

[27] Xu Bingkun. *Xianbei Sanguo gufen—Zhongguo Chaoxian Riben gudai de wenhua jiaoliu* [Three Kingdoms, ancient tombs—cultural exchanges between China, Korea, and Japan in ancient times], Liaoning Classics Publishing House, (1996): 140–53.

[28] Yang Hong. "Fengsufu mu madeng he Zhongguo zhuangjia de fazhan" [Stirrups of the Feng Sufu tomb and development of Chinese horse armor], *Liaoningsheng bowuguan guankan* [Journal of Liaoning Provincial Museum], Liaohai Publishing House, 2010: 1–6.

[29] Yü Ying-shih. *Trade and Expansion in Han China: A Study in the Structure of Sino-Barbarian Economic Relations*, (1967): 251.

[30] Zheng Yan, *Weijin nanbeichao bihuamu yanjiu* [A study of mural tomb painting in the Wei, Jin, and Northern and Southern dynasties], Cultural Relics Publishing House, 2002: 40–41.

[31] Zhou Xiaojing, "Fengsufu mu chutu de yuwan yu yuqian" [Jade bowl and jade sword unearthed from the Feng Sufu tomb]. *Liaoning sheng bowuguan guankan* [Journal of Liaoning Provincial Museum], Liaohai Publishing House, 2011: 14–19.

[32] Wu Gang, editor in chief, Shaanxi Provincial Classics Management, *Quantangwen buyi* [Addendum on complete literary works of Tang dynasty] (vol. 5), *Kanghui muzhi* [Epitaph of Kang Hui], San Qin Publishing House, 1998: 408.

[33] Zhu Zhifang, *Ji houyan longtengyuan yizhi de faxian* [Discovery of the Longteng Garden archeological site of Later Yan], *Dongbei difangshi yanjiu* [Study of Northeast Regional History] 1984.1: 7–8.

图书在版编目（CIP）数据

龙城之金：辽宁三燕文物选萃：337—436 / 海蔚蓝
主编；刘宁著. —沈阳：辽宁美术出版社，2024.9
　ISBN 978-7-5314-9778-3

　Ⅰ.①龙…　Ⅱ.①海…　②刘…　Ⅲ.①文物—概况—
辽宁—337-436　Ⅳ.K872.31

中国国家版本馆CIP数据核字(2024)第099713号

出 品 人：彭伟哲
出版发行：辽宁美术出版社
地　　址：沈阳市和平区民族北街29号　邮编：110001
印　　刷：天津市豪迈印务有限公司
开　　本：889mm×1194mm　1/16
版　　次：2024年9月第1版
印　　次：2024年9月第1次印刷
印　　张：18.75
字　　数：200千字
责任编辑：梁晓蛟
书籍装帧：马　欢　陈静思
责任校对：满　媛
责任印制：徐　杰
书　　号：ISBN 978-7-5314-9778-3
定　　价：280.00元

如发现印装质量问题，请与我社出版部联系调换。
出版部电话：024-23835227